287
SECRETS of
REINVENTING
YOUR LIFE

287
SECRETS of
REINVENTING
YOUR LIFE

BIG AND SMALL WAYS TO EMBRACE NEW POSSIBILITIES

By the editors of *MORE* magazine
and Dana Hudepohl

WILEY

John Wiley & Sons, Inc.

Published by John Wiley & Sons, Inc., Hoboken, New Jersey
Published simultaneously in Canada

Design and composition by Forty-five Degree Design LLC

For general information about our other products and services, please contact our Customer Care Department within the United States at (800) 762-2974, outside the United States at (317) 572-3993 or fax (317) 572-4002.

Wiley also publishes its books in a variety of electronic formats and by print-on-demand. Some content that appears in standard print versions of this book may not be available in other formats. For more information about Wiley products, visit us at www.wiley.com.

Library of Congress Cataloging-in-Publication Data

MORE magazine 287 secrets of reinventing your life : big and small ways to embrace new possibilities / MORE Magazine.
    p.   cm.
  ISBN 978-1-118-01262-8 (pbk.); ISBN 978-1-118-08794-7 (ebk.);
  ISBN 978-1-118-08795-4 (ebk.); ISBN 978-1-118-08796-1 (ebk.)
  1. Women—Psychology. 2. Women—Conduct of life. 3. Self-realization in women.
4. Success. 5. Career changes. I. More (Meredith Publishing Group)
  HQ1206.M6534   2011
646.70082—dc23

                                                                        2011024779

Printed in the United States of America

10 9 8 7 6 5 4 3 2 1

Contents

Introduction

Lesley Jane Seymour
Editor in chief, MORE

When my job as the editor in chief of a major fashion magazine came to a crushing end several years ago, I retired. Even though I was still in my forties, I was emotionally bruised and battered, disillusioned by the politics of corporate life and by bosses who gave orders, then suffered amnesia when things didn't exactly turn out as they'd hoped. Along the way, I also discovered a personal flaw: I was way too naive to successfully navigate the role of Monkey in the Middle between two business partners who distrusted each other. I was also physically exhausted. Spending sixty days a year on the road, traveling around the world, may sound glamorous in theory, but in practice it meant trying to pick winning covers for my magazine under the fluorescent lights of a hotel bathroom. Oh, and did I mention I had two young kids (JJ, now twenty, and Lake, fifteen) and a husband, Jeff, whose own working hours were insane?

Losing this frantic, dysfunctional, no-win job was emotionally painful and professionally terrifying—but also (secretly) a relief.

Because my husband and I are compulsive savers, we had put away a hefty nest egg, so I decided to reinvent myself as a full-time mom. When I worked outside the home, my kids had always guilt-tripped me that I didn't do the things other moms did— even though I *was* Class Mom two years in a row when they were in elementary school, attended every baseball and soccer game in middle school (plus the majority of practices), and was one of only three parents who actually showed up the day my daughter's creative writing teacher invited us to attend an afternoon reading. But *never mind*. Children, I have learned, are even bigger amnesiacs than corporate bosses and only remember what you did for them maybe an hour ago. So staying home full time would give me a first-class chance to redeem myself, I thought.

During the first few weeks, I still rose at 6:30 AM, scrambled into my three-inch heels and makeup, and rushed to . . . the kitchen counter! The change of pace was so dramatic that I felt as if I'd been thrown off an airport conveyor belt and skinned my knees. Truth was, my type A (or maybe triple A) personality couldn't let go of my old routine; for me, busyness itself offered a certain adrenaline rush. So I sifted my dry ingredients into a bowl the night before and turned out baskets of fresh blueberry muffins at 7:30 AM (Martha Stewart, step aside!) before driving the kids to school. I invited gaggles of their friends to dinner every night for casseroles of gourmet mac and cheese culled from that day's *New York Times* (take that, Rachael Ray!), led Lake and her fellow tweens on shopping excursions, and finally managed to unpack the last cardboard box from our move into our house eleven years earlier.

It was crazy—but gradually, with the help of friends and family, I learned to decelerate. I started going to the gym every morning after school drop-off and came to think of the regulars there as my new officemates. I learned to hit the beach midweek when most of the chairs were vacant. I hunted down a new wardrobe of casual pieces (good-bye, my beloved four-inch heels!) and became such a master of shopping the sales that I developed a personal philosophy of shoes (namely: the only thing standing between each of us and that perfect pair of wedges is time, not money).

Because I had no clue what my next act would be professionally—or if there would even be one—I explored the fantasies I'd never had time for. I took classes at a culinary school and learned to bake the perfect cake; I seriously considered opening a cupcake store near the local train station until my husband asked, "Do you really want to get up at three-thirty every morning to make muffins?" I joined the League of Women Voters and learned firsthand how many smart, dedicated people are working for change behind the scenes in America, and I tried my hand as treasurer of the book sale at JJ's school (let's just say that reconciling two different tally sheets of numbers is not my forte). I was even able to satisfy my giving-back gene by raising money for victims when a flood devastated the town next door to mine.

Most important, I was able to reconnect with my kids, who'd spent much of their time with nannies and au pairs since the day they were born. After they got over the shock of what a taskmaster their real mom was (unlike the babysitter, I *never* gave in to a pile of dirty clothes on the bedroom floor), they began to enjoy having me around. And I learned how to be present in my life. I learned to actually tune in to what my kids were saying when they spoke to me—because that constant buzz of thinking ahead about what-do-I-need-to-do-next had finally evaporated, as did my constant compulsion to check my BlackBerry. I was able to ask myself what I really loved about work. Was publishing great stories, some of which might change the world for the better, so satisfying—or did I merely crave constant motion that left little room for reflection on life's bigger issues? And why did I choose to write? Yes, it was a childhood talent, but was I trying to compensate for my years of silence growing up in a dysfunctional family? Or did I really have something unique to say? If the latter, then why had I started my journalism career in fashion—the ultimate high school lunchroom where you have to ingratiate yourself with the mean girls to succeed?

Eventually, I decided that I'd do a few freelance articles—but with the caveat that they wouldn't be shallow and flashy (like the yards of beauty copy I'd once churned out) but about issues I really *cared* about. So I spent a week in Rwanda writing about women who survived the genocide and were pulling their country together again by selling baskets, and I talked in *More* about how I was reinventing myself from corporate mogul to suburban mom. Surprise of surprises! My writing became fulfilling again.

When the opportunity arose to become the editor in chief of *More*, I was ready to embrace it. Unlike the fashion magazines I'd run, *More* is about the adventure of life, about getting to reinvent yourself with the benefit of the experience, confidence, and style you've acquired over the years.

And that, at last, was the genesis of the thinking behind this book. No matter what your stage of reinvention, there are tales in this book guaranteed to inspire you to action, urge you on, or cheer you during that final lap to the finish line. There are small reinventions—a woman who finally won a beauty contest at age fifty, and *ginormous* ones—such as the diplomat who ditched her job at the State Department to embark on a career helping sick people navigate the health-care system. There are famous-people reinventors—an award-winning novelist who was once a harried corporate executive, and quiet, behind-the-scenes reinventors—such as the harried mom who became a hard-core cyclist. There are reinventions set in motion by outside events, such as an earthquake that changed the career path of an American woman living abroad, and reinventions precipitated by personal events like a health crisis or a divorce. There are reinventions that began as expressions of love for animals or music or makeup. Or cheese.

There are reinventors who were terrified of the first step, and then there are serial reinventors who can't stop themselves.

Along with the inspiring stories in this book, you'll find something equally valuable: the concrete tips and tricks we've coaxed out of each person who was profiled. You'll notice that certain insights pop up again and again: *Be fearless. Don't wait—do it now.* The universality of certain beliefs and ideas holds all of these disparate stories together and ultimately delivers the message "No matter what your dream is, you can achieve it."

Feel free to dip in and out of these stories. You can start with the women who sought meaning in life by giving back (chapter 4, "Doing Good") or go right to the entrepreneurs (chapter 5, "Discovering Your Business Sense"). Or simply begin at page 1 and read straight through. No matter where you start, what you'll hear is the unbridled cheerleading, the just-do-it confidence of those who have succeeded and know that you can, too. What also becomes abundantly clear is that the only thing holding each of us back from finding her bliss is just a handful of excuses.

So get going, girlfriend, and know that I'll see you along the way. Because once I put this book down, I suddenly realized that despite all of the personal excavating I did, both during my career and then during my eighteen-month walkabout, these women make me feel like a novice. I'm newly convinced that I have no idea who or what I'll be when I finally grow up—but I'm ready to find out.

1

❧

Following Your Passion

Sometimes a hobby is merely a hobby, and sometimes it can redirect your life. In this chapter, you'll hear about women who jettisoned their original careers and chose a different future, channeling their enthusiasms—for anything from animals to food to connecting with nature—into work that is not only financially viable, but emotionally fulfilling.

Call of the Wild
Juliette Watt

On a dazzling September afternoon in southern Utah's dramatically gorgeous canyon country, while gazing at ancient cliffs shadowed in hues of vermilion and vanilla against a cobalt sky, Juliette Watt had an epiphany.

Watt and her husband, Jason, were one week into a volunteer vacation at Best Friends Animal Sanctuary, a 3,800-acre compound that's a last-chance haven for 1,700 dogs, cats, horses, pigs, and birds. Watt was working in Dogtown, Best Friends' canine quarters.

"I was cleaning out their kennels, scooping dog poop," she recalls. "I could see a hundred miles in the clear air. That's when I had what I call my Eckhart Tolle moment, a powerful knowing that we had to move here." Ready for change and burned out on East Coast big-city life, Watt felt nourished by the desert surroundings. She looked forward to sharing her revelation with Jason, who was toiling elsewhere in Dogtown.

Watt was already well into her fourth act when the urge to upend her life struck that day in 2002. Born and raised in London, she grew up with dogs ("We got the rejects breeders didn't want") and was such a good horsewoman that MGM studios hired her as a stunt rider for films such as *The Charge of the Light Brigade*. Before coming to the United States in 1976 and landing a gig as a chanteuse in Playboy clubs throughout the country, Watt had dealt cards in a casino and sung in cabarets in Turkey, Lebanon, and Belgium. In her forties, she settled in New York and thrived as an ABC-TV scriptwriter, turning out more than seven hundred soap opera episodes and earning a six-figure salary.

Watt met Jason, a voice-over actor fifteen years her junior, through a friend after her first marriage ended. They married in 1994 and bought a house in New Jersey. Not long after that, Watt fulfilled a long-held ambition to become a pilot and teach flying. As a flight instructor, she pulled in about $40,000 a year, sometimes taking her students, mostly doctors and businesspeople, up in her own four-seat Mooney. After the 9/11 attacks,

. . . .

The Most Important Thing I Learned

"When your gut, your instinct, your whole body are telling you to do something, even though it may seem like the craziest, most insane thing, do it. I used to ignore that; when my instincts told me to do something, I would always question it and talk myself out of it. Now it's sort of like the filter has gone."

. . . .

however, business waned, and her old restlessness returned. Then came the trip to Best Friends.

After a few days of volunteering, Watt felt a strong connection to the mission of the sanctuary (no animal is ever euthanized there, except in cases of painful terminal illness) and to the staff, many of whom had left behind successful first careers; there was a rocket scientist, a corporate purchasing agent, and a medical writer. Watt also loved the glorious high desert landscape just outside the town of Kanab. When Watt decided to move there, she had no idea what she'd do for a living,

......

The Most Important Thing I Did Right

"Trusting my instincts."

......

but that didn't faze her. "I'm a jack-of-all-trades," she says. "To work among the animals at Best Friends would be great, but I could also be a waitress or a flight instructor. I just knew this was the place I had to be. That evening I told Jason, 'We're moving.'"

Her husband balked. Jason loved animals and adored the beauty of southern Utah but didn't relish change and couldn't imagine that a voice-over actor would find much work in the area. "I was scared of leaving my comfort zone," he says. "But Juliette taught me to move outside it." Trusting his wife's instincts, he agreed to relocate.

After their vacation, they returned home to put their house on the market. Meanwhile, Watt continued to give flying instruction twenty-five hours a week, tracked Kanab real estate listings, and regularly checked bestfriends.org, hoping to find a suitable job opening for Jason. Her soap opera earnings had enabled them to buy their first house, so they decided that he would be the main provider now. One day she noticed that Best Friends had an opening for a videographer and that a beautiful cedar house near Kanab, with commanding views of the desert, was for sale. She took these as signs of what their future would look like. Jason, who'd studied filmmaking in college, applied for the position and was invited to Best Friends for a tryout. (The nonprofit requires many prospective employees, even previous volunteers, to work for two weeks at the job before it makes an offer.)

By July 2003, the pair were on the road to Utah with luggage piled on top of the car and their three dogs curled up in the backseat. The first week in Kanab, they took another big risk, putting down a chunk of their savings on the cedar house. With uncertain job prospects and two mortgage payments due (their New Jersey house still hadn't found a buyer), the situation looked perilous. Watt says she felt a stab of panic ("What if we're poor and homeless, and it's all my fault?"), but having already made several career changes, she had faith in her internal compass. "Most people don't listen to their inner voice, but if you do, everything works out," she says.

The couple had planned to live on Jason's new salary, but the amount hadn't been posted in the ad. When they discovered that if hired he would make only $37,000 (about a third of his voice-over earnings), Watt quickly applied for a volunteer-coordinator job at Dogtown, which paid $18,000. Her tryout went so well that after three days, Best Friends broke with protocol and signed her on. And at the end of his audition, Jason became the sanctuary's first official videographer.

With two mortgages draining their savings, however, their salaries weren't enough to live on. Eight months after the move and down to $300 in their checking account, the couple had a huge fight. "I believed we'd ride out the situation," says Watt, "but he saw my confidence as nonchalance, and that set him off." Jason moved into the guest room.

The turnaround came soon after the blowup, when the New Jersey house finally sold and Jason fell in love—with a feral Chihuahua. "Chaco came from a terrible animal-hoarding situation, a person who had more than 250 dogs," says Watt. "When we adopted him, he became Jason's best buddy."

With the couple's debt reduced and marital harmony restored, Watt reveled in her new job. During the next few years, her position expanded, and she's now the coordinator of volunteer groups and interns for the entire sanctuary—Piggy Paradise, Horse Haven, Cat World, and the bird and rabbit areas. Dozens of people help at Best Friends every day, most of them out-of-towners on volunteer vacations, and Watt matches their interests with work that has to be done, such as taking 140-pound potbellied pigs for their morning walks and cleaning the rabbit hutches.

In 2005, she was part of Best Friends' Hurricane Katrina response team, which rescued six thousand animals, mostly pets (including one emu) trapped in flooded homes and backyards. While Jason worked on logistics from the Kanab headquarters, Watt was deployed along with about twenty others to a rescue facility in Mississippi. "I spent seven months living in a trailer, being eaten alive by bugs," she says, "but when you save animals, there is no feeling like it in the world. Every night around midnight, a big truck would arrive from New Orleans full of dogs. We'd unload them, get them set up for the night, and, in the morning, process them through a makeshift clinic for vaccinations and medical care."

Back in Utah, workdays are less dramatic. On a typical morning at Best Friends, Watt is a blur of motion, ponytail bouncing as she oversees workers stacking wooden supply-transport pallets, rustles up shovels for heaving gravel into storage cans, and briefs volunteers on how to tidy an area outside Piggy Paradise headquarters. Patting shoulders as she bustles by, she calls everyone "darling" and swiftly molds a gaggle of California kids on spring break into a hardworking team. The students are here for a week, rotating through the various Best Friends neighborhoods. In Piggy Paradise, they fall in love with a potbelly named Sprocket and beg to take him on a sleepover to the house in Kanab where they're staying. Best Friends lets volunteers take animals home overnight, and Sprocket, housebroken and unflappable, is on the approved list. Watt calls the owner of the house for permission, arranges for a van to transport the pig, and asks her husband to send a photographer so they can post a story ("Sprocket Goes to Town") on Best Friends' website.

The constant motion of Watt's job serves her restless spirit, but Best Friends' rescued horses thrill her the most. "They're always monitoring what's going on around them," she says. "They reflect back the emotions you send out."

Living in Kanab has also enriched Watt's relationships with humans. "The silence of this place magnifies your inner self," she says. "There are no distractions, so you concentrate on friendships. I've made the best friends of my life here."

Of course, there's a sad side to working at an animal sanctuary. "A dog was turned in a few years ago because he didn't match the color scheme of the new house," she recalls. Many of Best Friends' inhabitants come from hoarders who amass hundreds of animals they cannot care for. Then there are the cruelty cases. "We did a rescue in Gabbs, Nevada, of dogs abandoned in pens in the middle of the desert." The sanctuary's success stories make the sadness more bearable. That so many animals, even gravely injured ones, can be rescued, healed, and placed for adoption inspires her to keep going.

Lately, Watt's work at Best Friends has led to an interest in natural horse training, a style pioneered by Pat Parelli, who runs a worldwide organization that teaches people how to become the animal's partner instead of its master. Now she wants to study the method, continue working at Best Friends, and eventually run a side business as a Parelli horsemanship instructor. "I can use my airplane to visit clients who want me to train their horses," she says. "It's a way to make the world a better place for humans and horses, working with different rescue groups and shelters, working with horses that are 'difficult'—I would like to make a difference in that area."

Will this be her last career change? Unlikely. When a visitor to Best Friends describes her as a serial reinventor, Watt cracks a big smile. "That's the nicest thing anybody's ever said to me."

·········· **My Biggest Mistake** ··········

"I could have been a little more conscious of Jason and his feelings."

From Executive Assistant
to Master Chef
Debbie Frangipane

For as long as Debbie Frangipane, forty-eight, can remember, she has been infatuated with all things Italian, and she's always loved to cook. So in 1996, when she started dating a work colleague, it felt like fate when she learned that he was a foodie who was 100 percent Italian.

When she married her match the next year, her new mother-in-law, who was born in Italy, began passing down centuries of prized recipes. The newlyweds immediately traveled to the mother country and returned at least twice a year for ten days at a time. They spent their days cooking with her husband's relatives, sampling cuisine at unadvertised hangouts, and getting to know the

········
The Most Important Thing I Learned
"I found my inner strength."
········

locals. "We weren't going as tourists," she says. "We immersed ourselves in la dolce vita." In 2000, they started renting apartments for their visits, and stayed a month each time.

Whenever they came home to Florida, Frangipane recreated the recipes they had tasted on their trips. Each time, though, she found it harder to return to her hectic American life. For twenty years, Frangipane had been an executive assistant to CFOs and CEOs. She liked what she did and was good at it, but her eleven-hour workdays were filled with pressure, and on bad days her commute lasted an hour and a half. She longed for the slow pace of Italy, where she could linger over a meal for hours with company or chat with passersby as she strolled to the market to buy fresh ingredients for the day's meal. So in 2004, when her husband, a computer programmer who could work from anywhere, suggested they move to Venice for a year, she enthusiastically agreed and resigned from her job.

In Italy, Frangipane spent her mornings in school, learning the language. In the afternoons, she picked a region out of her travel book, drove there, and discovered obscure neighborhood restaurants through word of mouth. "If I told the owner I loved the pasta sauce, it wasn't uncommon for her to take me back into her kitchen to show me how she made it," says Frangipane. She practiced new recipes on frequent visitors, both Italian and American, and showed them around the country. She was so good at both that an Italian relative suggested she start a business.

When she and her husband returned to the United States in 2005 after thirteen months abroad, they founded Savory Adventures (savoryadventures.com), a luxury tour guide company that centered on Italian culture and cuisine. To focus on building her new business, she left the corporate world behind for the flexibility of working as a personal trainer and nutrition coach. Dubbing herself Dolce Debbie, she gave Italian cooking demonstrations at a culinary school, and did a regular cooking segment on a daytime TV news program syndicated in more than one hundred markets nationwide.

......

The Most Surprising Thing about My Reinvention

"How natural the change has been, and the overwhelming support I've received from family, friends, and the general public."

......

.... **My Biggest Mistake** ....

"Waiting so long to take the path that I was meant to travel."

....

She and her husband hosted the first Savory Adventures tour in 2007. Frangipane cooked for the travelers and shared with them the hidden gems that she had uncovered during her own visits. "I got to travel *and* cook for people," she says. "It was my dream come true." She went on to host four Savory Adventures trips a year; now she does them only by request for private groups.

Two years later, Frangipane began taking classes at the Culinary Institute of America in Hyde Park, New York, to pursue formal chef training. "I had a hard time hearing people call me chef without, in my head, having earned that title," she says. "I'm always looking to take things to the next level." Now she's aiming to be the second woman ever to reach the status of Certified Master Chef, the highest and most demanding certification in the field. (There are currently only sixty worldwide).

In 2010, Frangipane took a break from hosting Savory Adventures tours so that she could focus on her culinary training. To build her chef résumé, she works at a restaurant in the Grand Floridian, a high-end Disney World hotel, cooks meals for clients in their homes as a personal chef, and has developed her own website, dolcedebbie.com, full of original recipes. She also teaches, makes guest appearances on TV and radio, caters events (she recently hosted a six-course benefit dinner in Manhattan to raise funds for amfAR), and is writing a coffee table book filled with menus and stories of relationships that have developed at her dinner table. "In Italy," she says, "the food and the table are the common ground where friends meet, relationships bloom, and families grow closer together."

Today Frangipane is just as taken by Italy as when she was a young girl, and she and her husband plan to settle there within the next ten years. "I used to daydream about being in Italy, and I hungered to experience what I saw portrayed in the movies," she says. "Doing what I'm doing is what I've always been destined to do. To say that I am blessed would be an understatement."

How much pain am I willing to endure to obtain the end
result? (Success doesn't happen overnight!)

Not Too Late for a New Degree
Babette Gladstein

Tired of her work as a stockbroker and an investment adviser,
Babette Gladstein needed a distraction, so she bought—and fell
in love with—an exotic Cornish Rex kitten. From that small
beginning, cats became her passion. During the next five years,
she purchased five more felines and started to breed and show
them. At the same time, she began to
work for her husband's venture capital
company and her family's auto-parts
business and eventually quit her job as
an investment adviser.

· · · · · · · ·

The Most Important Thing I Learned

"I discovered the possibilities of changing one's life.
I was married for fifteen years, and my husband's life
was more important than my life. I was the copilot. I
never thought that I would be the pilot. I'm not still
married to this man. I left him prior to going to vet
school. My life has taken so many turns, and those
options would never have been available to me if I
hadn't gone to vet school."

· · · · · · · ·

At home, Gladstein spent all of her
free time with her pets. When the kitties
came down with chronic diarrhea and
sneezing, she found a holistic veterinarian who cured them with a diet of homemade food. Watching him work,
Gladstein was intrigued. She'd discovered that she had a special gift for han-
dling animals, and she wondered what it
would take to become a vet herself.

At first, it seemed like a crazy idea
for a forty-three-year-old, especially after
she found out that getting into veteri-
nary school (typically, a four-year program) was possible only if she took the

required undergrad science classes, got top grades in most of them, and aced her GREs—a lot of big ifs. Up for the challenge, she spent three years taking organic chemistry, biology, physics, and calculus classes, while still working at least thirty hours a week. One year later, she was accepted into vet school—and felt a little stunned. "I never thought I had enough academic ambition to do this," she says. "It amazes me that I had the stick-to-itiveness."

> "By the time they hit their sixties, my mom and grandmother felt washed up. Now women have tremendous opportunities. It's our time."

These days, Gladstein (animalacupuncture .net) is involved in regenerative medicine, working with stem cells, publishing papers, and doing pro bono work with the Humane Society. She now earns about the same six-figure income that she did in finance, but she's far happier. "I get so much more satisfaction," she says, "and the animals are actually grateful. You get kisses!"

·········· **My Biggest Mistake** ··········

"Not focusing enough on my social life. But men aren't necessarily as appreciative of an ambitious woman."

Babette's Success Strategy

"Follow your passion—believe in something you feel strongly enough to pursue."

Homing In on a Hobby
Suzi Renehan

Suzi Renehan, fifty-one, always loved to cook, but she was never very crafty. "My Christmas cookies never looked like anything I wanted to give to anybody," she says with a laugh. So in 1994, when she came across a recipe for biscotti cookies, she thought that she and her two young boys could try their hand at those instead. They cranked up the Christmas music while she baked and her sons iced. When they gave the biscotti as gifts to family and friends, they were a hit. "It was the start of a family tradition," she says.

Renehan's biscotti quickly became famous among her friends. At Christmastime people looked forward to the treats, and she started to get requests throughout the year. Although she had a demanding executive job as a real estate trust officer for a national bank, she experimented after hours with different ingredients. She brought the new concoctions to her office for coworkers to taste-test. "I found it a great way to relieve the stress of my job," she says. "It was a fun little hobby."

In 2006, she was grabbing a cup of coffee at a kiosk in her office building when a colleague told the kiosk owner about her popular biscotti. The owner asked whether she could try selling them. Renehan was excited. "My family and friends had told me for years that I should," she says. Renehan held a family meeting with her husband and kids, and they settled on a name for the new venture: Uncanny Biscotti. The kiosk sold its first supply and ordered more. Renehan took samples to other coffee shops around town. By the end of the year, her biscotti were available at nine venues.

Although Renehan loved her new extracurricular activity, she became increasingly unhappy in her financial career. Stressed by changes in the company management, she wasn't taking care of herself physically, and her weight dropped to 95 pounds. "I drove home every day so miserable," she says. The final straw came one night after work when her husband was looking for the TV remote control and couldn't find it. Renehan reacted to this minor issue by screaming and crying, and once she calmed down, she realized she had a problem. "I said, 'This is not right, reacting this way.'" Something had to change, and she soon decided it was time to move on from her twenty-year career with her company.

When Renehan gave notice in 2008, she dreamed of doing the biscotti business full-time, but she wasn't sure it was realistic, so she pursued jobs in her field, sending out résumés and talking to recruiters. Everything changed a month later when she went to a wine-and-cheese tasting at a local cooking studio and brought along her biscotti. The chef loved the handmade goods and invited Renehan to do a presentation at an upcoming open house. "Before I knew it, I was getting orders from customers," says Renehan. "It was then that I went, 'Huh, maybe this could really work!'" The chef invited Renehan to use her commercial kitchen so she could produce biscotti on a larger scale. "It was scary taking that leap of faith," she says, "but at forty-eight, I decided it was time to cultivate my true passion."

Renehan went full throttle into finding new clients. Her older son, away at college, helped create a website, uncannybiscotti .com. Her younger son, in high school, assisted in production, pricing, and packaging. Friends and extended family helped whenever she needed them. "I had an incredible circle of support," she says. She put together sample packages of various flavors—from strawberry caramel balsamic to fig and fennel—took them into local shops, and mailed them around the country to gourmet grocery stores and coffee companies. She attended food shows and donated to charity events. "It made me feel good to give back to the community that was helping me grow," she says. "And we got a lot back from it as well."

....

The Most Important Thing I Learned

"When I started out, the only thing I focused on was baking and creating relationships with clients. As we began to grow, I realized that seemingly small details, such as paperwork, bookkeeping, research, and purchasing, could become full-time jobs themselves. I learned that in order to be successful, I couldn't do everything myself."

....

Renehan was always on the lookout for ways to market her product without putting money into advertising. She would hear of a potential opportunity while watching TV and then head to the computer to do research. She'd scour cooking magazines for names of stores to which she could send samples. Her efforts paid off when *Southern Living* magazine featured her biscotti right before the holidays. More than five hundred new orders poured in.

What started out as a fun family tradition is now a thriving family business that includes events catering, and they will soon be opening their own production facility and a new headquarters in Jacksonville. One of her sons is a chef, and the other is in web development. (Her husband, they joke, is in charge of research and development because he's not allowed in the kitchen.) The business has grown every year. It now offers twenty-seven flavors and in 2010 made deliveries to forty-seven states, Italy, and Germany.

"Recently, I was asked to prepare biscotti gift baskets," Renehan says, "and while I was making tissue paper flowers to decorate them, I just started laughing, thinking of how my life has changed. From the executive wearing expensive suits, heels, and hose to the girl in the kitchen in shorts, T-shirt, and tennis shoes making gift baskets. I never saw myself any other way than in the corporate world. When I sit back and reflect on what has happened since I walked out of that downtown building, I see that it was the best decision I could have made for my health, my happiness, and my family."

My Biggest Mistake

"Most of our clients for the first few years were small businesses and individuals. A corporate retailer approached us to sell the product in its stores, and we jumped at the opportunity to reach a wider audience, without carefully examining the real requirements to service a chain of stores. A retail store has a different set of needs from a coffee shop or a restaurant, and some mistakes were made as we learned what those were. Basically, we took on too big of an account too soon!"

Suzi's Success Strategy

"I send our biscotti out to different venues to obtain new clients and spread awareness. Many of these are cold calls and shots in the dark, and I don't hear back from everyone, but we put ourselves out there."

A Sea Change
Claudia Espenscheid

The sun was just peeking over the horizon. There wasn't a cloud in the sky, not a ripple on the Santa Rosa Sound in Pensacola, Florida. Ordinarily quiet at 6 AM, the beach was bedlam that June in 2006 when seventy-five women, ranging from nineteen to sixty-eight years old, clambered onto the dock behind Flounder's Chowder House.

Two dozen fishing boats (complete with captains) were in their slips, here a Pathfinder, there a Blazer Bay, a Ranger, a Yamaha, and a Mercury, each polished up and looking fine. Three by three, the women, all members of the then year-old angling club Fishin' Chix, climbed briskly aboard their assigned craft. The captains gunned the motors and varoomed a hundred yards out from the shore, waiting for the first annual Pink Rubber Boots Ladies Fishing Rodeo to begin.

Claudia Espenscheid, the founder of Fishin' Chix (fishinchix .com), which also sells women's fishing apparel and equipment and organizes regular angling excursions, was at her home, a shell's throw from the beach, dealing with some last-minute Fishing Rodeo business when the shotgun popped. It signaled the start of the competition, an event arranged to aid a local hospice, and for Espenscheid, a former financial adviser, there could have been no sweeter sound.

The benefit she had been working on nonstop for the previous three months, the benefit that everyone said would attract only twenty or thirty participants because women have zero interest in the sport, the benefit that everyone said would draw no sponsors because "These things take time, Claudia, don't you understand?" was officially on, with more than fifteen sponsors signed up. "When I have an idea and other people say it's not doable," Espenscheid says, "my attitude is 'Just wait and see, buddy.'"

· · · · · ·

The Most Important Things I Did Right

"Following my heart. Recognizing that this is about sisterhood. And fun. And getting out on the water and fishing."

· · · · · ·

In 2005, when Espenscheid, then forty and pulling down a six-figure income at Merrill Lynch, agreed to go on a daylong fishing trip sponsored by a mutual fund wholesaler, she was not exactly bullish on the idea. "I was concerned that I would throw up," she recalls, "and, truthfully, I had written off fishing as a redneck activity." To her surprise, she loved it.

"Going offshore in a big boat isn't only about fishing, it's about adventure," says Espenscheid—who, for the record, caught a 15-pound red snapper that day. She also caught the fishing bug and started heading out to a local dock a few days each week after work to cast her net and to cast about for a way to make this new passion a bigger part of both her personal and her professional life.

Espenscheid conceived of Fishin' Chix not only as a club but also as a pool from which to draw potential clients. The idea was utterly consistent with Espenscheid's MO. During her four years at Merrill Lynch, she put together wine tastings and dinner parties at a downtown Pensacola art gallery to attract new business to the firm. Then, in fall 2004, Hurricane Ivan hurtled into town. Espenscheid's office was destroyed, her neighborhood all but flattened. Her house, although still standing after the storm, sustained more than $400,000 in damage.

For months after the hurricane, Espenscheid and her family camped out at her mother's house. "I had seen nature at its worst," she says. "I wanted to be involved with something that was nature at its best." And, she adds, "I wanted an escape."

Espenscheid began to consider quitting her job. "I knew a lot of what I was feeling was post-traumatic stress," she says. "I can't tell you that only one thing made me want to leave. I just felt that life is too short."

A friend who was also a client encouraged her to take a step back and ask, "Can I picture myself ten or fifteen years from now sitting at this desk and talking to people about investments?'"

The answer was no. To be perfectly accurate, the answer was "Hell, no."

The problem: Espenscheid was the family's sole breadwinner. Her husband, David, a doctor, had undergone a triple bypass six years earlier at age forty-five and ultimately decided to give up his medical practice to become what Claudia gleefully calls a pediatric chauffeur for their daughters, Katarina, now fifteen, and Isabella, fourteen. "David was three when his own father died, and our two girls were very little when he had his surgery," she explains. "It changed our priorities."

Given her financial obligations, "it was extremely scary to make the decision to leave Merrill Lynch," says Espenscheid, who, contradicting the advice she routinely gave clients, liquidated her IRA and nipped at her 401(k) to shake loose $60,000 and later took out a $250,000 line of credit against the value of her house to help grow the business. "We lived on savings," she says. "We put it all on the line with the business."

"My husband and I are pretty big risk-takers when it comes to living life fully," she continues. "I don't mean stupid risk-takers. But we had been through so much, and it was time to embark on a new, fresh, positive endeavor." What sealed the deal was a class field trip to Tallahassee that Espenscheid took with her daughter Katarina a year after Hurricane Ivan. There, in one of the government buildings, she saw a display from the Florida Fish and Wildlife Conservation Commission. "I looked at the statistics, which mentioned that 29 percent of the fishing in the state is done by women," she says. Even more alluring was the research suggesting that the growth of fishing as a sport for women was explosive. "I guess that's when my MBA clicked in. I thought, 'There's a total niche out there.' There was nothing geared to women in apparel or equipment. I'm not a fashion plate, by any stretch, but I wanted to look cute when I went fishing."

To spread the word about Fishin' Chix, Espenscheid called all of her acquaintances, sent out a group e-mail, and put up flyers. She also relied on word of mouth—usually, her mouth. "I'm the sort of person who talks to everyone I see about what I'm doing," she says cheerfully and unapologetically. "I'll talk to strangers in elevators, to people at the next table in a restaurant. It drives my husband crazy. My first question to people is, 'Do you fish?'" If they say no, her second question is, "Do you want to?"

> "Reinvention equaled survival, at that point in my life. Failure was (is) *not* an option!"

While Espenscheid chatted up the Pensacola populace, a fashionista friend got busy designing the club's clothing line, which now includes T-shirts, Swarovski crystal–studded tank tops, shorts, hats, rubber boots, and flip-flops, many with the Fishin' Chix logo, a pink fish with Mick Jagger lips and a bejeweled body. The custom-designed equipment—conceived by Espenscheid with input from Wes Rozier, a fishing guide who consults for her pro bono—includes lures, rods, and reels. "We're going to 'girly-ize' tackle boxes," Espenscheid says. "They're going to have a water-resistant compartment for a cell phone and lipstick. And maybe a mirror."

Going from money management to fishing gear was no big leap, she says. "In my previous life, I was selling financial services. Now I'm selling adventure, excitement, and fun. And I get photos from women all over the country saying, 'I'm wearing your Fishin' Chix shirt, and look at the 60-pound fish I caught!'"

So far, more than two thousand women in forty states have paid $50 each in annual membership dues. New members net a Fishin' Chix hat or visor, a T-shirt, a decal, two pink koozies, and the O-fish-al Fishin' Chix gut rag. Members also get advance notice of the club's tournaments and fishing expeditions—inshore (for speckled trout, redfish, and flounder) and offshore (where red snapper and grouper are likely to be biting).

Back in 2006, when Espenscheid walked into Flounder's Chowder House for the lunch and the awards ceremony after the Ladies Fishing Rodeo competition, she says, "There must have been two hundred people wearing Fishin' Chix hats and shirts." Kids were running around with tournament shirts. Guys were wearing Fishin' Chix visors, tournament participants were carrying Fishin' Chix towels and, in some instances, clutching their catches of the day.

"I felt like, 'Oh, my God. I'm the catalyst for a revolution,'" says Espenscheid. This year, she expects to be able to draw a salary of around $80,000, and she's still working to expand her products' retail presence nationwide and get more exposure.

Now, she says, "People stop me in stores and say, 'Fishin' Chix!' Instead of *me* calling people every day to talk to them about investment opportunities, people are calling me, wanting to be a part of this. There's a camaraderie because of fishing. It doesn't matter if you're a physician or a janitor. You share a common bond. I'm part of something cool, and it makes me so happy."

.... **Claudia's Key Questions to Ask Yourself** ....

- Do I have a "Board of Directors" (successful business people and friends) whom I have asked to review and critique my business plan?
- How will this venture allow me to continually reinvent myself, so that I can stay excited and motivated?

Skills from the Past Can Create a Future
Elinor Griffith

In 2004, Elinor Griffith faced an unwelcome early retirement when the magazine company she worked for began to downsize. "One Monday, poof, no job," she says. At fifty-five, Griffith had been with the same company for thirty years and hadn't seen the end of her tenure coming. "I felt the same stomach-churning uncertainty of a teenager starting out," she says. "It felt really scary."

After three decades, Griffith had grown accustomed to a familiar daily routine and well-defined responsibilities. Unscheduled free time felt daunting. She knew she wanted to work again, but her severance would support her for almost a year, and she decided not to rush into just anything. "I wanted to let it breathe," she says. "I wanted to see who I was when I got rid of this identity that had been stamped on me." She met up with friends she hadn't been able to make time for when she was working. She got involved with her church council. When she couldn't figure out what else to do, she baked bread.

Through her publishing connections, Griffith got some freelance book-editing work, but the projects filled up only half of her time. Some days she'd power walk, catch a train into nearby New York City for an art opening, or practice yoga. "I had a wonderful yoga teacher who talked about risk taking and reaching into your highest self," she says. "The words started to take hold. I began to renew my sense of adventure and possibility." On a whim, she bought a rowboat with a friend. They'd float along the local reservoir, picnicking, and ignore the "no swimming" signs.

The Most Important Thing I Learned

"That pit-of-the-stomach, scared feeling when you're doing something new, really different, is actually good."

Two years later, during a family beach trip, Griffith's daughter, then twenty-four, made a suggestion that surprised Griffith. She had seen a TV show about an American leading culinary trips to Italy and said, "You could do that in France, Mom." Griffith, who had been a political science and French major in college, had spent her junior year in France and worked for her first seven years at the magazine company in French-speaking Montreal. Over the years, she had hosted French exchange students and traveled to France—she'd even rented a house there in the summer of 2004.

Although Griffith spoke the language and knew the country well, going in such an uncharted direction felt too out of character. "The idea caused my stomach to flip," she says. "How would I even begin such an undertaking?"

A few months later, Griffith had a reunion with college girlfriends she had lived with in France. She mentioned her daughter's idea, and they encouraged her to go for it. After all, her twenty-one-year-old son had moved to Paris a year earlier to study at the Sorbonne. "I took my inspiration from my kids," she says. "Be daring. Get into the front seat of your life." She started doing Internet research, and her future became clear when she found a chef in France who ran a cooking school in Provence and hosted groups there. The chef's name was Kathie Alex—a combination of the names of Griffith's daughter and son. "What was the universe telling me?" she asks. "You can't get much clearer guidance than that. Coincidence or not, I knew this had to happen."

In the spring of 2007, she launched Griffith Gourmet, a small customized cooking tour business. She and a group of four women took cooking classes with Alex at La Pitchoune, Julia Child's former rose-covered country cottage in southeast France, where the tiny yellow kitchen still sported stencils showing where the famous chef's pots and pans had hung. They poked around the cobblestone streets of the medieval village of St. Paul, visited

> · · · · · ·
>
> ### The Most Important Thing I Did Right
>
> "I followed my heart into something that I love: France *and* cooking. To that equation I've now added yoga, another of my loves."
>
> · · · · · ·

the Picasso Museum in Antibes, and
sipped champagne in the Michelin-
starred restaurant of the Hotel Martinez,
a hangout for movie stars during the
Cannes Film Festival. "I felt so much satisfaction in helping a group of women
do something that felt different and perhaps scary for them," she says. "I could
see their joy in accomplishing what they
thought never could happen."

Since then, Griffith has hosted one to
two trips a year. In 2010, she added yoga
to the cooking tour itinerary. "It's yoga
with a little bit of butter included," she
says. Although she's only breaking even,
financially, on the tours, she's developed
deep friendships and has come away from the kitchen with new
clarity about life (her favorite insight: innovation plus mistakes
equals new creations). "Cooking speaks to your higher self," she
says. "It has to do with getting out of ruts, evolving, and performing at a more interesting level."

Griffith has developed an ease in trying new things. At home,
instead of agonizing over whether potential publishing projects
and community service opportunities are absolutely perfect
before taking them on, she dives in headfirst. "Now," she explains,
"I say, 'Yes!' whenever I have a chance to."

In 2011, Griffith cowrote a book, *First Thing Every Morning*,
with a motivational speaker and, with another colleague, a coffee-
table book about the oldest church in New York State; she's currently writing her own book, *Salt for Luck, Thyme for Love: Stories
of Uplifting Family Through Food*. And, she says, "My dream of
cooking groups is playing out in ways that I couldn't have fath-
omed in my early days of palm-sweating and planning. My daughter says I look so much younger than I did ten years ago. When

you get out of a cocoon of safety, take more risks, and follow your bliss, you recapture that excitement and that glow. If something doesn't work right, you can correct it the next time."

Elinor's Success Strategy

"We thrive when we keep reinventing ourselves daily, weekly, monthly, and yearly."

The Sheep Farmer
Rebecca Denhoff

For Rebecca Denhoff, who was born and raised near Virginia Beach, Virginia, her contact with farms and animals was limited to stuffed toys and Little Bo Peep books—until she visited a great aunt who lived in the Blue Ridge Mountains. Awestruck by the beauty of the land, she vowed that she'd live in a place like that one day. She was five years old at the time.

Three decades later, she moved to the Blue Ridge area with her husband, a Boston lawyer. By day she worked as a registered nurse, eventually becoming a hospital administrator, and at night she read sheep-care books. Intent on buying a farm, she bolstered her savings with profitable real estate investments.

One day she adopted two orphaned lambs and bottle-fed them for eight weeks. They lived indoors, diapered, until she moved them onto the couple's two-acre property. That was the start of her flock, which grew from year to year. "I was happy as a flea, but my husband was not," she says. Then some farmland she'd long been eyeing became available, and she bought it that day. When she broke the news to her husband after the fact, he gave her a choice: him or the farm. Denhoff didn't hesitate. "The farm," she said. "If I give this up, my spirit will slowly die."

The Most Important Thing I Learned

"I shouldn't have been so blasted independent! Sometimes you need other people. Sometimes my being very independent didn't serve me very well, when I'm trying to get big projects done."

After her divorce, Denhoff kept her day job but fixed up Solitude Farm, a hundred-acre plot with no running water or electricity. She spent $250,000 on a well, a septic tank, fencing, and a barn. In 1996, she moved her twelve sheep onto the land, along with a trailer that became her new home. An experienced nurse, Denhoff gave the animals shots and wasn't afraid to "sew things up," she says. Nearby veterinarians showed her how to deliver and revive lambs and push back prolapsed sheep uteruses.

To prevent coyotes and wolves from threatening her flock, she acquired a Maremma, a dog bred to guard sheep. Then some local men vandalized her property, destroying the solar chargers that powered her electric fence. "They wanted to run me out of here. They'd never seen a woman driving a tractor before," she says with a laugh. "But I had it out with them, and now we get along. When their animals need a vet, they call me first."

· ·

The Most Important Thing I Did Right

"I followed my own conscience, my own path. For instance, when I started a women's retreat here on the farm, people asked, 'Why don't you just do a regular bed and breakfast?' I said, 'Because I live up here by myself, and I don't want strange men coming up here to retreat or whatever else.' I'm living outside the zone of 911, after all. I wanted to do something where I could meet other women and make friends. You just can't do that in a bed and breakfast as easily as you can with women who are coming together. I did what was comfortable for me, as opposed to what may have been more lucrative."

· ·

Today, Solitude Farm is home to sixty Leicester Longwool sheep, twenty head of cattle, and a dozen chickens. Denhoff hired a part-time worker and replaced the trailer with a house, which also brings in income as a retreat for women. Now fifty-seven, she continues to work the night shift as a nurse ("for benefits") and pulls in $30,000 annually from meat, wool, and the retreat (solitudefarmretreat.com). The sheep are Denhoff's passion, though.

During the lambing season, beginning every December, she always has a couple of orphaned lambs running around her house in diapers. "They're clean, and they smell good," she says. "They're easier than puppies. Sheep are peaceful and calming. They're the most Zen-like of animals."

.... **Rebecca's Key Questions to Ask Yourself** ....

- How well do you know yourself?
- Do you have the emotional and financial resources to do whatever you're going to do?
- Do you know what you would really like to do, what you want to accomplish in your life, and what you have an affinity for?
- Is this a temporary passion or a permanent one?
- How well do you stand up to criticism?

Rebecca's Success Strategy

"Know why you're doing it. You spend time and resources and money, and part of your whole soul goes into it. And I swear, if you ain't doin' it for the right reasons, you're going to be an unhappy person."

From Wags to Riches
Mimi Darr

Mimi Darr had been working in human resources and employee relations for eighteen years when, in 2002, she knew she'd had enough. At the time, she was traveling around the country for her company, handing out hundreds of pink slips, face-to-face. "I still remember the eyes of this seventy-five-year-old gentleman who had just lost his wife when I told him we were closing his facility and he no longer had a job," she says. "He just started crying. That was a defining moment for me. The shine of the six-figure salary had lost its luster."

Darr, then thirty-eight, was also in the middle of a difficult divorce, after years of trying to get pregnant had taken its toll on her marriage. Her life was in such upheaval already that she developed a "why not?" attitude toward changing things even more. So when word went around her office that layoffs loomed, she asked her boss to put her on the chopping block.

While she waited for the exit offer, she took training classes to be a life coach and planned her next step as a corporate business consultant. In 2003, she was elated to receive a severance package. During the next two years, she expanded her coaching clientele. In 2005, while working on a project with managers at her former company, she clicked with one of the clients over their joint passion for dogs. On their last day of working together, the client pushed aside her notebook and asked Darr, "What do you think about opening a pet wash together here in Atlanta?" She explained an idea that she had been researching to open a pet "spaw," where owners could get self-service or full-service baths for their dogs. "I told

....

The Most Important Thing I Learned

"How this would challenge the makeup of who I was. I had no idea about the personal areas I needed to finesse or improve, now that I was an employer."

....

her, 'If you are serious, let's not wait,'" says Darr. "Great ideas get buried by inaction."

The women met for three hours the next night. By their second glass of wine, they had the name of their new business: That Dirty Dog (thatdirtydog.com). Six months and two days later, they opened their doors. "With everything we did, it seemed like we were in the flow, and when you're in the flow, things just work," she says. "I had no fear whatsoever." Their opening was covered live by a local TV station, and their phone started ringing off the hook. As word got out, business took off. "We didn't know what we were doing," she says. "But we wanted to learn how to do it and do it really well." Having once worked for the Ritz-Carlton hotel company, she transferred that focus on fine customer service to her new venture.

The Most Important Thing I Did Right

"I had a strategy to survive financially while I paved the road with my business partner: I'd live on my severance package, leadership coaching gigs I'd lined up, and six months of extra savings I'd socked away when I knew I might be adjusting to a lower income."

Darr juggled That Dirty Dog with her consulting business, spending long hours at the shop between coaching calls. The first six months were rough as she learned to mesh with her new business partner. "We started out as acquaintances," she says, "and when you own a business with someone, you're practically married. We walked into it blindly." Darr discovered that her very direct approach didn't work with her more sensitive partner. "I can be aggressive and feisty," she says. "Opening That Dirty Dog gave me no option but to look at myself. I had to learn how to change." The two women soon figured out how to use their strengths to complement each other. "On stressful days, we'd glance over, laugh, and say, 'At least we're not wearing panty hose.'"

Darr's income was half of what her salary had been. A one-time über-shopper, she cut back on lavish spending. "Before I left my corporate job, my stress release was to go to Saks Fifth Avenue or Macy's, spend $500, and have no problem with that." She reexamined the clothes in her closet, many of which still had tags on them from her past-life shopping sprees. "My materialism and drive for money changed significantly," she says. "I wasn't making the take-home bacon like before, but the wealth came in the form of knowledge, confidence, creativity, and other intangibles."

· · · · · · · ·

The Most Surprising Thing about My Reinvention

"What started as a passion to work with animals soon morphed into more than simply a grooming 'spaw' for dogs; it is now also a life university for twenty-one employees."

· · · · · · · ·

She spent so much time at That Dirty Dog that in 2006, she stopped consulting. A year later, she and her partner opened a branch in a second location. Each year, their revenues increased, and they were named Best Pet Grooming Facility in the area. "Without realizing it, we had built a recession-proof model," she says. When the economy tanked, clients who could no longer justify grooming costs came in to use the self-service pet wash more frequently. "It was wonderful not having to lay anybody off," she says.

Darr started the pet spa because she was crazy about dogs, but the experience soon morphed into something bigger. She became intertwined with her customers, grieving with them over the loss of beloved pets or offering financial breaks when clients faced tough times. She also found herself serving as a role model and a confidante to her employees. "My employees are my family," she says. "Though I never had children of my own, this was God's way of saying that I definitely do. I had no idea That Dirty Dog would end up being a vehicle of awakening for me, about the effect I can have on so many people's lives. So many of us have preconceived notions about how we think life is going to turn out. I never saw any of this coming."

················· **Mimi's Key Questions to Ask Yourself** ··············

- Do I have a cadre of people who believe in my reinvention and will be there through the good and the bad?
- Do I have the mental stamina to manage the tough weeks and months, maybe years?
- Will the sought-after outcome of my reinvention result in my lamp burning bright, meaning will I be a better person and therefore better for the world?
- Am I cheerful and optimistic and do I laugh a lot (because I'll need to draw on that daily)?
- What is the intention behind my reinvention—is it free of bitterness, revenge, jealousy, or any other negative motive?

The Beekeeper
Marina Marchese

Marina Marchese was working as a designer and the creative director of a giftware company when her metamorphosis began. She had created a queen bee character named RosieB for her greeting card line. A neighbor saw her illustrations, and the neighbor's husband soon invited Marchese to tour the hives he kept in his backyard. Excited, she donned a beekeeper's hat and veil and braced herself for fierce buzzing and sharp stings. Yet when the neighbor pulled out one of the honeycomb frames, all that she heard was a gentle hum. "The bees seemed content and calm," Marchese says. Carefully, she reached into a cell to sample the raw honey. Divine, she thought. Maybe I could keep a hive.

Marchese had long desired a closer-to-nature lifestyle. That's what had led her to buy a home in the semirural Connecticut town of Westport. But the hour-and-a-half commute to her New

York City job had prevented her from fully exploring the possibilities of her land. There simply wasn't any extra time. Keeping bees seemed easy enough, however. "You don't need to be there every day," she says, and she envisioned doing most of the work on weekends. She ordered a beekeeper starter kit from a catalog for $125, plus a colony of twenty thousand bees for $72 from a Georgia bee farmer. When the kit, with its precut wood and nails, was delivered, she was ready with a hammer. "As a kid, I built tree houses," she says.

With her design work still paying the bills, Marchese devoted her leisure time to learning all that she could about apiculture. She read books, watched videos, and joined a local bee club. She found out how to rescue a hive when the bees "swarm" (abandon their nest) and how to "requeen" the hive if her queen bee disappeared. She fell in love with her honeybees, sitting in the sun to sketch them and marveling at the way they carried pollen balls and communicated through different "dances."

. . . . . .

The Most Important Thing I Learned

"Fearlessness and confidence."

. . . . . .

Two years later, Marchese had four hives ready for her first honey harvest. She'd planned to give away the wildflower honey, but after tasting it and thinking about how hard she and her bees had worked, she decided to turn her hobby into a business. Marchese created a label for her company, Red Bee (redbee.com), and began to experiment in her kitchen with products such as lip balm. (Her recipe, passed down by generations of beekeepers' wives, is, Melt beeswax and olive oil in a double boiler, whisk in honey, and add two drops of peppermint essential oil.) That summer she set up a table at a farmers' market, with jars of honey, beeswax skin-care products, and candles. On a good day, however, she usually made only $40. Disheartened, she thought, Guess I can't quit my day job yet.

Then, in 2006, a mysterious phenom-enon called colony collapse disorder destroyed many commercial hives. As the artisanal honey market began to swell, Red Bee started to get regular orders from upscale New York City restaurants and retailers. With the extra business, Mar-chese finally ditched her city work and wrote a memoir, *Honeybee: Lessons from an Accidental Beekeeper*, which was published in 2009. Today she grosses about $100,000 annually. "I love that I can combine my artistic background with beekeeping and nature," she says. "I've created a business that sustains my finances—and my soul."

· · · · · ·
The Most Important Thing I Did Right

"Being myself. Just listening to my creative spirit, and doing what I felt was right for me."

· · · · · ·

·············· **Marina's Key Questions to Ask Yourself** ··············

- Can I fly solo? A lot of people romanticize having their own businesses, working out of their homes, and doing exactly what they like. But can I live without a paycheck every Friday?
- Can I take chances?
- Do I feel confident?
- Am I a self-starter? Can I get up in the morning and make those phone calls and answer those e-mails without being distracted, without saying, "I'm going out to lunch with my girlfriends," or "I'm going shopping," or whatever?

Marina's Success Strategy

"Trust your instincts. Women, we never trust our instincts, and I think that's one of the biggest gifts I've given myself: to trust myself as a woman."

2

❧

Tapping Your Creativity

Turning your talent into a flow of income can be challenging. That's why many women with a gift for art, fashion, writing, or music end up in non-artistic careers which they may not especially enjoy. In this chapter, women find ways to reconnect with their creativity and use it to jumpstart their work life, rediscover a sense of purpose, and even heal from tragedy.

Fashion Saved Her Life
Jane Pennewell

Jane Pennewell's world began to unravel as she approached her fortieth birthday. By the time she was forty-two, in 1985, she'd had four surgeries in four years—one for TMJ (temporomandibular joint) problems, one for a nodule on her thyroid, and two for severe endometriosis that left her with monthly cramps that were as painful as childbirth. In addition to her physical challenges, she also endured emotional hardships. After twenty-three years of marriage, she and her husband divorced. Within months, their seventeen-year-old son, Scotty, was killed in a car accident.

Pennewell was devastated and sought normalcy by returning to her job at a Fortune 500 company. Yet as the months went on, her body, already vulnerable from the string of surgeries, shut down. Her legs felt so weak that she couldn't climb stairs. "At the end of the workday, I would go to the car and sleep," she says. "I had no energy even to drive home."

After a battery of tests, doctors diagnosed Pennewell with cytomegalovirus. "My immune system was shot," she says. Forced to leave her job and go on disability, she found that she couldn't get out of bed on most days and was overcome by pent-up grief over her son's death. "I went into a state of depression to the point that I didn't want to live," she says.

For the next six months, a friend came over almost daily to make her get up and get dressed. They'd pull together a flattering outfit and do her makeup, using techniques they'd learned a few years earlier while taking training classes in color and image consulting. "We would play dress up," says Pennewell. As the weeks went on, her friend convinced her to leave the house and go somewhere for lunch, which gave Pennewell a chance to interact with outsiders. She got a lift when strangers smiled at her or complimented her outfit or when she caught a glimpse of her well-dressed reflection in a window. "The world seemed a little more hopeful," she says. "Looking good made me feel better. It was so healing."

As she recovered emotionally, Pennewell began to improve physically when she started on an intravenous protocol drug to

. . . .

The Most Important Thing I Learned

"That you can survive anything if you have faith, friends, and a purpose in life."

. . . .

boost her immune system. She lay in bed getting treatments and thought about the possibility of going back to work. She decided to start her own color and image consulting business. Having already had formal training, she believed that making others over would prove meaningful for her. "I knew the impact because I had experienced it myself," she says. "I wanted others to feel that same joy. I realized it was more than a business. It was a mission to make people happier." In 1986, with an IV in her arm, she started JP Image Consulting (www.jpimageconsulting.com).

Pennewell took business classes and met her first client at a networking meeting. While shopping for clothes to outfit the client for an upcoming business conference, Pennewell met her next customer—in the store's dressing room. Her client pool grew quickly through word of mouth and came to include top executives, politicians, and journalists. She worked with budgets of $500 up to $20,000 to build a compact, high-quality wardrobe with colors and textures to flatter each individual. Clients credited her with helping them feel more confident, secure promotions, and even find love. "It gave me a whole new lease on life to know that I was making a difference in other people's lives," she says.

Pennewell shopped with clients in New York City, Paris, Italy, Berlin, China, and Bahrain. In 1998, she expanded her business to include home décor. As the years went on, many of her early clients became her closest friends. She supported them through personal crises, helping one friend choose wigs when she went through cancer treatment and another cope with the death of her husband. "My own life experiences have made me feel compassionate about events in other's people's lives," she says. "When I work with clients, I really take the time to sit down and talk, listen, and understand where they are coming from."

In 2004, Pennewell faced another family tragedy of her own. She had just finished shopping with a client at Neiman Marcus when she got a phone call: her twenty-two-month-old grandson had drowned. The client drove her home and called several other clients who came over and made reservations for her to fly to Florida the next day. Some even came to the funeral. "I had the most wonderful friends who stepped up to the plate," she says. "It was amazing."

Today, Pennewell still gets monthly infusions of the drug that boosted her immune system. For New Year's, she hosts an annual party for clients where the women share poster boards they've filled with positive words and images of how they'd like to live their lives. Pennewell keeps her past posters on hand so she can review them. "In all of the tragedies I remained positive," she says. "The sadness that is a part of me today also reminds me to seize every moment to live life to the fullest because it can all be taken away in the blink of an eye. For twenty-five years I've helped people reshape their wardrobes, their homes, and sometimes their lives. You can say it's just fashion or color, but it also helps the soul. By making a difference in other people's lives and living my life well—with passion and purpose—I feel as if I am honoring my son."

················ **Jane's Key Questions to Ask Yourself** ···············

- What does your heart say?
- What does your head say?
- If your heart and head aren't saying the same thing, can you somehow reconcile the two and be able to provide for yourself and your family?

A Headhunter Rediscovers Painting
Linda Holt

As a graduate student getting her master of fine arts at the University of Pennsylvania, Linda Holt went to the studio and painted all day. Yet when she graduated in 1976, art didn't seem like a viable career path. She went to work for Lord & Taylor in New York City as an assistant buyer, a fast-paced executive-training job. "It was the genesis of my corporate spirit and my entrepreneurial soul," she says. "I loved every minute of it."

She transferred to Boston where, in 1980, she left the retail business and became an executive recruiter, finding employees for companies such as Nabisco and Ralph Lauren. She worked for a large firm with two hundred offices nationwide and became one of the top headhunters. At her next job, "One of my bosses told me I could sell ice to the Eskimos because of my enthusiasm," she says. "I wasn't afraid to cold-call anybody."

Still, any time Holt was in the vicinity of a museum or a college campus, she found herself lingering in front of paintings or the art department. "I always missed painting," she says. "It was my first love." But her career kept her too zapped of time and energy for artistic pursuits. "I dabbled in art, nothing more than that," she says.

In 1988, she was laid off. Instead of looking for another executive recruiting job, she started working part time at an antiques store and discovered that she had time to devote to painting. She also had the guts. "At this point, I knew I could sell anything," says Holt. "Once I had that confidence, everything else fell into place." While going through old photographs to find something to paint, she stumbled on five snapshots of exotic, oversize koi fish that she had taken while on a business trip to Maui. "Their vibrancy mesmerized and inspired me," she says. She pulled out her easel and supplies and did an oil wash on paper, capturing the underwater movement of the bright red, gold, and orange fish

· · · · · · · · · ·

The Most Important Thing I Learned

"How valuable the skills I developed working in previous positions could be in a completely different career. I didn't realize how useful I'd find the marketing, organizational, and sales skills I honed as a headhunter to be in my career as an artist."

· · · · · · · · · ·

in the dark lagoon water. Through the help of a friend, she sold the work right away.

Holt spent her days painting, researching galleries, networking with dealers, and marketing. "My life as an artist began to evolve, taking shape one stroke at a time," she says. The corporate world where she had spent decades of her life now wanted her paintings to hang in lobbies and company boardrooms, which led to exposure and credibility. "The koi fish is supposed to bring happiness and good luck," says Holt. "People loved those paintings. They seemed to strike some deep, resonant chord." In 1995, she began showing her work at the Beth Urdang Gallery on high-profile Newbury Street in Boston. In the first newspaper review of her work, the *Boston Globe* called her "a painter to watch." The timing was right. "I don't think I was ready for it right out of college," she says. "I needed to be seasoned, more mature."

Holt loved painting koi, but she didn't want to be one-dimensional as an artist. On a whim, in 1997, she painted Pinky, her cocker spaniel, who was always with her in the studio. When her dog groomer saw the painting, she asked Holt to paint her dog, Jerrie. Another friend asked her to paint her Rhodesian ridgeback, and another, her Norwich terrier. Soon strangers were finding Holt through word of mouth and commissioning her to paint their dogs, too. Before painting a new dog, Holt spent time with the pet to get to know its personality, did an extensive photo shoot, and painted from the pictures and memory. "Once I have the eyes I've got the soul, and I go from there," she says. "So many people have said I have captured their dog's essence."

. . . . . .

The Most Important Thing I Did Right

"I believed in myself."

. . . . . .

. . . . **My Biggest Mistake** . . . .

"Assuming I wouldn't make mistakes!"

Twenty-three years after an ancient Asian fish serendipitously shaped her resurrection as a painter, Holt continues to get joy out of bringing to life the koi's vibrant colors, dancelike movements, and tranquil environment. Today her paintings hang in galleries, exhibitions, and the offices of more than three dozen corporations, and she's been commissioned to paint twenty dogs and counting. Holt's private commissions have expanded her repertoire to include new subject matter, including portraits of dog *owners* with their dogs; soon, she expects to be painting a portrait of a horse.

Now, at sixty-three, she's working on building her reputation beyond Boston (see her work at lindaholt.com). "I feel good about what I've done, but I have always been very driven, and I have more that I want to do," she says. "It has always been important to me to bring beauty to people. I read somewhere, 'Don't die with a song still in you.' If you have a talent, it's your obligation to share it."

From Entrepreneur to Best-Selling Novelist
Karen Quinn

In 2001, when she was forty-five, Karen Quinn was unexpectedly laid off after working for fifteen years in advertising at American Express. This didn't cause a financial crisis; her husband was a lawyer at a brokerage firm, and she received a substantial severance package. Still, she says, "I was devastated. I remember thinking, I've had this job for so long. How am I ever going to do anything else?" Then she realized she did have one qualification that could translate into paying work: she had gotten her kids accepted into private schools in Manhattan.

To most parents, that doesn't sound like a major accomplishment, but anyone going through the process in New York City knows that competition for spots is unbelievably tight. "You feel so judged," Quinn says. "I hated the experience. I thought, If I can help people through this and make it better for them, maybe there's a business in it."

She paired up with another mother at her children's school, and together they got the operation up and running. After a couple of years, though, Quinn could no longer stand the drama and the excess she witnessed. She remembers one woman, a single mother, who hired an actor to pretend to be her husband as she went through the process. "It worked," Quinn says, "but the next fall she had to pretend to go through a divorce." On another occasion, Quinn was helping a little girl cram for an entrance exam when the child held up her hands and said, "Stop! Can't you see I'm only four?"

Quinn sold her share of the company to her partner and started to cast about for another career. She had always fantasized about being a writer, and it occurred to her that she had a lot of juicy material from her school adventures. "*The Nanny Diaries* had just come out," she says, "and I figured, well, that was a best-seller, maybe I can write one, too."

. . . .

The Most Important Thing I Learned

"The learning never ends. You can't just say 'I've reinvented myself and I'm done.' It's all a journey. You're going to go in one direction, and it will take you somewhere you never expected to be."

. . . .

. . . . **My Biggest Mistake** . . . .

"When I sold my first book, I had a lot of different publishing houses trying to buy it, and I went with the one that offered me the most money—instead of the one that had published a similar book and had done fabulously well with it. I should have gone with the house that had the experience, as opposed to the higher-paying one. Even though my first book did very well, I think it would have done even better had I done that. But I didn't know enough about the publishing industry."

The Most Important Thing I Did Right

"I followed my heart in terms of what strongly interested me. Following my heart and following my passion have always led me to things that I'm excited to get up every day and work on. Even after I wrote my fourth novel, I had a desire to write a nonfiction book, *Testing for Kindergarten,* because I felt as if I had all of this knowledge inside me that I wanted to share. I'd never done nonfiction before. I wasn't an expert. I wasn't a PhD. I was a parent who had a passion for the subject. I wrote the book anyway because I was so interested in it. That took me to the website because I wanted to help the parents who were e-mailing me. Wherever my heart opened up, I just went in that direction."

She and her husband agreed that she would work on the manuscript for three months before looking for another job. So she sat in front of her computer for ten hours a day, plugging away on a humorous story about a woman who—you guessed it—gets fired from the corporate world and starts a private-school consulting firm. As it happened, a friend of Quinn's had a connection to the *Nanny* editor, so when Quinn finished a draft, she called her. "The editor had me drop off the book at her company's mail room," Quinn recalls. "There were bins and bins of books—thousands of manuscripts people had sent in that were all being returned with rejection letters. For the first time I thought, Maybe I won't get published after all."

The editor initially rejected the manuscript, but she did recommend that Quinn make the main character more likable. It took Quinn another month to do the rewrite. When she finished, she told the good news to her babysitter, who turned out to have hosted play dates for the son of a literary agent. The agent took Quinn to lunch, and before the check arrived, the woman had agreed to represent her. Around the same time, Quinn's husband mentioned the book to one of his acquaintances—who turned out to have edited the book *The Devil Wears Prada*. "I sent her the manuscript," Quinn says. "When she e-mailed to say she'd read it, loved it, and wanted to publish it, that was truly one of the most exciting moments of my life."

Her agent set up an auction for the book, and in September 2004, almost six months after Quinn started writing, the novel sold for a price in the mid six figures. *The Ivy Chronicles* was released in the spring of 2005 and became a national best-seller; Sarah Jessica Parker has signed on to play the lead in a movie version. Quinn,

. . . .

The Most Surprising Thing about My Reinvention

"It's led me to meet the most interesting people. When you're in this place of reinvention, and you're excited about what you're doing, it just opens up doors and new people walk in."

. . . .

meantime, has published three other novels—*Wife in the Fast Lane*, *Holly Would Dream*, and *The Sister Diaries*—as well as a nonfiction book, *Testing for Kindergarten*, a practical guide that prepares children for kindergarten testing. Last year she launched a website called testingmom.com, for parents who want support and strategies to help their children ace school admission tests.

"A lot of people didn't believe I could do it at the beginning," says Quinn, who now lives in Miami. "You have to listen to that inner voice that says, Yeah, *I can*. You may end up somewhere you never could have imagined."

How a Beading Class Set Her Free
Pam Older

When Pam Older was an art major in college, she talked her way into a job at a small jewelry store that wasn't hiring. During her year there, she learned from the artisans. Inspired, she set up a workbench in her basement and sold her creations at craft fairs to help pay off school loans.

After graduation, she put jewelry making behind her when she moved to New York City and landed a production job at a magazine. During the next twenty-three years, she worked her way up to senior management, eventually heading production for *Time* magazine and the *New Yorker.* "I had a very big salary and generous perks," she said. "I always considered myself a creative person deep down, but I had a nose for business." She loved her work, but as the years went on, she became disillusioned with the daily grind and office politics. She longed to have more time with her two teenagers. In 1999, she decided to quit. "It was an agonizing decision, but I was just so miserable," she says.

The Most Important Thing I Learned

"That I could develop my craft to a professional level. I knew I had a certain aesthetic, but I had a long way to go, and I didn't know how long it would take to get there. And I didn't know how many ancillary expenses there would be (labor, insurance, supplies, printing, professional services, website, etc.)!"

The following year, she says, after a family vacation in Italy, her husband of nineteen years dropped a bomb. He wanted a divorce. Older became depressed, cried constantly, and couldn't eat. "I fell apart," she says. "The divorce practically paralyzed me. I couldn't do much of anything except get up and take my son to school and crawl back into bed." A friend helped her get back on her feet by offering her a job consulting for a publishing company. After that, she tried head-hunting and technology consulting, but none of those paths felt right. "I needed to do something, but I didn't have the passion or the fortitude to go back into a high-powered publishing job," she says.

My Biggest Mistake

"Not being bolder and investing more money in the business. I've never done worse than break even in any year and have gotten my investment back many times over, but I'm still not as confident as I should be about investing more. I'm just now convincing myself that I can afford to grow a bit."

Then, in 2001, she signed up for a beading class at the local high school and felt an instant high. She beaded in every spare moment. "I'd be at the beach, and while my friends were relaxing and drinking wine, I'd be stringing necklaces," she says. She started selling right away, at first to acquaintances and private clients. A few months later, she was on her way to dinner with friends in Manhattan when she spontaneously walked into a boutique and showed the owner the necklace she was wearing. She loved it and wanted to sell it. "She told me, 'Take it off!'" says Older.

The boutique owner put the necklace in her case, sold it, and asked Older for more jewelry. After that, Older cold-called and sold jewelry to stores wherever her life took her, such as Brookline, Massachusetts, where she was visiting a friend, or West Hartford, Connecticut, where she stayed with relatives. She didn't have enough hands to keep up with all of her design ideas, so she advertised for art interns through the Youth Employment Service at a local high school.

In 2005, another bomb dropped: Older learned that she had breast cancer. Her mother had died of the disease when Older was seven, so she was on guard and detected it early. Through fatigue-filled days of surgery, chemotherapy, and radiation, she continued to develop Pam Older Designs. "Some of the days following chemo I would work in my bathrobe because I was so exhausted," she says. "The girls who interned for me kept my spirits up and kept my mind somewhere else."

The Most Surprising Thing about My Reinvention

"That I have been able to reap modest financial rewards from a relatively small investment, and that I achieved my goal of being proud of the designs I produce."

The year 2010 was a breakthrough for Older when some of her jewelry was chosen to be in the *Sundance Catalogue*. "Now people know I'm not just another jewelry designer who is selling beads," she says. She has expanded to work with metal and continues to sell in small shops and online (pamolderdesigns.com). She sets up displays at trade shows, craft shows, and charity events and has a wide range of products and price points (from $28 to $1,500) for wide appeal. "All of the things I did in publishing—sales, customer service, design, and production—are at play in my business," she says.

Today, instead of the monetary perks of her former career, she thrives on not having a boss, on buying gorgeous gemstones, and on designing beautiful things that people enjoy. "For twenty-three years, I wasn't painting or drawing or doing anything creative," she says. "I'm in a new realm. I don't have to fit into a mold anymore. I've been able to achieve this on my own terms with my own sensibility."

At fifty-eight, Older says, "I like the freedom. But the most rewarding thing is the feedback I get from people saying how much they like what I do and how many compliments they get. I'll see a woman on the street pass by wearing my jewelry, and I'll smile. *That* is my definition of success."

Pam's Key Question to Ask Yourself

Do you realize that 20 percent of your time may be spent working on your passion and 80 percent on the more mundane things, such as making sales calls, ordering supplies, and collecting money?

Handbags Helped Her Heal
Jayne Dearborn

When her third son was born, Jayne Dearborn left her job creating corporate employee health promotion programs to stay home with the children she calls her three amigos. "It was a happy time, for sure," she says. "I was consumed with being a mom." Three years later, in 2000, she took her middle son, Max, to the doctor for some constipation issues, and the specialist felt an enlarged spleen. Max was diagnosed with leukemia and after seven difficult months lost his battle with the disease. Dearborn, then forty-one, was emotionally crushed. She couldn't walk into his bedroom. "I was in so much grief and pain that I had checked out, floating through my days in a fog," she says. "Everything I had known about life, my sense of safety, no longer existed."

It took almost five years for Dearborn to feel ready to embrace life again. She felt as if she had to start over. "I kept asking myself: *What is my purpose? Why am I here? What excites me?*" she says. She turned to spiritual books, signed up for a women's triathlon, and took classes in watercolor and pastels. She had never thought of herself as an artist before, but she had loved arts and crafts as a girl and had sewn stuffed animals, pillows, even drapes and tablecloths. "I decided to reconnect with my creativity as a source of healing," she says.

In a small corner of Max's room, Dearborn set up an easel and started to paint. It helped her feel close to him. Following a suggestion in one of her books, *The Artist's Way*, by Julia Cameron, Dearborn went on a solo "artist's

The Most Important Thing I Learned

"I didn't realize that I was starting a reinvention in the beginning. I was trying to find a way to heal from the loss of my son and turned to creativity as an outlet. One of the most important things that I have learned is to trust the process, to believe in myself and that all of our past experiences have made us who we are today."

date" to find and nurture her creativity. For her date, she chose to visit a fabric store. "When I walked in and saw all of the gorgeous fabrics, I felt a sense of joy I hadn't felt in a long time," she says. "I felt like a kid again." She thought of a small handbag with a handle that she'd seen her friend carrying. She felt inspired to try to make one herself and walked out of the store carrying a load of fabric.

Clearing away more space in Max's room, Dearborn sketched, made patterns, and sewed a few small silk bags with beaded handles. It felt therapeutic. "The work was an outlet, other than being with my grief," she says. When friends saw the one-of-a-kind purses and wanted to buy them, she made more. Within a few months, she was selling the bags at local trunk shows. The feedback was so positive that she decided she had a business in the making. "A big motivation was that by sharing my story, I could give hope to others about overcoming tragedy," she says. She hired a seamstress to help with patternmaking and sewing. Even though the selling part of the project scared her, she met with boutique owners to share her collection.

At times, Dearborn felt deflated by the huge learning curve she faced and the difficulty of getting stores interested in her bags. "I felt as if I was working harder than I had ever worked in my life," she says, "and I wasn't seeing the fruit of my labor." One day she seriously considered quitting and prayed for guidance. That night Max came to her in a dream. "It was his little face and his little voice saying, 'Mommy, don't give up. Keep on going,'" she recalls. As Dearborn persisted on her purse-making path, she says, Max showed himself in other ways. Years earlier, Dearborn's good friend had had a dream about Max that involved blue butterflies. Dearborn began to see blue butterflies everywhere: on a calendar in the fabric store, all around her at an aquarium exhibit, in garden art peeking from the dirt that she stepped on when she went for a walk. Once, as she was driving and mulling over whether she was making the right decision, a car pulled in front of her with Max's birth date on the license plate.

Two years after starting her company, Dearborn decided to create a nonprofit to raise research funds to fight the aggressive form of childhood cancer, acute myeloid leukemia (AML), that Max had faced. "My husband thought I was crazy. He said, 'Doing a business is enough. How can you think about doing a nonprofit on top of that?' I told him, 'We need to suck it up and make this happen.'" They created Max's Blue Butterfly (bluebutterfly campaign.org) and began to donate a percentage of her handbag profits. In 2010, Max's Blue Butterfly held its first fund-raising event, a golf outing and a silent auction, and raised more than $40,000. After extensive investigation, Dearborn and her husband handpicked Cincinnati Children's Hospital, where doctors are doing cutting-edge AML research, as the recipient.

Today, Dearborn's little fabric purses with beaded handles have evolved into manufactured all-leather handbags sold in boutiques across the country and online at jaynemax .com. She has also just signed on with "Accessories That Matter," a showroom on New York City's Fifth Avenue; this will be her new headquarters for corporate sales. Her husband, a twenty-five-year veteran in the technology business, left the corporate world to become the company's VP of sales and chief operating officer. Dearborn has transformed Max's room into her studio. His 8 × 10 photo rests on her studio windowsill, and she still feels connected to him when she's in there alone, creating.

· · · · · · · · · ·

The Most Important Thing I Did Right

"I persevered! Part of what has helped me the most is my belief that Max is still with me on this journey. Our relationship continues, it's just in a different form."

· · · · · · · · · ·

·········· **My Biggest Mistake** ··········

"I didn't trust my own intuition enough."

· · · · · · · ·

The Most Surprising Thing about My Reinvention

"I have gone from barely surviving to thriving! I have rediscovered myself and realized that I have strengths and abilities that I did not know were there."

· · · · · · · ·

Ten years after Max's passing, Dearborn's goals are to grow the company internationally and to help fund AML research. "It's more than a business and a nonprofit—it's about serving a purpose," she says. "For me, my reinvention was about finding myself, putting myself out there in the world again, and becoming the person God intended me to be. In a way, I feel like it's the second half of my life. If we can make a difference in these kids' lives and keep their families from suffering, I would feel as if I have served my purpose. I wish I could have gotten to this place with Max here, but I believe this was the way it was supposed to unfold."

Jayne's Success Strategy

"I don't see obstacles as a reason to stop."

Giving Up Money for Music
Kim Cameron

"Music has always been my true passion," says Kim Cameron, forty-four. She was the lead singer in a high school band, and, later, a backup singer for a group that regularly performed in Washington, D.C. Fresh out of Wichita State University with a journalism degree, she went into radio. "Then I stumbled into information technology, making training videos." The monetary rewards kept growing, along with her IT expertise. At her last job, she made more than $200,000 a year. "Once I got a taste of the good life, with my corporate career, I was too insecure to leave it," she says.

Then, in March 2007, her brother-in-law was diagnosed with liver cancer. Overwhelmed with emotion, Cameron wrote her first song, "Never Forget," which launched her transformation into a full-time singer-songwriter. People who heard the song were so encouraging that Cameron realized she had a real talent. Fourteen months later, she'd pulled together a repertoire of songs, a band called SideFX (a play on "side effects" used in recorded music), and a business plan. In 2008, she quit her IT job. It was hard to walk away from the money, she says, but "if you're going to pursue your dream, you should do it 100 percent."

She hired a promoter, a website developer, a public relations person, and an executive assistant. During the first few months, she would often run *Rocky*-style up the steps in front of the Lincoln Memorial to burn off her anxiety. "Sometimes I would break down in tears, thinking, What have I done?" Yet by February 2009, performing for active servicemen and military veterans in New York City, she looked every bit the confident, sexy blues-rock star. She introduced her song "My Hero," telling them about her conversation with a soldier who had just returned from two tours in Iraq. She found his story heart-breaking, and this song was her response. "His courage and strength/Kept us safe," she sang. "I'll still call him my hero."

· · · · · · · · · ·

The Most Important Thing I Learned

"To go with my gut. In the last few years I've found that if something doesn't quite feel right, it usually isn't. "

· · · · · · · · · ·

·········· **My Biggest Mistake** ··········

"Trying to produce my own album. I'm not a producer. If I had just stuck to songwriting and gone directly to a good producer, I could have saved about $40,000. That was a very expensive lesson. I think everybody's got a role, and now I'm really comfortable with mine."

The next month, she celebrated the debut of her first album, *Contradictions*, at the legendary Blues Alley Jazz and Supper Club in Washington, D.C. ("a genre-shifting album that seamlessly introduces an intoxicating blend of late night jazz, smooth blues, catchy funk, easy rock, and gentle groove-driven pop," raved one critic).

Today, Cameron's songs are played on more than a hundred radio stations and on Sirius—and her brother-in-law is cancer-free. She sells her CD, as well as SideFX T-shirts, caps, and ring tones, on her website, sidefxband.net. She is working on licensing her music and has toured the United States. "I could have done this before, but I didn't have the confidence," she says. She has a three-year plan to help her turn a profit. Getting just one song produced, she says, requires $5,000, not including marketing. "I don't need to be Madonna to make a living," she says. "There's a lot of room for women like me."

· · · · · · · · · ·

The Most Surprising Thing about My Reinvention

"I've learned how to do things that I never thought I was capable of. While I've always been a performer of some kind, I'm really out there now. I mean, *really out there.* I never thought I could do that."

· · · · · · · · · ·

············ **Kim's Key Questions to Ask Yourself** ···············

- What is your true passion?
- Can you reinvent yourself on your own two feet? People don't like change, so if they see you change, they'll want to hold you back to what they knew you as before, even if they support the change.
- Are you ready for disappointment? Reinvention will turn your world upside down. You will get disappointed. You will get discouraged. And you're going to fall down. I've fallen down so many times, I have scars on my knees.

Kim's Success Strategy

"Lay out some goals—not huge ones, but baby-step goals so you can have small victories along the way to keep yourself motivated."

She Ditched the Corner Office
Lalita Tademy

In the early 1990s, Lalita Tademy, then in her forties, was earning in the mid six figures as a vice president at Sun Microsystems, a multibillion-dollar computer company in Silicon Valley. On a typical day, she'd rise at 5:30 AM and commute thirty-five minutes to work. There she would endure a crush of back-to-back meetings, constant phone calls, and as many as 150 e-mails—all while cramming down lunch at her desk and dealing with endless logistics—until she left the office nearly twelve hours later. Dinner would consist of prepared meals delivered in plastic containers to her front step. Often she was so exhausted and so hungry that she just stood at her kitchen counter to eat, then dropped the empty containers back on her front step to be picked up. She was single but not dating. Once a three-times-a-week racquetball player, Tademy no longer even knew where to find her racquet. She gained forty pounds.

So, in 1995, she quit her job.

"I'd loved it for a really long time," she says. "I loved doing deals. I loved the challenges and proving the impossible could be done. But it was no longer feeding me. Something in the back of my mind said, 'This is not enough.'" After a career that had taken her from Philip Morris to Xerox to Sun, from New York to Los Angeles and back to the Bay Area, where she grew up, she could have scaled back or taken a leave. In her heart, however, Tademy knew that she had to make her move in such a way that there could be no escape back to corporate life. She had a financial cushion for three years, but she allowed herself only one year to take a deep breath and find a new direction. "I made a contract with myself that I wouldn't take any work, no matter which head-hunter called or what opportunity came up," she says. If she couldn't think of something else to do, she figured she would then have two years to find the right job.

Of course, what had felt like a sensible decision on her final Friday at work was absolutely terrifying when Monday rolled around, and she woke up to a bafflingly empty schedule. She began to phone the people she wanted to reconnect with and found that (no surprise) they weren't available in the middle of the day. "Suddenly," she says, "I had to find something to do with eighty hours a week." What emerged from Tademy's daunting new leisure was time to think. She had always been fascinated by her family's history in a small Louisiana town called Colfax. She started spending time at her local branches of the National Archives and the Mormon Family History Center and along the way amassed roughly a thousand documents—land deeds, census records, birth certificates, and newspaper articles—that informed her about the generations of slaves and slave owners, massacres and injustices, repression and ascension that formed her family's history. As she read the documents, she says, "The stories started to pop out and dovetail with the things I had heard as a child."

· ·

The Most Important Thing I Learned

"I knew how difficult it is to achieve balance, but I'm not sure that I appreciated fully *how* challenging it is. One thing that I wanted to do with my reinvention was to open myself up for experiences that I knew very little about, such as having a personal life, but I didn't appreciate how overwhelming the urge would be to continue with my same pattern."

· ·

In the 1950s, Tademy's father, Ted, had formed a loose association of five African American families and purchased land, through a white front buyer, in a white suburb of Oakland, California. His intention had been to build houses for each of the newcomers, but his own family, the first to make the move, was shunned. The new neighbors were so resistant to the integration of their town that they pooled their money and offered to buy back the land—at a higher price than Ted Tademy's association had paid. He declined the offer. "We were the lone black family there for a while, and it was very tough," Lalita Tademy says. "The kids I made friends with were constantly being snatched away because their parents forbade them to play with me. I found that books were my friends."

Tademy went back to that childhood love of stories and, using her stacks of research, put together a collection of character sketches and family trees. When she presented her first efforts to her niece and nephews, their eyes glazed over. "I thought, If this doesn't pass the test with my own family, I've got to do it in a different form," she says. So she tried fiction as a way of bringing the experiences to life and found that she was drawing on the discipline she'd developed as an executive. "I had a lot of rules," she says. "I had to write for three hours a day, whether it was good or bad, even if I threw it away." After nine months, Tademy had a first draft of a novel she would eventually call *Cane River*, a reference to the area north of New Orleans where her mother's family had come from. When she sent it to literary agents, the rejections—thirteen in all—were crushing. "If I was lucky, the agent would give me a criticism I could use, such as the characters weren't developed or there wasn't sufficient tension," she remembers. After each rejection, Tademy allowed herself twenty-four hours to pout. "I could crawl under the covers, go to back-to-back movies, whatever was required. But at hour twenty-five, I had to be back in my chair, rewriting, so I that could send it out again."

Finally, Tademy realized that she needed some guidance. She

signed up for a course at UC Berkeley Extension with novelist Donna Levin, who was immediately impressed by the uniqueness of Tademy's subject. "When Lalita mentioned that she had found the bill of sale for her great-great-great-great-grandmother," Levin says, "that just made me shudder."

Tademy worked on the book extensively under Levin, who introduced Tademy to her own literary agent, Jillian Manus. With Manus's input, Tademy rewrote the book again; in all, she produced fourteen drafts. When Manus finally sent the manuscript to editors, Tademy says, "I braced myself for the same experience. A ton of rejections."

The manuscript went out to fourteen editors on a Friday, and on Monday the offers started coming in. "There was a bidding war!" Tademy says. It was won by Jamie Raab, the publisher of Warner Books. "I adored it," Raab says of the manuscript she read that weekend. "I loved the characters and wanted to have a part in making sure their stories were read."

······················· **My Biggest Mistake** ························

"I'm not sure I would have thrown myself so headlong into 'I think I'll become a writer now,' but I think it's what I needed to do to come out to a gentler other side. Now I do have the space to make some choices that are not as harsh or dramatic. I just got back from a month in Italy with my husband. We rented a farmhouse in Umbria, and the deal was that for two weeks we would do the tourist thing and for two weeks I would have my head down, and I was going to make tremendous progress on this book. Well, I wrote in the morning, but every afternoon there were hill towns to explore! There was wine to be drunk, and there was food to eat, and there were new things to see. I had to make a very conscious effort while I was there to say, 'Get a grip. When are you going to pass this way again?' You just have to dial it back."

The book was published in 2001 and was doing relatively well—and then Oprah called. Winfrey got right to the point. "She said, 'I think it's an important book, and here are the reasons why,'" Tademy recalls. "We talked for a while, but I was in such shock, I don't remember what I said." *Cane River* became the summer 2001 selection of Oprah's Book Club, and sales skyrocketed.

Today, Tademy is living an entirely different life. She still wakes up early, but not because the alarm clock is ringing. She might spend some time lying in bed, thinking about what she is writing. "Then I figure out what I'm going to do: reading, errands, going to the gym," she says. She likes to clip things in her garden to tidy it up, and she eats out often (no more meals at the kitchen counter). Time with friends, once devoted to work-related problem solving, is now more likely to involve hiking the trails in the nearby hills. "Whatever comes, comes," says Tademy, who still writes for three hours at a stretch but no longer, "because my brain just collapses in on itself." She admits it isn't a very structured life. "The truth is, I don't like to have more than three things in a day to do."

. . . .

The Most Important Thing I Did Right

"Throw myself on the mercy of the universe—not to hold onto taking a sabbatical or hedging my bets. Had I not made a clean break, I don't think I could have ended up with a second career."

. . . .

Those aren't the only changes she has made. Tademy had assumed that she would never marry, but eight years ago she met Barry Williams, a corporate executive, at a friend's house. Williams is "a larger-than-life kind of guy," Tademy says, insisting he's as extroverted as she is introverted. The two married in 2004. During the period she now refers to as "the crazy years," she says, "I had neither the time nor the mental flexibility to develop or nurture a relationship. I'm not convinced that I could have appreciated Barry or found the time to try."

Tademy is realistic about the financial realities of life as a writer. Even phenomenally successful first novels are seldom followed by equally lucrative second books, and this was the case with her next effort, *Red River*, about an 1873 attack on a black community in Colfax. It was published in 2007 and sold only modestly. "I had a huge financial success with the first book, but I will never hit those heights again," she says. Nonetheless, "the second novel's story was something intensely important to me, so I'm grateful I had the chance to do that." She's now at work on a third historical novel.

Changing careers was never about money for Tademy; she knows she would have earned much more if she'd stayed in the corporate world. "I couldn't have gone on in business without what I think of as great soul damage," she says. "Writing is what I know I have to do, regardless of the economic consequences."

·············· **Lalita's Key Questions to Ask Yourself** ··············

- Can you deal with the unknown?
- Are you willing to be happy?
- Can you change from always saying no to saying, "Uh-oh, what do we do now?"

A Dream Built on China
Alexanne Albert

As a struggling single mother and emergency room nurse, Alexanne Albert could never afford to buy heirloom-quality china, but "the beauty of it really touched my heart," she says. One day, she saw some cheap jewelry made with china pieces, and she thought she could do better. She imagined how beautiful the delicate patterns would look if they were set into silver: "I could turn people's broken china cups and plates into accessories they'd want to wear." The problem was, at age forty-seven, she had never designed anything and had no idea whether anyone would buy this kind of unusual jewelry. So she took a one-semester metal arts class at a nearby community college and learned the fundamentals. "Many women get stuck by having too many obligations," she says, "but if you want to have a dream, you have to take time to discover what your dream really is." Her first solo attempt during the course— a silver ring set with blue willow china—showed that she had an eye for design and the skill to execute her ideas. It also kindled her entrepreneurial spirit.

The Most Important Thing I Learned

"You really can't depend on the financial institutions that are in place. I feel as if we've built this business despite the financial obstacles that have come our way. I didn't realize that it's smart to borrow money when you *don't* need it."

The banks, however, did not share her enthusiasm. When she went shopping for a loan, they all told her a version of the same thing: "We don't see how you can make money selling this stuff." She disagreed. So, while still working in the ER, she made the risky decision to cash in a $17,000 retirement plan and then racked up about $50,000 on credit cards, buying used jewelry-making equipment and random pieces of china from flea markets and estate sales. Next, she invited her daughter and daughter-in-law to join the business, which she named China Baroque.

At first, Albert says, "the three of us worked in three different garages in three different Texas cities": Albert in San Antonio, her daughter in Austin, and her daughter-in-law in Houston. They coordinated their work, turning hand-cut china chunks into belt buckles, pins, necklaces, and bracelets, which they sold for $30 to $260 at Junior League benefits throughout the South and at the Houston rodeo. Albert later relocated to Houston, and in 2008 the company grossed in the mid six figures. The women continue

· · · · · · · · · ·

The Most Important Thing I Did Right

"We have a very accommodating customer service policy. If you're ever unhappy with anything about China Baroque—for example, if the custom order didn't turn out the way you thought it would, or the pattern rubs off— we'll exchange, refund, or do it over, whatever it takes to satisfy you."

· · · · · · · · · ·

to sell original pieces at various shows, as well as through their website (chinabaroque.com), and by taking custom orders—many from people who were distressed after breaking a piece of their family's valuable china. "We will do our best to turn your loss into a newfound treasure," promises the site.

Until August 2010, Albert still worked two twelve-hour shifts each week as an ER nurse in order to keep her health insurance. Now fifty-nine and retired from nursing, she devotes all of her time to China Baroque. "I've always been an optimist, and now the things I've visualized have come to fruition," she says. "I have the honor of being involved in creating precious memories for families, starting with a dish that someone loved."

· ·

The Most Surprising Thing about My Reinvention

"We really have the means to be independent because of this business. I'm talking about more than financial independence. No one in our company has to beg somebody for a Friday afternoon off to see her child play sports or be in a play. We can be in control of our own time. That's the most valuable thing to us: our time."

· ·

············ **Alexanne's Key Questions to Ask Yourself** ············

- Ask yourself, What's the worst thing that could happen? I asked myself that, and my answer was, I'll lose some money. I decided I could live with that.

- Then ask, What's the best thing that can happen? My answer was that my girls would know what it's like to own a business, which is not an experience that most young women have.

Her New Life Was in the Cards
Kathy Davis

It's a bright Friday morning in Ambler, Pennsylvania. Kathy Davis (kathydavis.com) sits at the head of a conference table, her company's president and creative director crouched on either side of her so that all three can review the designs that kicked off her 2009 product launch. Just in time for Mother's Day, a new line of home accessories (quilts, pillows, vases, and picture frames) featuring Davis's designs hit four thousand gift shops, drugstores, and grocery chains across the country, followed by the publication of her new motivational book, *Scatter Joy*. The following summer, she rolled out a collection of 108 new Kathy Davis–branded greeting cards.

Known for her sunny, nature-inspired watercolors and the unapologetically emotional quotations and verses on her cards, Davis keeps an eye on each element of the business, from plans for the annual stationery trade show in New York to the four-foot-tall store displays. Are her press kits friendly enough? ("I want them to feel personal, not corporate," she says.) Has the blue on one of the e-cards been toned down? ("It was a little too fluorescent," she notes.)

In 2007, despite a cratering economy, Davis's designs generated $15 million in revenue; since then, her retail sales have more than doubled. Her business partner, American Greetings, the giant manufacturer and distributor of "social expression" products, expects Davis to build on that success and hopes her messages will continue to inspire.

With the bravado of the business mogul she's become, Kathy Davis walked through the doors of New York's Jacob Javits Convention Center for the stationery trade show last May. Yet she doesn't forget her thirty-six-year-old self, the one who attended that same event twenty-four years ago clutching an old Godiva chocolate box filled with homemade card designs and a watercolor of the apple tree in her backyard. Paying the $20 artist's entrance fee was a stretch for her, and her confidence hit rock bottom as she took in the hundreds of booths already staffed with designers. She couldn't help but think that her desire to become a professional artist might be a huge mistake.

Ever since she was a child taking art classes, Davis had loved painting and designing, but her passion fell prey to that most common of roadblocks: insecurity. "I was not confident about my ability," Davis remembers. "I sat next to a boy who painted so beautifully." Later, she taught English and science for six years and got married. She earned her master's degree and certification to teach art, but it wasn't enough. "I remember being in class one day, thinking, I want to be sitting with them, not standing up here. I want to be creating."

After two more years, she left teaching and had children, Ben and Katie. At first, Davis thought she could paint during the children's naptime. "But the naps were never long enough," she says.

With no time to work on big acrylic paintings, Davis took up calligraphy. Soon she was using watercolors to illustrate her own writing and creating homemade Christmas cards each year.

Then, when she was thirty-six, her marriage unraveled. Davis realized that she was facing single motherhood and a big mortgage with no income to speak of.

. . . . . .

The Most Important Thing I Learned

"How much time it takes to run the business of the business."

. . . . . .

"Everyone assumed I'd go back to teaching," she says, but she couldn't summon the required passion, so she cobbled together an income from occasional freelance art assignments, designing restaurant menus, and working part time as a graphic designer. At night, she taught calligraphy. She paid her bills, but her crazy routine of waking up at 4 AM to get it all done wasn't sustainable. One day, she went to the grocery store and realized that she didn't have enough money in her wallet or checking account to cover even milk and toilet paper.

A turning point came when she got a call from a friend who'd received some of her homemade Christmas cards. Davis recalls her friend saying, "Girlfriend, you and I need to check out the National Stationery Show. With your talent, you might just find your niche!" The first day of the event, the two of them wandered the floor posing as retailers, hoping to learn about the companies that were hosting booths and what they wanted from artists. "All of the old feelings of not being good enough came back: I felt as if no one needed me, that there was too much competition," Davis says. Yet she returned the next day, determined, her chocolate box filled with ideas and hand-lettered business cards. "I was embarrassed, but I thought my work was a little different," she says. The art directors at the show agreed, especially when they saw her watercolor. "I had thrown it in the bottom of the box, and an art director said, 'Why didn't you show this to me first?' I learned that day that watercolors are softer and more connecting." She'd found her style.

Davis began freelancing for six different card companies and two years later got her big break when one of the larger firms ordered six card designs for $1,800. "That's when I felt like I'd made it," Davis says. It was June 8, 1990, and she was about to turn thirty-nine.

Gradually, Davis became known as that rare designer who could produce original art and messages for cards that really resonated with consumers. Despite working full time creating cards, however, she could barely meet her expenses. To slash costs, she sold her house and moved into a condo.

···················· **My Biggest Mistake** ····················

"Taking other people's advice instead of listening to my gut."

Freed of the financial stress, Davis focused on her career and flourished. During the next dozen years, she licensed her designs to numerous manufacturers. By 2002, Davis, now married to Peter Walts, a publisher whom she'd met at a stationery show, had a line of licensed products that included stationery, scrapbooks, bank checks, calendars, address labels, and gift books.

During this time, she opened a card and gift store at the local mall, but the place gobbled up all of her time and didn't turn a profit. "I had to ask myself, Do I want to be a retailer or a designer?" she says. She made the painful choice to close up shop. From then on, she would never forget to delegate business tasks so that she could focus on designing.

In 2007, Kathy Davis Studios began to discuss a possible partnership with American Greetings, but even with fourteen employees, seven designers, and $15 million in annual revenue, Davis wasn't taking anything for granted. The night before her official pitch meeting at the organization's headquarters in Cleveland, Davis had an attack of the jitters. All that she had to promote herself were posters with a collage of designs representing a mood, a lifestyle, a product line. To Davis, the challenge felt both familiar and scary, like walking into that first trade show all over again.

The next day, however, in front of seventy people, her faith in her message took over. "We are a brand about

···········

The Most Important Thing I Did Right

"Seeking help from other experts for things that are not my expertise. I hired an accountant for the books, a lawyer so that my decisions were grounded in good legal advice, and an administrative person. If you own a business, you continually need to delegate things that are not your core strength."

···········

joyful living. About connecting and inspiring," she said to the group. Afterward, the president told her how impressed they were. "I remember feeling as if it were an out-of-body experience and wondering, Who is he talking about?" Davis says.

Now when she walks into the National Stationery Show, Davis reflects on how different the visit is from that fateful excursion she made years ago. "I'm a late bloomer," she says, "but I finally figured out that there is always going to be someone better than you, and, at some point, you just have to say, That's okay, I still have something to offer."

············ **Kathy's Key Questions to Ask Yourself** ············

- What are you most passionate about? I got the book *What Color Is Your Parachute?*, and the exercises it provides really helped me drill down to what specific things had given me joy over the years, and how to fashion that for myself.
- How patient can you afford to be for that to pay off?
- What are your strengths and weaknesses? Be honest about how you will maximize the first and compensate for the second.
- Are you willing to stay open to possibilities and adjust your path as you need to? Happy surprises will come your way. You need to stay open to them, so that you can take them in a direction you may not have seen.

Write What You Know
Alexandra Kathryn Mosca

As a child, Alexandra Kathryn Mosca always had her nose in a book, whether she was in the backseat of the car, under the covers at bedtime, or outside during recess. She even cut school to go to the library. By high school, she—and everyone around her—knew her destiny was to be a published author. "I didn't dream of a gala wedding and the proverbial white picket fence but of signing my name in a book at the local bookstore," recalls Mosca, fifty-four.

Sticking to her plan, she declared English as her major in college. To help pay for books, she took a job as receptionist at a funeral home. As the months went on, she was given an opportunity to shadow her boss, accompanying him to the health department to file a death certificate or to the morgue to move a body and helping him do cosmetic work on the deceased. "I found it fascinating," she says. It was also a huge challenge. Not only was she facing her fear of death (her mother had died while giving birth to her), but she was also getting an insider's view of a male-dominated profession.

· · · · · · ·

The Most Important Thing I Learned

"How much I like the solitude of writing, and how it gives me a sense of control over my work and the way I spend time."

· · · · · · ·

As Mosca neared graduation, she let go of her writing dream—it seemed too risky—and plunged into the more practical challenge of breaking into a career in funeral service. "At the time, this was one of the most nontraditional careers for women imaginable," she says. "I wanted to be one of the groundbreakers." She went to mortuary school for a year, did an apprenticeship, and took a job at a small funeral home. Five years later, she started her own funeral firm. "I loved it," she says. "Working with grieving clients, I was convinced that I was doing important and meaningful work."

At first, she tried to keep her hand in writing. She wrote a short column with funeral advice for the local paper, but that side gig faded away. She searched for other outlets to offset the heaviness of her work. "Every day is somber," she says. "You have to get away from it." She took acting classes and did some modeling. On a lark, she sent photos to *Playboy*, along with an article about her career, which she hoped the magazine would publish. It didn't publish her writing but did run a revealing eight-page photo spread titled "The Lady in Black." "It was quite shocking to many of my colleagues," she says. "People said, 'You may not work again.'" But she was resolved to remain a funeral director. "I wasn't unhappy with my career or looking to leave the industry. Rather, my experience with *Playboy* was just the glamorous respite I needed from an occupation that can take a huge emotional toll."

As it turned out, Mosca's business didn't suffer, but her experiences made for good journaling material. Her desk was littered with pieces of notepaper filled with daily observations. She didn't intend to use these notes for any greater purpose; note taking was simply a habit that she had developed during childhood. "My notes about my workday were a catharsis for all of the raw moments I saw on a daily basis," she says. "They were also the building blocks of the book I hoped one day to write." Eventually, during downtime at the funeral home, she began to piece together the notes into a fictional story about a female funeral director.

As the years passed, Mosca grew resentful that she was too busy working to find enough time to fully develop the book. "At forty, I was a far different person than I had been at twenty-one. I felt that I had chosen a career early on that no longer suited me," she says. "I knew I would never be happy until I published something. 'If not now, when?' began to echo loudly in my head."

> ....
>
> ### The Most Important Thing I Did Right
>
> "I continued to work at my job while pursuing my writing career. I stayed determined, as well as undaunted by naysayers."
>
> ....

Mosca decided to follow the rule "Write what you know." She published an article with funeral-planning advice for a consumer publication. On a high after seeing her story in print, she followed up with numerous funeral-related queries to editors. "The rejections showed that death was not the most popular of topics," she says. She persisted. At forty-one, after more than twenty years of working in the funeral industry, she landed a cover story in a funeral trade magazine, one that she had been reading since she took her first job answering phones at the funeral home. "That's when I felt like a real writer," she says. Soon she became a regular contributor to the magazine. "I had found my niche," she says. "I felt that a new part of my life was beginning."

Invigorated by her dual career, Mosca set out to pursue her writing dream. She pulled together a proposal for the book, which she had reworked into a memoir, and mailed out close to fifty copies to agents and publishers. She faced a string of rejections. Then in 2001, a publisher, New Horizon Press, called and said they'd changed their minds and wanted to publish her book. *Grave Undertakings* came out in 2003 when Mosca was forty-five. "I really felt as if a weight had been lifted," she says. "I thought, *I can die happy now.*"

Since then, Mosca has scaled back her small funeral business to make time to write. In 2008, Arcadia Publishing brought out her second book, *Green-Wood Cemetery*, a pictorial history of one of America's most famous burial grounds. She continues to freelance about death, funerals, and cemeteries. She is also writing a biography and searching for a publisher for the fictional book that she started so many years ago. "Being published has made me look at my role as a funeral director with a new appreciation," she says. "My work taught me lessons about life and death and the importance of being remembered. Working in the funeral industry makes you think a lot about endings, and I feared that at the end of my life, my biggest regret would be not having pursued my writing goals. At times I've said, 'Maybe I should never have become a funeral director,' but now I realize it's the best thing I could have done."

· · · · · · · ·

The Most Surprising Thing about My Reinvention

"How my written work has influenced others to enter the funeral industry. I have become a role model for some women."

· · · · · · · ·

3

Finding Your Place in the Limelight

Some of us need to be coaxed onto center stage, while some of us were born for it. If you fit the latter description, you know that an affinity for the spotlight will not be denied—yet becoming a performer or a political leader isn't easy. For inspiration (and pointers), read these success stories.

A Suburban Mom's Road to TV Stardom
Kathryn Joosten

When Kathryn Joosten's mother lay on her deathbed at age forty-nine, she told her daughter that she regretted deferring her career plans. "She was going to get to them later, because somebody always needed something," says Joosten, who was twenty-three at the time. "It was an object lesson for me." Almost two decades later, when Joosten was a single mother of two young children, the memory of her mom inspired her to risk everything for her own dream: an acting career.

Now Joosten, seventy-one, is an Emmy winner, best known for her roles as Karen McCluskey, the crotchety neighbor on ABC's *Desperate Housewives*, and Dolores Landingham, the secretary to the president on *The West Wing*.

. . . .

The Most Important Thing I Learned

"That success comes in degrees of small achievements, not as one big giant step."

. . . .

Her journey to TV stardom began at age forty. After years as a doctor's wife in the Chicago suburbs, she was divorced and unable to jump back into her previous career as a psychiatric nurse. She took whatever odd jobs she could find to pay the bills: hanging wallpaper, selling advertising. "I had no babysitter, no backup," she says. "We had times when the utilities were turned off, and I went on public assistance. The wolf was always at the door."

Then, remembering her mother, she decided to just go for it. She joined a community theater group and took her children with her to rehearsals and performances. Joosten landed her first role at forty-two, then auditioned for as many local shows as she could squeeze into her schedule. One day, when she was playing Tessie Tura in *Gypsy*, she met an agent scouting child actors. The agent decided to represent Joosten instead.

"There was this incredible luck," she says and then corrects herself. "Luck is where preparation meets opportunity. I was prepared, and the opportunity came along."

With an agent on board, auditions for commercials followed. In 1992, a decade after her stage debut, she signed with Walt Disney World in Orlando for a role as a street performer. The improv skills she'd honed in community theater paid off: "I played a character named Annie Hannigan, an Irish cleaning lady to the stars." She was finally making a living as an actor. After the yearlong contract ended, she took a bartending course and moved to L.A., where she supported herself with her new skill. Then she landed a two-line guest spot on *Family Matters*, playing a grocery clerk. By age fifty-seven, she was in great demand, garnering guest roles on *Roseanne, Murphy Brown, Seinfeld,* and *Frasier,* and a recurring role on *The West Wing.* Her spot on *Wisteria Lane* led to Emmy Awards in 2005 and 2008. Now there's talk of a new show in which she would star with Lily Tomlin, who plays her sister on *Desperate Housewives.*

> **The Most Important Thing I Did Right**
>
> "I always kept in view the fact that I could go back to what I was doing before if the next step didn't work out. This gave me the freedom to try for the next goal and know I could survive."

Her *West Wing* character gave a big boost to Joosten's financial stability. During her 1999 to 2001 run as the no-nonsense Mrs. Landingham—a character so beloved that when she died, dismayed fans sent angry e-mails to NBC, and a California legislator paid her tribute on the assembly floor—she earned up to $6,000 per episode, with a guarantee of at least 10 appearances. On *Desperate Housewives* she earns $15,000 per show, but says that for each of the last two years, she's made in the high $200,000s, thanks to residuals, recurring roles, and commercials.

During her *West Wing* tenure, Joosten was diagnosed with lung cancer and had surgery in December 2001. It barely slowed her down, and she began speaking to cancer groups. Recently, a new cancer appeared, and she's now cancer-free for a second time.

She remains positive. "I don't see myself necessarily as a survivor but as

> **The Most Surprising Thing about My Reinvention**
>
> "The two Emmys and the realization that I earned them."

managing my life," she says. "Some people are passive. I want to get out there and drive the damn thing."

Kathryn's Success Strategy

"Don't be afraid to follow your dream—you don't know where it will take you. And know that there is no 'there' there; it is the journey that is the achievement, not the goal."

The Cop Who Became a Comedian
Gina Scarda

Did you hear the one about the nice Italian girl from Long Island who joined the New York City Police Department and was asked to work undercover as a hooker? Her family was horrified at the assignment, but as she tells her listeners, she was excited: "I already had the wardrobe." The audience at the popular Long Island bar Katies of Smithtown erupts with laughter. Many of them know that the comedian they came to see used to be a police officer. And Gina Scarda was the real deal.

A member of New York's finest for twenty years, nine of them on patrol, Scarda went undercover to battle underage drinking and to arrest prostitutes and johns. With her long blond hair, curvy form, and stiletto boots, she was the perfect candidate for the assignment. Now fifty and a retired sergeant, Scarda has used her cop capers to reinvent herself as a stand-up comic (ginascarda .com), spinning riffs that in December 2008 earned her the title of Long Island's Funniest New Comedian.

Growing up, Scarda had only one police officer in the family: her older sister's husband, who turned her on to his world. (She jokes that while other girls played with Barbies and had tea parties, she was cuffing Ken and guzzling coffee and doughnuts during stakeouts.) When a girlfriend took the police test, Scarda followed suit and won a spot at the Police Academy. During the first weeks, the physical workouts were so grueling that Scarda says she would come home "crying in pain." Her then-boyfriend-now-husband, Tom, said, "You'll never get through," but that only made her try harder.

Once promoted to sergeant, Scarda conducted investigations and provided support for the bureaus of narcotics and organized crime. "I had an amazing career," she says. In 2007, she was eligible for a full pension after twenty years on the force, but as the date loomed, she thought, I'm still young. I could do other things.

She got certified as a personal trainer and a holistic health counselor. For two years, she ran her own franchise food business. Meanwhile, something more intriguing caught her attention. In late 2007, she enrolled in a stand-up comedy course, "totally for the fun of it." Scarda was hooked. "I took unpaid performing jobs wherever I could, to practice," she says.

Blessed with a buoyant personality and a laughter-studded conversational style, Scarda bases her routines on her life: growing up Italian, being a cop, being married to the same man for twenty-one years. "You take something true and exaggerate it. My life is funny."

· · · · · · ·

The Most Important Thing I Learned

"When I was younger, I thought that everybody was always looking at me and judging me— I learned that's just not true, which is why I'm able to do this stuff now!"

· · · · · · ·

My Biggest Mistake

"Not pursuing this earlier. Even though it's always been a secret dream of mine to be an actress and a comedian, I never thought in a million years I would have done it. And now I feel like I've let a lot of time pass me by."

Her break came in the summer of 2008, when she joined the Italian Chicks comedy troupe. Today, she tours the United States with them and makes frequent solo appearances. In July 2010, she appeared on NBC's *Last Comic Standing*, and can be seen playing Loretta Nuzzolo on the web sitcom series *Something about Ryan*. Scarda has also acted in four independent films and performs with the SEE Saw Comedy Repertory Company, a Long Island–based improv group.

"I'm making money, which is kind of unheard of for someone who has been in comedy such a short a time," she says. Last year, she took home around $20,000 on top of her $50,000 annual police pension. "I hope to make a living at this, but meanwhile I'm having a great time." If she were still in her twenties, she'd be too terrified to try comedy, she says. "When you're young, you're afraid of what people will think. When you're older, it's time to live for you, not anyone else."

················ **Gina's Key Questions to Ask Yourself** ···············

- Are you proud of your life?
- Are you going to regret anything at the end of your life?
- Do you have dreams you never realized?
- Are your children going to be proud of what you've done?
- Does your life bring you joy?

She Discovered She Was a Leader
Grace Diaz

Back in the Dominican Republic, Grace Diaz had worked for the president of the country and for the mayor of her city, and she had owned her own store. Yet after her marriage turned sour and her store was burglarized, Diaz decided that the United States was her best option for a happy future. In 1990, she moved to Providence, Rhode Island, where she had a friend. She spoke not a word of English and had only $40 in her pocket and two dresses in her suitcase. The day after she arrived, she got a job working the door at a disco. "I was embarrassed," Diaz says. "In the Dominican Republic I had never been to a club, and here I was at the door."

She had left her four children behind with her mother, so she devoted herself to saving enough money to buy a house and bring them all to Providence. "My dream was to support my kids," she says, and she began by taking English classes and training to be a certified nurse's assistant. She then found a job at a nursing home so that the children would have health care when they arrived, and she took a second, part-time job for extra money. In 1992, she remarried and got her resident card; three years later, she bought a house. By the time she went home in 1995 to bring back her kids, the youngest of whom was seven, she had been away from them for five years. "One of the happiest days of my life was when I reunited with my children," she says. "Christmas was never Christmas without them."

In 1996, Diaz became an American citizen and the following year got a job as a certified nurse's assistant; two years later, she brought her mother to live with her. Now that she had reassembled her family, she wanted to spend more time with them, so she went back to school and trained to be a licensed child-care provider. In 2002, she started a home-based business,

· · · · · · · · · ·

The Most Important Thing I Learned

"I didn't know anything about politics in the United States! I had some background from the Dominican Republic, but I didn't have a clue what my responsibilities would be as a state legislator. When I began this journey, it was like, 'Where am I? Am I able to do this?' But eventually I took advantage of all of the good friends around me, who invited me to learn. My only option was to do my best. And I think I did."

· · · · · · · · · ·

Teddy Bears Under the Rainbow, and also became an active member of Local 1199, the home health workers and child-care providers union. "The providers were isolated," she says. "They didn't know how the system worked or how to protect themselves."

Diaz started to advocate for them at community meetings, and before long, her peers were urging her to represent them in a different way, as a state legislator. She threw herself into campaigning and in 2004 defeated a two-term incumbent. "It was a crazy moment!" she says. "It was unbelievable. My family called, friends called, people from all over the world called." In winning, she became the first Dominican American woman elected to state office in the United States. At her swearing-in ceremony, the Speaker of the House called her the perfect example of the American Dream. "During the election, I was able to inspire a lot of people by harnessing the energy of those around me," says Diaz. "They pushed me through to where I needed to be."

Despite her achievements, Diaz still had financial worries. State legislators in Rhode Island work only three days a week, six months of the year, and are barred from taking a job at any organization that receives state money. "For almost a year, I was struggling," Diaz says. "I couldn't pay all of my bills and sometimes had services cut off." She found work as a part-time diabetes outreach coordinator for the Latino community while taking college courses; at fifty-one, she earned a bachelor's degree in human services. She went on to finish her master's degree in organizational management and leadership in 2010.

········· **My Biggest Mistake** ·········

"Not going back to college earlier, because that would have given me more opportunities to perform better. I graduated high school in 1977, but life took over. I had responsibilities. I had children. I couldn't make the time before."

Her political success continues. She became a superdelegate to the 2008 Democratic National Convention and currently chairs Rhode Island's Commission on Child Care. "I say someday I'd like to settle down and work less," she says. "But I know that circumstances will put me in some kind of leadership position in the future."

················· **Grace's Key Question to Ask Yourself** ···············

Can you go deeper, can you go beneath your skin to find what is special in you, what makes you unique? What are the things that only you are able to do?

Mika's Do-Over
Mika Brzezinski

It's five o'clock on a Wednesday morning at MSNBC's Manhattan studio, and Mika Brzezinski is trying to tell a story. It's difficult because she's also getting her hair washed and reading the day's newspapers on her BlackBerry. Head back, she holds the device above her face while a stylist scrubs. In a circus-worthy feat of multitasking, Brzezinski, who has to be on air in an hour, starts to talk—while still reading and being lathered—in almost perfect, ready-to-print sentences.

She describes how in 2005 she had to face the most stressful day in a TV newswoman's life: her fortieth birthday. It didn't help that Brzezinski was not, as she is now, the cohost of both a highly rated morning show and a nationally syndicated radio program, as well as a book author (her first, *All Things at Once*, was published in January 2010; her second, *Knowing Your Value*, in May). Her glory days at CBS News, as a correspondent for *60 Minutes* and an anchor for the *CBS Evening News*, were over. She was, to put it plainly, well on her way to being another bit of blond roadkill on the TV highway.

Although even before makeup she looks like one of those golden, gorgeous creatures who thinks a business obstacle is having to give up the corporate jet, the reality is that Brzezinski's path to TV celebrity status has been complicated. In 1997, when she was twenty-nine and the mother of a two-year-old, Brzezinski landed a plum gig: anchor of CBS's national overnight news program *Up to the Minute*. She was confident that she could balance a high-powered job and family life the way her parents had—her dad, Zbigniew Brzezinski, was the national security adviser to President Jimmy Carter, and her mom, Emilie Benes Brzezinski, was a successful artist—but having it all turned out to be cruelly stressful. "I was weeping every day," she says. Then, only months into the new job, she got pregnant again.

During Brzezinski's six-week maternity leave, WABC in Manhattan hired her husband, television journalist Jim Hoffer, as an investigative reporter. This meant that when Brzezinski returned to work, both parents were pulling crazy, intense hours. "Jim never slept. I never slept," she says.

Two months later, Brzezinski's exhaustion took a horrible toll on the family. She had hurried home to relieve her nanny so that the woman could take a well-deserved afternoon off. "I rushed upstairs and grabbed the baby," she says. "I was talking a hundred miles an hour, and I walked right off the top of the stairs. I fell down the complete flight."

Brzezinski landed on top of her daughter, Carlie, and quickly realized that the baby wasn't moving from the chin down. Brzezinski says she instantly began to tell herself, "'She's got to be okay. She's got to be okay,' because I knew Carlie wasn't okay." She tears up even now, years later. "Her cry was all wrong. I thought she had a head injury. I took her straight to the hospital."

There, doctors strapped Carlie to a board and began tests. Brzezinski realized that they thought the child's back was broken, which meant she might have made the prognosis worse by moving her daughter. "I fell apart," Brzezinski says. "I slid down the wall. My face was on the floor, and I wept." It took eight hours for the medical team to determine that Carlie's main injury was a broken femur.

Still, the incident was serious enough that child protective services investigated Brzezinski on suspicion of child abuse. She felt so guilty that "when the social worker came to our house," Brzezinski says, "I told her, 'Put the handcuffs on me.'" The social worker interviewed her nanny and her husband, inspected the home, and examined the children. Then she closed the case, recommending to Brzezinski that she get some rest.

That was it for Brzezinski, who told her husband that she was quitting her job. "I had it all worked out," she says. "We would downsize to an apartment, and I'd be a stay-at-home mom." Hoffer agreed that a huge change was necessary but believed that if she up gave up the work she loved out of guilt and exhaustion, she'd be miserable. "We've been cheap," he told her. "Now we're going to get all of the help you need. If after six months you still want to quit, you can, but you can't quit like this."

"So we got help. And I started spending less time with my daughters," Brzezinski says, to go full-throttle on her career. "I missed things. School things. Moments." There were times when her kids were "on the back burner," she says. "That's a hard thing for a woman to admit. But that's what I started doing."

The rewards came swiftly. Rival network NBC hired her away in 2000, and in 2001 CBS snatched her back.

. . . .

The Most Important Thing I Learned

"My value. It's one thing to know it and another thing to actually be able to say it. Getting fired was a hard fall. It hurt and I cried a lot, but it taught me exactly who I was, as a professional and as a parent. As a professional, I'm far more real and honest than I was before I was fired from CBS, and as a parent I'm more real and honest."

. . . .

Soon, she was working with every news show at the network. "I felt like such a bright, shiny penny," Brzezinski says. "I would bring in my young daughters, and they'd play under the desk while I anchored the news. I thought it was cute. I drank the Kool-Aid."

Before long, it turned sour. In 2006, CBS News hired Katie Couric to replace Dan Rather as anchor of the evening news. That week, the network told Brzezinski it was not going to renew her contract, which was set to expire six months later. At the same time, Brzezinski heard that someone at the top of the company didn't find her attractive. "I don't think that played a part in my being let go," she says. "But it is a hard thing to hear when you're in TV and you're thirty-nine, and you've just been fired."

For the record, a spokesperson for CBS News says that neither Katie Couric's arrival nor Brzezinski's looks had anything to do with the network's decision not to renew her contract; the network's on-air needs simply changed. "TV news is an unforgiving craft," says Dan Rather, who was the CBS Evening News anchor for twenty-four years. "It's filled with mysteries and unexplained things." Bottom line, he says, "there are only two kinds of correspondents: those who have been fired and those who are about to be fired."

Maybe it was growing up around politics or maybe it was having spent years covering them that caused Brzezinski to spin her story to her children. "Mommy has good news," she told her daughters, "Mommy is going to leave CBS. I'm going to have more time with you!"

"No, no, no. You can't do that," Emilie, then eleven, said. "That's the only reason the library lady likes me!"

The next day, her younger daughter's school called, saying eight-year-old Carlie was lying on the floor in the fetal position. Brzezinski drove over immediately, leaned down to her child, and whispered, "Honey, what's wrong? I'm here for you."

"That's actually the problem," a teacher said. "Your daughter told me you're leaving your job, and she's very upset."

"Mommy, you love [work] so much," Carlie said. "I don't want you to have to leave your job."

There are probably a dozen ways to analyze these mother-daughter scenes. The way Brzezinski interprets them is, "Kids can see that their mother is more than mom or wife, that she has things that define her and make her happy and bring her joy, and they want her to be able to have those things."

Brzezinski, who has been an avid runner all of her life, tried to get back in stride. Her agent succeeded in setting up high-level interviews, but, one after the other, executives would sit Brzezinski down and instead of talking about a new job would ask, "So what really happened at CBS?" Brzezinski had no dastardly tale. "In the news business, having no story . . . well, what use are you?" she says.

She knew she could either fall into a pit of depression or dive into what she did have—time to bestow on those she loved. She dove. Her family became her project and distraction. "My daughter Emilie had an issue with her vision," Brzezinski says. "My husband's mother was diagnosed with ovarian and stomach cancer. Caring for the family helped me feel alive."

Meanwhile, Brzezinski explored other fields. In late 2006, she got to the final round of interviews for a six-figure public relations job. "I'm sitting there thinking, Salary! Salary! Salary! I can't wait to tell my husband I got this job!" But she had zero interest in PR. In the last interview, she blurted out that she knew someone better for the position.

The friend she recommended got the job. As bad as Brzezinski felt about letting the opportunity go, it made her realize how much she wanted to be back in TV broadcasting. Brzezinski asked her agent to find her any TV job, even if it was low on the ladder: "Assistant to the assistant. Cleaning toilets."

The agent promptly lined her up for an on-air, entry-level position at MSNBC as a substitute graveyard-shift news update reader. The job paid less than one-fifth of what Brzezinski would have made at the PR firm. Despite that, "I was thrilled," she says. She read updates on then congressman Joe Scarborough's weeknight program, at the end of which she'd lower her voice to a sardonic purr and say, "Now back to—Scarborough Country."

In April 2007, when Scarborough was in New York putting together a morning show, the two met for the first time. "I know you're making fun of my show every time you toss back to me," he said.

"How can I make fun of a show I've never watched?" she retorted.

Scarborough's next thought was, I've found my cohost! They were both smart-asses. His conservative politics plus Brzezinski's Democrat bona fides had the potential for stunning TV.

. . . .

The Most Important Thing I Did Right

"I thought for myself. I thought for myself in terms of transitioning from a free-lance job to *Morning Joe*. I stayed in my field and was willing to start all over again. I was ready to start from the bottom. I took a job that I would've laughed at fifteen years ago."

. . . .

The position was freelance, essentially a tryout, but Brzezinski went for it. When the red on-air light blinked on for their first show, "I was, like, 'Wow. Of all the thousands of wavelengths out there, we are on the same one,'" she says. "I felt as if I'd known him for twenty years, and he was like one of my brothers at the dinner table, fighting the way we fought in our family."

Brzezinski isn't exaggerating. Weeks into her gig, she did the newscaster equivalent of sucker-punching the host. She refused to read the lead story about socialite Paris Hilton's release from prison after serving five days for driving with a suspended license. "I hate this story," she said on the air, "and I don't think it should be our lead." The now-legendary YouTube footage of her trying to set the script on fire with a cigarette lighter and, later, running it through a shredder turned her into a news hero. Brzezinski told the network, "No more tryout. You need to marry me."

······················· **My Biggest Mistake** ·······················

"Trying to be everyone's friend. That's not what business is about. True friends don't come in large numbers. And you can't be a good mother if you're friends with everybody."
··

"She got the contract she wanted," says *Morning Joe* executive producer Chris Licht. "Right away."

"Joe is extraordinary, but Mika makes him even better," says Rick Kaplan, the current executive producer of *CBS Evening News*. "She gets under his skin. She is a catalyst for some of the show's most interesting conversations."

When the red TV studio light goes off to end the show at 9 AM, the cohosts—having bantered and bickered for three hours—depart without a word to each other. Brzezinski clicks down the hall in her four-inch heels to her closet-size office, where she wiggles out of her skirt and into size 4 jeans. Then she clicks back down the hall and onto an elevator, which she takes to a radio studio. There she eats two bowls of cornflakes and prepares for the two-hour *Joe Scarborough Show* with Mika Brzezinski, which starts at 10:00 sharp. All on five hours of sleep, which she says is all she needs.

"I probably still couldn't do this unless I loved it," say Brzezinski. "But I really love my job. And I didn't think this could happen again."

Nonetheless, she doesn't meld family and work the way she used to. The girls come to MSNBC's studio at 30 Rockefeller Center "maybe once in the summer," she says. If she loses this position, she doesn't want her kids to get upset again. "All these TV jobs are very bad boyfriends," she says; the network could decide any day that they are not that into her. At the same time, she takes comfort in the fact that some of the most visible high-level anchors have been women over forty: Katie Couric, Meredith Vieira, Ann Curry, Barbara Walters, Campbell Brown, Diane

Sawyer, and, yes, Mika Brzezinski. She knows that no penny can shine forever, but she's too busy reading her BlackBerry to worry about that now.

················ **Mika's Key Question to Ask Yourself** ···············
Do you know your value and who you are?

Becoming Mrs. Oregon at Fifty
Debra Gilmour

Debra Gilmour had two breast biopsies at forty-eight, and for a few months she suffered soreness from the three-inch incisions, which weren't healing properly. She relied on ibuprofen to deal with the discomfort, never realizing that the over-the-counter medication was burning half a dozen holes in her stomach. "I was bleeding internally and lost four pints of blood, half of my blood volume," she says. "Had I waited any longer to go to the doctor, I would have bled to death."

The emergency diagnosis at the hospital was a wake-up call for Gilmour. She had gained thirty-five pounds since her early thirties and she was feeling bad about letting herself go.

The Most Important Thing I Learned

"My ability to accomplish anything lies solely within me. While it's nice to have the support of family and friends when undertaking a sea change in your life, it's not required. The only thing required is belief in yourself."

She decided to set a tangible goal that would motivate her to get back in shape—something fun, challenging, and memorable. "So many women around me looked at turning fifty with indignation, planning facelifts to fight that process of aging," she says. "I was looking for a positive way to enter into a part of life that most people were dreading." So, at fifty, she signed up for the Mrs. Oregon International Pageant. She'd been a contestant before and a successful one: In 1988, she'd been crowned Mrs. Oregon America, the youngest woman at that time ever to hold the title. Her next twenty years had been spent far from the pageant world. She'd divorced, remarried, and focused on her two daughters and her career as a registered lobbyist and policy adviser.

Gilmour was especially drawn to the "platform" aspect of the Mrs. Oregon International Pageant: the part of the program in which contestants were asked to speak about a cause they supported. When Gilmour was nineteen, her parents and youngest brother had been in a horrific car accident caused by a drunk driver. "The chance of gaining a lot of attention for this issue—drug and alcohol abuse and prevention—at the pageant was off the charts for me," she says.

The Most Important Thing I Did Right

"I put time into research. I had a pretty good idea of how to proceed, but talking to some industry professionals gave me valuable information that helped me make changes in my approach."

Yet although promoting her cause would be a bonus, her specific goal was to win—not so much the Mrs. Oregon title, but the pageant's fitness competition. Instead of putting contestants in swimsuits, this pageant judged how fit the women looked in aerobic wear. "I wanted to prove you can be in shape at fifty," she says. "I've been telling my daughters their whole lives that they can do anything they set their minds to, and it was important for me to show them that they never need to be limited by age."

.... **My Biggest Mistake** ....

"A couple of times I second-guessed myself, wondering what on earth I was thinking in setting this goal. Great friends and my treadmill reminded me that I had no time or energy to spare for second-guessing!"

During the next twelve months, Gilmour pumped light weights with her arms while she pedaled on her recumbent bike, watching the Travel Channel to amuse herself. She cut empty calories from her diet. She worked with a coach to help her feel comfortable with the personal interview component of the competition. She shopped for a pageant gown. "As a lobbyist, my closet was full of suits in navy blue and black," she says. "Aside from getting a mother-of-the-bride gown for my daughter's wedding a few years earlier, I had no idea how to go about buying that kind of thing anymore." She ordered her normal size, but because pageant gowns were sized smaller than other clothing, the dress turned out to be an entire size too small. With little time left before the competition, she had to step up her exercise regime even more to make the dress fit. "There were days I tried it on, and I still had a pound or so to go, and all I could say was, 'Oh, good Lord, what was I thinking?'" she recalls.

One week before the pageant, Gilmour attended a workshop with the other contestants to pick numbers for who would go on stage first. "As I looked around the room, I thought, I'm the oldest person here!" she says. "One of the girls was younger than my youngest daughter, and here I was a new grandmother." Insecurity grabbed her on the day of the pageant as she changed into an aerobic top and shorts for the fitness competition and saw that many of the other women, all in their twenties, thirties, and forties, were in phenomenal condition. As she stepped on stage, though, she reminded herself that she had already reached her real goal. She'd been determined to get into the best shape she'd been in for years, and she had. "If you lined up the women and said, 'Which one has the best body?' I was not that person," says Gilmour. "But I had a confidence about me that said, 'I am who I am. I've worked hard for this, and here it is.'"

The rest of the pageant entailed an evening gown competition and five individual interviews. At the final ceremony, various awards were presented as a lead-up to the crowning of Mrs. Oregon. When they came to the prize for the fitness competition, Gilmour waited for the inevitable. Though pleased that she had made a good effort, she was sure that the winner would be "the drop-dead gorgeous lady standing next to me who had never had children." Then she heard the emcee announce her as the fitness winner. "I just stood there in shock," she says. "I thought they got it wrong."

The time came to announce Mrs. Oregon 2008. As the runners-up were named, one by one, Gilmour tried to figure out who else was left. Then the winner was announced—"And it was *me*!" she says. At fifty, she had become the oldest woman ever to win the pageant. "When my husband crowned me, he had to hand me his hanky," she says. "I kept saying to him over and over, 'Can you believe it?'"

· · · · · · · · · ·

The Most Surprising Thing about My Reinvention

"My story has inspired others to take a chance and embrace who they want to be."

· · · · · · · · · ·

Gilmour went on to represent Oregon in the Mrs. International Pageant and in 2009 won the Beauties of America Pageant for women over fifty. Now, in addition to her work as a lobbyist, she coaches other women whom she's inspired to pursue their own pageant goals. "I never knew that in setting my own reinvention goal, it would have a ripple effect well beyond my own personal success," she says. "I've proved that age is no excuse. I knew the odds were against me. What I didn't realize was that the confidence that comes with age and experience also resonates tangibly. You can't buy it in a bottle, potion, or procedure. It takes those added years to really cultivate an appreciation for the inner beauty that comes with age."

········· **Debra's Key Question to Ask Yourself** ·········
What does success look like? How do you picture myself as successful in your goal?

Soul Survivor
Sharon Jones

Between opening for Prince and going on tour with a 2010 CD that, as she puts it, "had everyone talking" (*I Learned the Hard Way*, which she recorded with her band, the Dap-Kings), soul singer Sharon Jones is having a very good year. "I did a duet with him at Madison Square Garden," says Jones of the superstar, who joined her in what one reviewer called "a collaboration about as amazing as you would expect it to be." Now her focus is on the next album, which she wants to release before the year is over. Things are happening fast for Jones these days—but until the band really started to break through with the 2007 CD *100 Days, 100 Nights*, the road to fulfillment had been long. She started performing in her twenties—which means that, at age fifty-five, this small (barely five feet in her stage heels), strong-looking, immensely charismatic woman has been seeking success longer than many of her current fans have been alive.

Now she has found it. Performing with the Dap-Kings—who once backed up British star Amy Winehouse on a CD that went multiplatinum—Jones has spent the last few years playing sold-out shows in the United States and Europe. In 2007 she made her screen debut, playing a juke-joint singer in the Denzel Washington film *The Great Debaters*. ("Harvey Weinstein invited me to walk the red carpet at the premiere with Denzel and all the cast," Jones remembers. "You can add that to my 'most amazing things' list.") In other words, at an age when many musicians' careers go ice cold, Jones's is definitely hot.

The youngest of six children raised by a single mother, Jones was born in Augusta, Georgia, but moved to Brooklyn at age three. She started singing young, in church choirs and school cho-ruses. "People always told me I had the voice to make it professionally," she says. In her twenties, she performed with sev-eral neighborhood bands but never hit it big. "One guy at a record label told me I was too black, too short, too fat, too old," she recalls. "I was good enough to be in the background but not to be the star."

The Most Important Thing I Learned

"No matter what life throws at you, never give up. I've always felt that my singing was meant to be."

By the time Jones turned thirty, she knew she needed a better way of paying the bills. "I took the police test," she says. "I took the post office test. I was one of the first women in New York City to go for the garbage test." For several years she was an armored-car guard for Wells Fargo. "I carried a .38," she says. "I got praised for my marks-manship." She also worked as a prison guard for two years, at New York City's Rikers Island.

One night the inmates found out about her former career and wouldn't return to their cells until she sang the Whitney Houston ballad "Greatest Love of All." "I knew they were probably playing with me, but they refused to lock in until I sang," Jones says. "So I stood up front and did one verse and the chorus." She shudders at the memory, then admits that the experience taught her some-thing about stage presence—just one of the things she learned in that job. Never showing fear was another.

Jones left Rikers in 1990 and spent the next decade surviving on weekend gigs as a wedding singer. "Anytime I got on that stage, I knew that God had given me a gift and that if I used it, someday it would work out," she says. In 1996, a boyfriend introduced her to a group of musicians who were reviving 1960s soul, Memphis style, and soon Jones was a fixture with the band, the Soul Providers. In 2000, after a bad breakup and tight on money, she moved in with her mother in a housing project in Queens. The band, now called the Dap-Kings, struggled on until 2004, when their luck finally changed.

Winehouse, then twenty-one, had just signed to do an album—her first—with Island Records, but there were problems. "The producers were looking for a certain sound and couldn't get it," Jones says. Winehouse's producers heard the Dap-Kings in New York and took them—without Jones—to play on the CD *Back to Black*. Jones could have allowed the experience to crush her, but she'd gotten smarter since her first try at a music career.

While the Dap-Kings played with Winehouse, Jones hired a manager, continued working as a backup singer, and then landed the movie role. When she and the Dap-Kings reunited, the band's connection to Winehouse helped them get major press attention and brought in new fans. "It would have been great if they could have put Amy and me in a duet," Jones says. "But that's not the way it is." Although she admits that being left out of the Winehouse maneuver had made her angry at first, Jones now sounds genuinely at peace with the way it played out. "I realized it was okay, you know? You have your blessings, and other people have theirs," she says. "Keep doing what you're doing. If it's right, good things will come to you, too."

Today, Jones can count many twenty-somethings among her admirers, but plenty of influential industry types as well. One of them is Harvey Weinstein, at whose wedding she performed. "I was singing 'At Last,' and I looked over and saw Marc Anthony and Jennifer Lopez dancing in their seats!" Jones says. "They were so cute."

Despite such moments, the last few years have been tough for Jones personally. In 2007, twenty-four of her friends and family members died, including a brother, and her mother had a minor stroke. Now her mother has been diagnosed with cancer, and Jones is buying her a house in South Carolina so she can live there, with Jones's sister, during her treatment.

Through it all, the stage has been her outlet. "That's where the passion and energy come out," she says. And the audience is responding. "Our first record out, we sold fifty in the first week," she says. "Second record, we sold five hundred in the first week. Third record, we sold five thousand in the first week." Jones feels as if she's learned a lot of things the hard way (to quote her latest album title), including this: "You have to hang in there—have patience. You have to *hang*. I'm grateful that I stayed with what we're doing now. Even when there was no money, I didn't try to jump around—'Oh, well, maybe I'll do a pop song with somebody.' You know, go to the mainstream. You have to have trust, you gotta believe in the dream."

My Biggest Mistake

"This is what I've learned: You have to really look out for you. I'd still do what I've done in my life in terms of taking care of my family, but I think you must focus. You've gotta stay focused on your life. Sometimes it's so easy to let someone sway you. You have a man, and he's like, 'Baby, we can do this together.' And most of the time, once they get their dream, you end up with nothing. So I think my biggest mistake was not looking out for myself sooner, not standing my ground a little sooner."

Sharon's Key Questions to Ask Yourself

- Is it worth it?
- Why are you doing it?

- Who are you doing it for? I think a lot of musicians and actresses get it in their heads that it's all about them. But you've got to be true to your fans. I'm definitely doing it for me because I have the talent to do it, but I also do it for the people who love my voice and love what I'm doing.
- And this is the main thing: Do you have it in you to finish what you start?

4

Doing Good

Maybe you've been extremely successful in your job but are now feeling the urge to "give back." Or you've always been restless at work, wishing you could make a difference in the world. Or you've just awoken in the middle of the night and felt a calling. The women in this chapter are all role models for reinventing themselves around one powerful desire: to reach out to people in need and offer help.

Her Restaurant Breaks All of the Rules
Denise Cerreta

Denise Cerreta still remembers how her mouth watered when, as a child of eight, she gazed longingly at heaps of plump strawberries at a farmers' market in Atlanta. She asked her dad if she could have some, but he said no, they were too expensive. As the family returned to their car, a young man bounded up to her father, holding out a pint of the sweet-scented fruit. "Sir, I hope you don't mind," he said. "I bought these for your daughter."

That stranger's impulsive act of kindness made a lasting impression on Cerreta. Forty-one years later, at age forty-nine, she's on a similar mission. As founder of One World Salt Lake, a pay-what-you-want restaurant in Salt Lake City, Utah, Cerreta is determined to change the way restaurants do business and to bring delicious, healthful food to everyone, even those who can't pay. Although skeptics told her that a restaurant based on customer donations could never survive, the enterprise is debt-free and had its eighth anniversary in June 2011.

Located in a converted two-story red brick building not far from the University of Utah, One World Salt Lake serves organic, freshly prepared dishes, buffet style, in four cozy dining areas decorated with bright hangings and hand-carved statues from India. The menu changes daily and includes options that impress even the most sophisticated eaters. A hand-lettered notice asks customers to "donate a fair, respectable amount," similar to what they'd pay in other restaurants. Anyone too strapped to make even the most minimal payment can volunteer to wash dishes, cut vegetables, clean up, or garden (one hour = one meal), and rice and dal are always free. Since the recession took hold, the number of customers earning meals through volunteering has doubled, with the average donation about $6 to $8 per meal, and the sixty-seat eatery attracts as many paying diners as in the past.

· · · · · · · · · ·

The Most Important Thing I Learned

"The strength of community, or the strength of a community. A huge part of my growing awareness is just the need and the beauty of people working together to accomplish something."

· · · · · · · · · ·

Here, tourists, judges, businessmen, and even the mayor of Salt Lake City dine alongside single mothers, laborers, college students, and street people. Cerreta says she's seen lasting friendships form as strangers sit down together at tables seating two to six people. When they go to the buffet counter to be served, there's only one rule: don't ask for more than you can eat. Food is never wasted, because every scrap is either consumed or composted. (Meat bones are thrown in the trash only after being boiled for soup.) That's unheard of at conventional restaurants, where diners' leftovers are thrown away.

"We have three Dumpsters outside our restaurant," says a Salt Lake City restaurateur who manages a branch of a $28 million seafood chain (and who asked to remain anonymous). "After the weekends, they are filled to the brim with garbage, at least half of which is food." At One World Salt Lake, on the other hand, by the end of an average night, there's a quarter of a ten-gallon can of garbage and one or two five-gallon buckets of food scraps, which are composted at a nearby community garden that also serves as a site for educational programs. Cerreta says that the savings from this lack of waste enable the restaurant to be self-sustaining.

A curvy woman with luminous hazel eyes and a broad smile, Cerreta had zero experience running a restaurant when she jumped into the food business. She'd moved to Salt Lake City to open an acupuncture clinic in 1997, after studying acupuncture and herbal remedies at the International Institute of Chinese Medicine, in Santa Fe. The clinic was very successful. She saw from twenty to twenty-five clients a day and made good money. Yet at forty-one, after running the business for five years, she "hit a spiritual glass ceiling," she says. She'd come to believe that most of her patients were lonely, rather than ill. "Loneliness is an undiagnosed disease in this country, and I wanted to change that," she says. A café where customers could socialize seemed like a worthwhile enterprise.

In 2002, with no idea what she was getting into, Cerreta opened a small coffee and sandwich shop in the building that housed her clinic. She called it Smoochy's One World 7-10, envisioning it as a healthy alternative to 7-Eleven stores. She hired five people and funneled all of the profits from her acupuncture practice into running the shop. Six months into the venture, however, the shop wasn't attracting enough customers to cover costs.

Realizing that she couldn't run two businesses at the same time, she folded the clinic, let the coffee shop staff go, and ran Smoochy's herself. She opened an hour earlier than before, hoping to bring in more customers. "I honestly wasn't sure what was coming next," she says. "It was like throwing myself down the Grand Canyon." For the next four months, she struggled, doing all of the food preparation, shopping, and cleaning. She maxed out her credit cards and could barely pay her rent. Then came the lowest point: her car was repossessed. Concerned friends told her she was crazy to keep the shop going.

One particularly stressful day, when Cerreta had run out of sandwich meat and had no money to buy more, a local street person named Doggers entered the shop and handed her $50. "He said, 'Denise, I have some money but no place to cook. If I buy you some food, will you make it for me?'" Cerreta remembers. She walked with him to the grocery store, and when she explained her predicament, he offered to buy her the roast beef and the turkey she needed. "Now he can eat at One World anytime he wants for free," Cerreta says. "It's amazing how the answers to your prayers aren't what you think they're going to be."

A few years earlier, Cerreta had learned to trust her intuition and listen to what the universe, or her own subconscious, was trying to tell her. She'd been training in martial arts and was about to take a test for her yellow belt when she had an overwhelming feeling that something would go wrong. She went ahead with the test anyway and ripped a muscle in her groin so badly that her left thigh turned black from bruising. Cerreta thought she'd be bedridden for weeks, but she promised herself that if her leg healed sooner, she'd never again ignore such a strong feeling. The leg healed in ten days.

That's why Cerreta paid attention in June 2003 when, about a month after her experience with Doggers, she had what she describes as a *Field of Dreams* moment: a strong feeling that she needed to let customers pay whatever they wanted. "It was such an unusual phenomenon, and it hasn't happened to me since," she says, laughing at how unlikely it sounds.

Cerreta recalls the first customer who came in after her revelation. "Just price your own food," Cerreta told her. The woman looked shocked but dropped her money into a basket on the counter, smiled, and left. Cerreta, not checking to see how much the woman had paid, felt a surge of recognition, thinking, Oh my gosh, this is my purpose.

The event marked the beginning of Cerreta's economic turnaround. Operating a coffee shop on a pay-what-you-want basis was so unusual that people flocked to it. Encouraged, Cerreta expanded beyond sandwiches and started to offer one dish cooked with fresh, local produce every day. At first, the news about the restaurant spread by word of mouth, and then in September 2003 the Associated Press wrote a news story that said the cafe "breaks two of the most fundamental rules of the restaurant business: It has no menu and no prices." The article was picked up by newspapers across the country and gained her both local customers and interested tourists.

· · · · · · · · ·

The Most Surprising Thing about My Reinvention

"This model has been replicated in so many communities. It's like we're creating a family of community kitchens. It blows me away."

· · · · · · · · ·

It took Cerreta two years to get back on her feet financially. Then, with her charitable goals of fighting hunger and educating people about waste uppermost in her mind, she sought nonprofit status, which the IRS granted in 2006. In effect, Cerreta gave the enterprise away. "It's not mine anymore," she says in a voice both triumphant and wistful. It's now a community kitchen, part of the One World

Everybody Eats Foundation (oneworldeverybodyeats.org), with a board of directors that oversees operations. Until 2008, Cerreta was a paid employee, receiving a $50,000 annual package that included a monthly salary of $1,200 plus room and board, insurance, and a few other perks. Besides running the community kitchen, her job description included doing outreach to nonprofit groups around the country, speaking about food waste and world hunger, and mentoring small business owners.

As part of her mission, she spent a month in Denver mentoring the founders of the nonprofit SAME Café (So All May Eat), which opened its doors in 2006; and she helped create a sister community kitchen called One World Spokane, which launched in 2008. Cerreta also advised a no-waste, pay-what-you-want commercial eatery called Potager, which opened in 2009 in Arlington, Texas. Like-minded groups in Washington, D.C., and York, Pennsylvania, are planning to open community kitchens this year. She also urges other commercial restaurant owners to reduce waste by allowing patrons to choose from small, medium, and large portion sizes.

In 2008, Cerreta left the restaurant. "We passed the café on to our head chef, and I waived all income from there." She now splits her time between Florida and Ohio, consulting for the foundation. To date, there have been thirteen spin-offs nationwide. Although Cerreta says she makes less money now, she is comfortable with how she lives. Because of her travel and charitable work, people sometimes think she has a trust fund. She doesn't. "I sold everything I owned," she says, "and moved out of Salt Lake to be more available to the people and groups I am mentoring and to spend more time with my mother, who's eighty-six now." She is currently working on a book and other projects that she hopes will supply more income this year, but leaving One World was definitely a leap. "I knew it was the right thing to do. And it was a lot easier because of that first leap I took in 2003."

Despite Cerreta's success with One World Everybody Eats, the nonprofit has had its share of growing pains. In October 2008, after a series of bookkeeping and accountability snafus plunged the organization into debt, the board of directors fired the long-time general manager, and three angry staffers staged a highly publicized walkout. Cerreta promptly went to work in the kitchen herself until the board hired new staff. The organization is solvent once again.

Cerreta now has a dream big enough to fill the rest of her life. "If we could eliminate waste in restaurants, agriculture, grocery stores, and wherever food is served or harvested," she says, "I believe we would have enough food to feed the world."

············ **Denise's Key Questions to Ask Yourself** ············

- If money were no object, what would you be doing right now?
- If you were to die tomorrow, how would people remember you?

The Book Farmer of Botswana
Pam Shelton

In the modest assembly hall on the campus of the senior secondary school in Maun, Botswana, about fifty students, teachers, and librarians are poring over stacks of books of every description. It's a sweltering day in October 2008, but the visitors are wearing their best attire. In one corner, three teenage girls are absorbed in the pages of a romance novel, hands covering their mouths as they giggle. In the middle of the crowd, a tall boy flips through a Hardy Boys novel. Petite, blond Pam Shelton, dressed in khaki shorts and a T-shirt (all the better to lug around piles of books), thrusts a hefty paperback into his hands. "You like the Hardy

Boys," she says to the student, "so I'm sure you'll enjoy this thriller. If you promise to read it, you may take it home without a donation." The young man hesitates; it's a thick book. Shelton bounces rapid fire into a plot summary, and two minutes later, he is smiling, nodding, eager to dive in.

Shelton, the founder of the Botswana Book Project (BBP; botswanabookproject.org), is doing what she loves best: matching people and books. It's the second day of a five-day book-choosing marathon, and the books, shipped from the United States, are the star attraction; about 25,000 of them are heaped onto rows of folding chairs and stashed in boxes lining the walls. The Batswana (as the people of Botswana call themselves) make their choices, give a small donation, then take the books back to their schools, day-care centers, hospitals, AIDS clinics, and homes. Since the program's inception in 1999, countless individuals and 458 institutions have received a total of 320,000 books through the BBP, which is fueled almost entirely by Shelton's relentless desire to promote the mind-expanding power of reading. Once a children's librarian, Shelton describes herself as a "book farmer, seeding Botswana with books and waiting for a crop of readers."

Fourteen years ago, Pam Shelton was forty-six, long divorced, and feeling decidedly restless. She was just finishing up her twenty-third year as head librarian at the Shelburne Village School, in Shelburne, Vermont, where she'd built a successful reading program for the school's nine hundred children in grades K through eight. That fall, her only son would be heading back to Harvard, and Shelton wasn't really looking forward to the start of another school year. When friends who were working for USAID in Botswana invited her for a visit, she quickly bought a ticket.

Within days of arriving, she met a safari guide, and romance blossomed. She also fell in love with the lifestyle and the good-humored courtesy of the Batswana, now well-known to many Americans through Alexander McCall Smith's *No. 1 Ladies' Detective Agency*. Shelton wanted to learn about village life, so her boyfriend-guide arranged for her to spend a week in Marutsa, a tiny, remote place in the north. Shelton arrived with a sleeping bag, a mosquito net, water, crackers, and canned tuna, and she slept in a small round hut with a mud floor. Her bathroom consisted of nearby bushes. When she helped village women fetch water from a stream, they had to hide from thirsty elephants. It was extreme culture shock, "terrifying and exhilarating at the same time," she recalls. "I felt more alive than I had in years."

With the exception of one man who translated for her, the villagers spoke only Setswana (one of the national languages), despite the fact that English is the official language of the country.

Marutsa had no school, and the women told Shelton that their greatest wish was for their children to learn to read. Wanting to return a bit of the friendliness she'd been shown, Shelton held a story hour every morning in a dusty clearing under a tree, acting out the tales, to the delight of every child within walking distance. "I smiled so much, my face felt sore," she recalls, "but it really is true that a smile is a universal language."

Back in Shelburne that summer of 1997, Shelton couldn't settle down. "I felt I belonged in Botswana," she says. She asked the school for a year's leave so she could return there and perhaps begin a literacy project. "When my request was denied, I made an impulsive decision," Shelton says. "I quit." Her safari guide, who had called frequently, arrived for a visit and helped pack up her belongings. She cashed in some investments, rented out her house, and bought a ticket to Maun.

When she arrived in Botswana, however, Shelton felt lonely and isolated. She briefly considered leaving, then rejected the idea. "It was time for some risk-taking. I said to myself, You wanted to be here, to learn about the culture, help with literacy—get going!" She bought a beat-up Toyota, found a house-sitting job, and set about making a life for herself. She formed a consulting company offering literacy services, then told everyone she met that she wanted to learn about the country. "Soon, new friends were sharing so much about the land, the customs, language, history, animals, birds," she says. "I felt like a sponge!"

One morning, she dropped off her CV at the Maun Education Centre, the administrative office for schools in northern Botswana, and met with the director, Mma Olga Seretse. (*Mma* is the female honorific in Setswana.) Shelton offered to volunteer as a primary school librarian, then discovered there were no primary school libraries. "I was startled," Shelton says, "but I remembered that when Botswana got its independence from Britain more than forty years ago, the country started from scratch." As it turned out, she was talking to exactly the right person.

Mma Seretse had been praying that the country's primary schools would get libraries. The two women vowed to make it happen. "God made us meet, and we jumped with the same zeal!" Mma Seretse says. "For how can children grow up to be informed citizens if they have no libraries and no books?"

Books are extremely expensive there, but after a month of research, Shelton discovered that Books For Africa, a nonprofit agency based in Saint Paul, Minnesota, would send donated books to Botswana for only the cost of shipping. "The day I told Olga that I hoped to get twenty-five thousand books if I could come up with $5,000 for shipping, we danced around her office, laughing," Shelton recalls.

· ·

The Most Important Things I Learned

"How strong I am. There were some moments that were so low—where I had to slap myself and say, 'Come on, you're bigger than this. Just get on with it.' And I did. And it all worked out. That's another thing that I know now: in the end, everything always works out.

"Another thing I learned: Don't put your tent underneath a Marula tree when the fruit's in season. The elephants come for it, and they'll stand over the top of your tent."

· ·

The first book container, funded by Shelton's father and a few friends, arrived in 1999. For the next three years, Shelton traveled with Mma Seretse to about two hundred primary schools to introduce the concept of Parent-Teacher Organizations. At each school, the teachers agreed to give up their staff room so that it could be converted into the school library. Enthusiastic mothers made brick-and-board bookcases. Then the Botswana Book Project began to fill the shelves.

Eventually, Shelton was contracted to update the Maun Secondary School Library and train librarians. Shelton also taught puppet-making and mapped game reserves to earn cash. By living on $10,000 a year and selling her Vermont house, she could devote huge chunks of time to the BBP.

When books by such writers as Agatha Christie and Dr. Seuss turned up in the new libraries, children discovered reading for fun. Soon reading ability and English language test scores among those students skyrocketed—so much so, that in 2000, the Botswana Ministry of Education sent someone to investigate whether the schools were involved in a cheating scheme. Two years earlier, the students had registered some of the lowest standardized test scores in Botswana, and now they approached the scores of the country's elite private schools.

The day a ministry official visited Matlapana Primary School, in Maun, he was at first unimpressed as he listened to the children read for him in English. "Clearly, he thought that the first child had been handpicked, so he randomly kept pointing to one child after another," Shelton says. Each read better than the last. Shelton saw the official glance up at the display of neatly written book reports—something else new to the schools. She vividly remembers how his face showed astonishment and finally unabashed delight when he realized the scores were real. Until a few years ago, any school could receive a hundred free books if it attended BBP's book-choosing day, and each student who came also got one free book. Shelton would then box up all remaining books and send them to the schools, the hospitals, and the clinics that were unable to attend. In the last few years, however, the shipping costs have tripled, so attendees are asked for a donation of one to five pula (15 to 75 cents) per book—a bargain, considering that most of these books would sell for 100 to 400 pula ($15 to $60), assuming they were even available.

········

The Most Important Things I Did Right

"I listened. And admitted that I knew nothing. And realized that, in Botswana, I needed to step back. You don't run up to someone and say, 'I need this.' You just come and you greet people, and you look them in the eye. You take the time to really smile, not a little quick thing. *Nicely* is their favorite word. You want to do things nicely."

········

On this broiling October day in Maun, no one at the book choosing is complaining about the donation. Many of the visitors have walked, hitchhiked, or bounced along in a public bus for up to ten hours to get here. An air of purpose pervades the room. There is no breeze, and no water or snacks are available, but nobody seems to notice. "You have to see Pam to believe her," says David Tregilges, an educator in Botswana. "She is this little fireball of a woman, fast-talking, passionate, and undaunted by obstacles." Thanks in large part to Shelton, he says, during the last decade reading for pleasure has become a possibility for thousands in Botswana. In 2007, Shelton received a James Patterson PageTurner Par Excellence Award for her devotion to cultivating readers.

By sundown, every head in this sand-swept town on the edge of the Kalahari Desert is gray-tinged and gritty. As the Maun headmaster locks the doors, Shelton is grimy, hungry, and pleased. Today has shown her, once again, why she's a book farmer. Tomorrow she'll get to work on new ideas, such as developing teen book groups ("we need teen novels and health books," she says). She'll also comb the Internet for potential grants.

Shelton, who calls her work a lifestyle hobby, does not collect a salary, nor does she own a home. She lives off an inheritance from her father, as well as the largesse of friends. Her personal overhead is zero, she says, although she sometimes hosts fundraisers to offset organization expenses such as shipping. Her financial situation is fine with her. "I'm sharing my greatest joy, the love of reading," she says. "What could be better?"

·············· **Pam's Key Questions to Ask Yourself** ··············

- Is the timing right?
- Who really needs you right now? Because reinventing yourself is often a bit of a selfish thing, you really have to look at how it affects the people around you. I couldn't have done this when I was raising my son because I wanted him to have stability in his life.
- Do your friends have their own agenda? When my friends responded to my reinvention with "You're crazy, you can't do that," I asked them why. Half of the time they said, "Well, because I'd like to do it!"
- Can you be by yourself? There was a lot of all-by-myself time in there—whoa, was it lonely at the beginning! In the end, you have to trust your own instinct.

Crisis Is Her Business
Elisabeth Schuler Russell

When Elisabeth Schuler Russell's phone rings at seven o'clock one evening in October 2010, she braces herself. As the founder of Patient Navigator (patientnavigator.com), a company that advocates for people facing medical problems, she is prepared to hear a heartbreaking story. Yet this phone call turns out to be especially wrenching. "My nephew had an accident," says the weary, halting voice. The day before, the boy and several of his fellow college freshmen had piled into an SUV and headed to a school event. He was riding in the cargo area without a seat belt when the vehicle flipped, then skidded forty yards.

"He's in intensive care, paralyzed from the waist down," the aunt says. He also has a broken jaw, six fractured ribs, and a punctured lung. Doctors think he will live, but his parents, the Marshalls (not their real name), can't bear to leave his bedside. They've asked his aunt to get information about the best spinal cord rehabilitation facilities. Are there any for young patients near their hometown? Can Russell help them?

Russell's own teenagers are downstairs doing homework. She feels tears welling up but wills herself to sound calm. "Yes, we can find all of that for you by tomorrow afternoon," she says. Then, at the aunt's request, Russell runs through a quick explanation of Patient Navigator's fee structure. The woman agrees to the firm's $125 hourly rate and a two-hour retainer. Russell has put off her usual litany of questions about doctors and insurance, because at this point what the family needs most urgently is research. Only later, in the kitchen with her husband, does she let herself experience the intensity of the sadness and compassion she is feeling.

The next morning, Russell phones Debora Harvey, the contract employee who works for her on call, and asks her to compile a list of spinal cord rehabilitation facilities within a hundred-mile radius of the Marshalls' home, with recommendations for the top four.

Russell describes herself as a problem solver. For more than twenty-two years, she practiced her skills not in the health-care system but as a diplomat working for the U.S. Department of

> ··········
>
> **The Most Surprising Thing about My Reinvention**
>
> "Creating a profitable business is a lot harder than I expected. This is an emerging profession, so there isn't much inherent demand. You have to create public demand, then meet it."
>
> ··········

State. During stints in Washington, D.C., the Ivory Coast, and Nicaragua, she worked with host-country officials, reported on economic and political events, and guided congressional delegations, often acting as interpreter.

Now, as the founder of Patient Navigator, she uses those same talents to assist people caught in the confusing, frustrating, sometimes desperate situations that result from illness, accidents, or aging. "People can get lost in the complexities of our system," she says. "They see doctors but are not necessarily heard or helped."

Russell's job changes day by day. She is sometimes the linchpin in a client's health-care action plan, making appointments, filling out insurance paperwork, even interviewing and hiring in-home caregivers. She once negotiated with a nursing home to reduce the fees for an injured woman whose insurance benefits ran out, and she saved another client $14,220 by winning an insurance appeal. One woman, who suffered from a rare disease, approached Russell because she was in constant pain, needed surgery, and felt that she wasn't being listened to by her team of thirteen doctors. Russell typed up a summary of the woman's history so that the doctors wouldn't have to wade through her voluminous files, found a pain specialist near the patient's home, then tracked down (in another state) the surgeon who had the best record for the needed procedure, and persuaded the woman's insurance company to pay, despite the distance. The result? A great reduction in the patient's pain and the beginning of her recovery. For another patient with a rare, painful disease, Russell located a leading authority on the affliction, in the Netherlands. She e-mailed him, sent a narrative, and quickly received an action plan. Today the woman's pain is under control.

Russell's discovery of this new career came out of a traumatic health challenge in her own family. When Russell and her husband left Nicaragua and moved with their two young children back to Washington, she continued to work for the State Department, pioneering the organization's first-ever job-sharing arrangement.

· ·

The Most Important Things I Learned

"That God has a plan for my life. In terms of business, the most important thing I learned is that the world of entrepreneurs is amazingly flexible. I can do what I think needs to be done without requiring seven layers above me to approve it. The State Department does its work very well, but I'm an out-of-the-box person, so it was always a little hard for me. Now I don't have to report to anybody; I feel as if I finally have wings to do what I want."

"I also learned that success comes in degrees of small achievements, not as one big giant step."

· ·

Six months later, on the evening of September 18, 1998—"a date engraved in my memory," she says—her nanny reported something odd. Russell's daughter, Claire, then two years old, had begun to drag her left leg and couldn't walk normally. Russell immediately phoned their pediatrician, who instructed her to bring in the child the next morning. From there, Claire was rushed directly to the hospital for a CT scan. The next hours were a blur of tests and ominous, unfamiliar phrases, such as *high intracranial pressure*. Finally, a doctor gave them the news: "Your daughter has a brain tumor."

"I fainted," Russell says. "I remember the scent of smelling salts."

All day she and her husband received bursts of terrifying and sometimes conflicting information. First, they were told that Claire's life was threatened because the tumor was on her brain stem, which controls motor functions such as breathing and swallowing, but that surgery could remove it. Then a surgeon declared that the tumor was not on the brain stem but embedded in it, which meant it was inoperable.

"We were being asked to make decisions that could cost Claire her life or possibly save it," Russell recalls. At first, she went into brain freeze, a kind of mental paralysis that can befall those slammed with horrible news. Yet within twenty-four hours, she moved into problem-solving mode. She phoned the offices of pediatric neurologists and surgeons in Washington and New York City, using sheer persistence to push through layers of receptionists and nurses. Before a week had gone by, her research had convinced the Russells that they had to treat Claire's tumor with radiation, or she very likely would die.

Claire, who by then couldn't even stand up, began radiation treatment five days a week. A nurse inserted a surgical port for medications into her chest. Nausea made it difficult for Claire to eat or drink, so Russell learned to administer the saline drip when she was dehydrated. Once the radiation was over, they waited. For three months, MRIs showed no change in the tumor.

Then one day, new test results came in. "I'm sorry, but the tumor looks bigger," said the doctor, Glenn Tonnesen, MD, of Fairfax, Virginia. He offered chemotherapy as a last-ditch effort but suggested waiting a little longer to see further radiation results. Claire started to feel a bit better. "She wasn't walking, but she could stand," Russell recalls. In late May, eight months after the terrible diagnosis, an MRI showed that the tumor was smaller. "That gave us our first hope that Claire would make it through this alive," she says. Subsequent tests showed more shrinking, and so it went, until what was left appeared to be only scar tissue. Claire survived, but no one understands how. "Most children with brain stem tumors do not survive, although some do. Some live a year, some more, some less. We don't know why," Tonnesen says now.

As her daughter was being treated, Russell met parents of other gravely ill children and swapped stories with them in waiting rooms and online. While sharing any useful information she'd acquired, she learned a lot herself: which doctors specialized in which types of children's cancer, where research trials were being held, where parents could find support groups. Her coworkers helped as well. Thanks to a State Department program that allows staff members to donate vacation hours to colleagues facing an emergency, she continued to draw a salary. "My coworkers gave me more than nineteen hundred hours—so many that, combined with my own accumulated vacation and sick time, I never had to take unpaid leave," Russell says.

By the time she went back to work, dealing with the health-care world had become a new skill. When it became apparent that her daughter was tumor-free, a conversation with her pastor inspired Russell to turn that skill into a vocation. "I asked him, 'Is Claire's recovery a miracle? What am I supposed to do? How can I possibly give enough thanks to God for this?'" she says. The pastor answered, "Help other people, one by one."

Determined to meet that challenge, Russell considered retiring from the State Department, but what, specifically, would she do? She had run grief support groups for a local hospice as a volunteer, and although she admired their work, it didn't feel right for her. Then one day she took a walk with a colleague. "He told me how hard it was to get health care for his ailing aunt, that just the insurance troubles alone made him feel as if he had stepped into an alien universe," Russell recalls. "I thought, That's what I want to do. I'll help people navigate the health-care maze." In 2004, while still at the State Department, Russell founded Patient Navigator and began moonlighting in her new field.

. . . .

The Most Important Things I Did Right

"I was smart to start the business while I still had a full-time, paying job. By the time I retired, four years later, it was all set up, and I already had some experience under my belt. My husband thought I was crazy not to wait until I retired, but I didn't want to wait. I'm very glad I didn't—if for nothing else, just to prove him wrong!"

"I always kept in view the fact that I could go back to what I was doing before if the next step didn't work out. This gave me the freedom to try for the next goal and know I could survive."

. . . .

Her line of work now turns up in "hot career" lists under a variety of names: patient advocacy, medical or health advocacy, health-care consulting. Russell receives about twenty-five inquiries a month from people wanting to get into the business, and the demand from patients and clients is expected to rise, says Laura Weil, the director of the master's degree health advocacy program at Sarah Lawrence College.

Russell's first clients found her through family and friends. As she assisted them, she taught herself the basics of Internet marketing, bookkeeping, and invoicing. Toughest for her was dropping her volunteer mind-set and thinking like a business owner. "I found it hard to set a realistic fee, because I feared it would close the door to many who needed me," she says. "I had to learn that what I do for people is valuable and that they are willing to pay for it."

A year after Patient Navigator launched, Russell teamed up with fellow advocate Debora Harvey and in 2006 hired a freelance cancer-care specialist. In 2008, after more than twenty-two years in the State Department, Russell retired and took the helm of Patient Navigator full time, working from a tidy home office.

Because much of Russell's work can be done by phone or online, she casts a wide customer net, with about two-thirds of her clients coming from outside the D.C. metro area. "The only thing I can't do for those who aren't local is go to appointments with them," she says. Besides her hourly fee of $125, Russell offers monthly or annual retainer agreements with some long-term clients. To date, a substantial portion of her income has gone to pay freelancers and cover marketing costs, while she has leaned on her State Department pension. This year, however, she expects to start racking up enough profits to pay herself a salary.

Russell says it was her boots-on-the-ground knowledge of how the health-care and insurance systems work that enabled her to build the business successfully. "I know where the power lies and who makes the decisions," she says. During Claire's treatment, she learned to speak what she refers to as doctors' lingo so that the physicians would feel comfortable talking with her. Mostly, though, she calls on her diplomatic skills—-listening, working with all sorts of people, collecting and interpreting information, finding solutions. "Diplomats are advocates. I just do my advocacy in a different setting now," she says.

She recently advocated for a family she calls the Davidsons. The husband, Jonathan, suffers from debilitating anxiety and needed a series of neurological tests. The family found Russell via the Internet and hired her to identify a team of specialists in Washington and supervise his care. At a recent appointment, Jonathan sat hunched over in a waiting room chair, elbows clenched to his body, radiating nervousness. With calm efficiency, Russell checked in with the nurses, who knew her from previous cases, then returned to his side. "The doctor is reading your summary, so you won't have many questions to answer," she said. "The real business today," she continued, "is finding out which tests the doctor recommends." Yet Jonathan's agitation persisted: he was worried that he would embarrass himself during the testing. "I'll make sure the doctor prescribes something that will keep you calm during the scan," Russell told him. "No need to worry about it. You'll take something, I'll drive you, it will be fine." Jonathan brightened.

·················· **My Biggest Mistake** ··················

"Being naïve about protecting my own intellectual property. I was with the State Department for twenty-two years, and our job was to serve the public. We gave away our knowledge, free, to the taxpayer. So it was hard for me to get out of that mind-set; for a long time, I gave away my knowledge for free and couldn't ever say no to people."

These days Russell's daughter, Claire, is a thriving high school freshman. She enjoys soccer and hanging out with friends, like any other teen. Russell is still emotional about her recovery, but when it comes to Patient Navigator, Russell has taught herself to put her own feelings aside as necessary. "I can compartmentalize and get the job done, even when tears are lurking," she says. "It isn't my nature to sit around weeping. I want to make things better."

·········· Elisabeth's Key Questions to Ask Yourself ··········

- What is the passion in your life? What would give your life real meaning?

- Do you have the money to support yourself for at least a year? At first, I had my salary from the State Department; now I have my retirement pension. Which I need, because I still don't make much money. Last year was my biggest: $20,000 in revenue.

- Who have you talked to about your idea? I would say, "Talk to a lot of people." Most will shoot you down—"Well, you can't possibly make money doing that." But talk to a wide range—business people, others doing the same thing, close friends—and you'll find a turning point. For me, it was my pastor.

- Have you assessed your own level of risk-taking ability? How much risk will you bear versus how much security do you need? The business world is dog-eat-dog, so you need to know: What are you most afraid of? Is it fear of failure or of going broke?

- At your funeral, what do you hope people will say that you did in your life? Is your second act what you want to be remembered for? Is it that important to you?

The Up Side of the Down Side

As an entrepreneur, you have no security at all, and making money is difficult. And finding an investor who believes in what I do is impossible. But I love it. I wake up evey day and can't wait to get to work, because I know that it's all on me.

The Earthquake Avenger
Marla Petal

Five days after a magnitude 7.4 earthquake hit Izmit, Turkey, in August 1999, the city lay in ruins, with piles of rubble where factories and houses had once stood. Bulldozers roared and clanked. Volunteers sifted through the debris, seeking survivors among the flattened structures. Jeeps and ambulances rumbled, bearing away the thousands of dead.

California native Marla Petal walked slowly past what had been apartment towers, the floors now pancaked and sliding, furniture spilling out through crumbled walls. She lived sixty miles away, in Istanbul, with her Turkish husband (an urban planner) and their daughter, and the couple had driven into the disaster zone to see if there was anything they could do to help the victims.

A year earlier, Petal, then forty-three, had followed her husband to Turkey, envisioning a luxurious break—"going to lunch with the other expat wives," she says—from her hectic life as a social worker in California. Yet having no job, few local friends, and minimal Turkish at her command, Petal soon felt lost and homesick.

Now, in the street, she made eye contact with a blank-faced woman in her late fifties. The stranger stumbled into Petal's arms and crumpled in anguish, wailing. Petal quickly learned that the woman had lost two children during the quake. It was a powerful

moment that helped set Petal on her path: to protect the world's
children from the devastation of earthquakes. More than a decade
since that day, Petal has made good on her vow and is now one of
the world's foremost earthquake safety
education advocates. "When you have
been through something that devastating
and had to witness the suffering, it drives
you," she says.

> **The Most Important Thing I Learned**
>
> "The importance of being open to what life brings. I wasn't going for an intentional reinvention; I was just open to opportunities when they literally jumped in front of me."

Safeguarding children is more complicated than it sounds, though. Children
spend more time at school than anywhere except their bedrooms, and it
turns out that schools around the world—
including some in the United States—
are exceptionally vulnerable to quakes,
hurricanes, and floods. Many classroom
buildings have not been built to code; others have never been
retrofitted to meet current safety standards. Plus, says Petal,
"schools are often assigned to unsafe locations, such as the bottom
of a landslide-prone hill or a floodplain where others don't want
to build."

The May 2008 earthquake in China's Sichuan Province, in
which apartment buildings stood undamaged next to destroyed
school buildings, is a terrifying example of how poorly many
schools are built: Almost seven thousand schools collapsed, by
some reports killing ten thousand children. Heartbreaking images
flew around the world on CNN International: students perched
on tipping slabs, waving to show rescuers where classmates were
buried; parents, weeping and frantic, clawing at the rubble.

Soon afterward, the Earth Institute at Columbia University
calculated how many U.S. children might be at risk for a similar
disaster and found that 4.2 million attend schools in earthquake
zones throughout the nation. In 2007, Oregon's Department of
Geology and Mineral Industries released a report that examined

thirty-three hundred education and other public buildings, and deemed thirteen hundred of them to have a "high to very high" probability of structural failure in a quake. These statistics infuriate Petal. "Schools should be safe," she says, unequivocally. "We should not put kids' lives at risk to educate them."

Petal is a child of two earthquake zones. She was born in California and spent some formative years in Japan, so she learned to "drop, cover, and hold" (the standard earthquake instruction) as a routine part of her school day. When she was eight, the 1964 Niigata quake struck a hundred miles from her house in Tokyo. Petal tried to run upstairs to bring her baby brother to safety, but she couldn't reach him because the steps were shaking too much. (He was unhurt.) When the 1994 Northridge earthquake hit northwestern Los Angeles, she was there with her husband and daughter. They all jumped out of bed and rode out the temblor clinging to door frames. Petal's family came out of it unharmed, but she acquired a deep respect for the unpredictability and brute force of quakes.

Petal has always had an interest in helping children. Starting in the early 1990s, she worked as a consultant for disabled kids and their parents, helping them claim hard-to-access government services; in addition, she worked as a child abuse prevention specialist. Still, she willingly gave up her career when, in 1998, her husband proposed relocating the family to Turkey for his work. The following summer, sideswiped by the loneliness of being unable to speak the language and the self-doubt of having no job of her own, Petal took her daughter back to California for a long visit with friends.

·············· **My Biggest Mistake** ··············

"Not studying the Turkish language seriously from Day One. And thinking that without having language ability, there was nothing meaningful I could do."

Ironically, as it turned out, they used some of their time to gather disaster education materials: Petal's daughter, then eight years old, had joined an Istanbul Girl Scout troop, and Petal had an idea—based on her childhood experiences—to create an earthquake-safety badge. The trip went so well, they extended it a week, switching their departure tickets to August 20, 1999. On August 17, Petal heard that an earthquake had rocked northwest Turkey and torn Izmit apart. Two days after her return, Petal and her husband entered the ravaged city.

Petal was perfectly suited to her new mission. She had lived through earthquakes without being debilitated by the trauma. She knew how to help people talk to one another, even about very sensitive issues. And she had just stuffed her suitcase and her head with critical disaster-preparedness knowledge. Back in Istanbul, Petal immediately created an earthquake safety workshop for other expat women. She expected a dozen to attend; about a hundred showed up. Demand grew quickly. She put on workshops for another women's group, expat schools, and local businesses. Her Turkish neighbors became interested, and she taught them, too, through a translator. She began to understand that the simple protective steps that every Californian picks up in childhood, such as fastening furniture to walls and not hanging heavy objects over the bed, were rarely discussed in Turkey. People didn't understand how vulnerable they were, and there was no widely disseminated source of earthquake safety information.

News of Petal's seminars quickly spread. The American Friends Service Committee—an international relief organization—asked Petal to draft materials that community organizers could distribute throughout the neighborhoods. A Turkish magazine wrote admiringly about her efforts. In 2000, Istanbul's Boğaziçi University, the home of the national earthquake research institute, asked her for help in developing the Istanbul Community Impact Project; the resulting curriculum educated four thousand teachers about what to do during an earthquake, how to prepare buildings to reduce the chance of injuries, and how to organize first responders. The lessons those teachers passed on to their one million students during the next three years were so well received that the Turkish Ministry of National Education asked Petal to expand the program so that twenty-five thousand more teachers could attend. More than a decade after Izmit, the woman who once felt alienated from Turkey had helped protect and educate five million Turkish students.

Petal didn't limit her message to only one country. She quickly saw the need for governments worldwide to teach earthquake safety techniques and to improve the construction of school buildings. Petal joined the Coalition for Global School Safety, an international group of engineers, architects, social scientists, and disaster workers from forty countries. With disaster preparedness expert Ilan Kelman, she founded RiskRED (Risk Reduction Education for Disasters; riskred.org), a virtual nongovernmental organization that she runs from New York, where she and her family moved in 2010. Funded by grants, donations, and consulting fees, Petal and her RiskRED colleagues work with governments and nonprofits worldwide to develop the plans that will save students' lives in emergencies.

In 2008, the United Nations released a report that Petal wrote, about disaster prevention in schools, to the education ministries of 168 member countries. UNICEF used her earthquake safety checklist in China to help shape a major public awareness campaign after the Sichuan earthquake. In Turkey and Central Asia, the courses Petal developed—which include slides, safety manuals, and booklets—have been used to train almost thirty thousand teachers. She has written chapters for engineering and urban planning textbooks, as well as articles for dozens of professional journals and magazines. Petal also directed and produced twenty short public-awareness films, which have been translated into various languages and are shown in education workshops and on television.

Despite her international involvement, Petal hasn't forgotten the risk to children in the United States. In November 2008, she and her RiskRED colleagues participated in the Great California Shakeout, a massive earthquake drill that included five million people and hundreds of schools. The state asked Petal to evaluate how well the government helps children survive disasters.

In 2009, the American Red Cross awarded RiskRED a grant to develop a comprehensive online training program for school disaster management in Turkey. Partnering with the Turkish Ministry of National Education, the program expects to train ten thousand teachers in an online self-study program in 2010–2011. The portal and the curriculum will be available to Red Cross/Red Crescent Societies, nongovernmental and governmental partners internationally, and will allow everyone to learn from one another's experience.

Petal now works as a consultant, earning in the range of $60,000 to $75,000 a year. She is retraining herself for what she hopes will be her next and perhaps final career: becoming an instructional designer, re-tooling her messages for large-scale, Web-based, and mobile delivery. "By the time a disaster happens, it's too late," she says, before she gets off the phone so that she can catch her next plane. "The time to plan is *now*."

············· **Marla's Key Questions to Ask Yourself** ·············

- What do you care about?
- What are you good at?
- What do you want to get better at?
- Whom can you ask for help?
- What are you waiting for?

She Dreamed of Africa
Vivian Glyck

As the plane touches down in Entebbe, Uganda, Vivian Glyck unfolds her long, tanned legs with relief. She has just traveled ten thousand miles from California to East Africa on three lengthy flights during two long days, economy class. She collects her bags while porters swarm around her, as determined as the mosquitoes that start biting even before she leaves the airport. Outside the terminal, she's greeted by smells redolent of African evenings— charcoal cooking fires, open sewers, the acrid pollution generated by aging vehicles damaged by lousy roads, all mixing with the heady, sweet perfume of night-blooming jasmine.

Glyck still manages to look fresh, which is more than can be said for most of her fellow passengers. And she's not done yet. After a dusty three-hour van drive over bumpy washboard roads due north, she arrives at the Bishop Cesar Asili Memorial Medical Center, in Luwero, to be greeted by a coterie of African nuns who are thrilled to see her. She is, in their words, a miracle worker.

Glyck's commute used to take her from her San Diego kitchen, black coffee in hand, to her home office, where she worked as a marketing consultant to such high-wattage clients as Dean Ornish and Deepak Chopra. In May 2006, however, when she was forty-five, she visited Africa, looking for a way to help; when she saw the hospital in Luwero, she had her answer. The fifty-bed facility, a series of one-story buildings with chickens scratching in the yard, was practically the only one serving an area that was home to 650,000 people. It had no running water and lost electricity for weeks at a time. This meant no refrigeration for medicines and vaccines; women gave birth by the light of a lantern. Worse, there was no doctor, in a region where malaria and HIV/AIDS are rampant.

The Sisters of Mary Mother of the Church, a Ugandan Catholic order, were running the facility on the tiniest of budgets. "They did the very best they could, but conditions were heartbreaking," Glyck says. She asked the center's administrator, Sister Ernestine, what she needed most. "A generator," the nun replied, expecting Glyck to go home and forget about it.

Back in California, however, Glyck promptly raised $30,000, the price of a generator, by appealing to everyone she knew. She also formed a foundation, Just Like My Child (justlikemy child.com), because she saw that the hospital needed so much more. Then she hit her first roadblock: her own nascent board objected to wiring $30,000 to Uganda before the charity's structure was solid. Launching a Glyck charm offensive, she smiled and

The Most Important Thing I Learned

"The complexity of really making a difference in a country, as opposed to putting a Band-Aid on the problem by bringing in bed nets or medical supplies. Our model is to create sustainable long-lasting solutions that empower people to solve their own problems. If we just give a handout and don't offer people the know-how to lift themselves up, we're only making ourselves feel good."

told them, "Yes, but the hospital needs electricity *now.*" She won that battle; today the precious room-size generator, which supplies electricity to the hospital and the small adjoining convent, sits inside its own heavily barred shelter, where it is safe from thieves.

"I can't tell you how surprised I was when Vivian promised things and then delivered," Sister Ernestine says. "This had never happened before." The generator was only the beginning. A few well-placed phone calls led Glyck to a California doctor who was willing to sponsor a Ugandan doctor's salary; soon an MD moved from Kampala, the capital, to join the staff. In order to receive antiretroviral drugs from the government, the hospital also needed a CD4 diagnostic machine, which determines when HIV has progressed to AIDS. A new machine costs upward of $100,000. Glyck exhaustively lobbied the Clinton Foundation in New York until it gave her entrée to a company that donated a long-term lease on a refurbished one.

"How could I not make the effort?" Glyck asks. "More than 17 million Africans have died from AIDS, and there are almost 25 million infected with HIV. That's more than the Holocaust, more than the tsunami. I've got twenty-plus years of marketing and business experience to do what I'm doing: making connections, using the Internet to generate interest and money." Glyck visits Uganda several times a year; at home, she telecommutes and holds "friend-raisers." Although she never formally quit her consulting business, she let it dwindle. "Just Like My Child is more than a full-time job," she says.

. . . .

The Most Important Thing I Did Right

"Working with community leaders and asking them about how we could help the local familes affected by AIDS. Through the hospital we're working with, more than 3,500 patients are now on AIDS treatment and are coming back to life as a result. We also suggested microloans but they were suspicious of money and interest rates and didn't think that they were going to be able to pay it back. So we created Project Grace, which is basically a livestock exchange program that gives sets of pigs or chickens to families where a parent is on AIDS treatment, so they can start to build a sustainable business.

"Now we learned that we've got to qualify the people whom we're working with. You can't just sprinkle fairy dust and hope that everyone will understand how to take advantage of what's being offered. So, as a result of our rigorous qualification program, we interview the patients and the families and see what their motivation is to build their businesses, which is why we've been really successful with this project so far. We asked the communities and worked with them, to find out what would stick there."

. . . .

Glyck herself is surprised by how she ended up doing charity work. She was forty-two when her son, Zak, was born in 2002; she and her husband, Mike, a technology consultant and an Internet marketer, wanted another child. "I had back-to-back miscarriages," she says. "After the third one, I couldn't do it again. I got very, very down. People tried to comfort me, but I went to a dark place. I'd find myself sitting in my car at traffic lights, sobbing inconsolably."

At about that time, both Bono and Angelina Jolie were in the news for their humanitarian work in Africa. "I found myself thinking, if *they* can do something to help, so can I," Glyck says. One night shortly afterward, she sat bolt upright in bed, woke Mike, and told him, "I have to go to Africa." Soon after that, Glyck was in Senegal with a local church group when an Italian photographer told her about Sister Ernestine. Next stop, Uganda.

The Bishop Cesar Asili Memorial Medical Center sits on a road leading to a childhood home of Uganda's despotic former ruler Idi Amin. After Amin's regime fell, Luwero District, still reeling from the dictator's genocidal purges, was the site of a brutal six-year bush war in the 1980s, during which thousands died and piles of human skulls lined the roads.

Today Luwero is a sleepy backwater baking in the sun. Red soil covers everything in a thick dust. Surrounding the hospital is a shantytown of corrugated-iron shacks and tiny impoverished stores selling a few cookies, homemade snacks, and used bicycle parts. In her denim miniskirt and black tank top, which set off her exercise-toned body, Glyck is a dramatic counterpoint to Sister Ernestine in her blue-gray habit. Fast-talking and quick-thinking, Glyck bends and bobs to greet adults and children alike.

Malaria is the number-one killer of children in Uganda. "It's insane that they don't have bed nets," Glyck says. While a lifesaving insecticide-treated mosquito net for a hospital bed costs $10 and for an ordinary bed as little as $6, these prices are prohibitive in a region where most people are subsistence farmers. So Glyck went into battle again, contacting the President's Malaria Initiative, Malaria No More, and the United States Agency for International Development, all of which had nets but didn't have the Luwero hospital on their radar. Now they do. USAID told her to buy some nets herself first to prove the hospital was serious about preventing malaria. Glyck found an American donor who anonymously gave her $50,000 to do just that. Several large donors, including the Clinton Foundation and Mildmay International, an HIV charity, invested to create an AIDS treatment program.

Glyck has also pledged to supply antiretrovirals for the HIV-positive mothers who come to counseling sessions at the hospital. In addition, she has come up with funding for a mobile health-unit ambulance and is closing in on a surgical suite. "We're also going to start some microfinancing projects," she says.

Glyck believes in holistic philanthropy: focusing on all of the interrelated needs of a community. To that end, she intends to move beyond health care into education. "The UN has consistently advocated for the education of girls, which has the single largest impact on the developing world," she says.

One girl in particular grabbed Glyck's heart: Nyangoma Recha, who was nine when Glyck first visited Uganda and met her, in the destitute village of Kikoiro, some thirty miles from the hospital. "I couldn't forget her face," Glyck says. "She was so full of love, playfulness, and promise, yet she had never been to school." Thanks to Glyck, construction of a public school is now under way. "I hope Nyangoma will be able to avoid early sex, pregnancy, and AIDS," she says.

....

The Most Surprising Thing about My Reinvention

"Feeling as though I have firsthand knowledge of how development works at the grass-roots level [in developing countries]; I'm now a bit of an expert, and I never really expected that."

....

························· **My Biggest Mistake** ·······················

"Thinking that everyone was going to be honest. We came really close to working with a partner of a village who didn't have the same motivations that we had. There's a lot of desperation, and desperation breeds all kinds of distorted motivations."

Her inspiration remains Sister Ernestine. "She makes me very committed," Glyck says. "I once asked her if she ever despaired. She replied that she had learned you can't waste anything. That she'd seen a drop of water bring someone back from the brink of death."

In turn, Sister Ernestine says of Glyck, "When I met her, I could see she had a vision. Before, I felt so frustrated. I told her many times, 'I don't want to go into the villages, because I'm empty-handed.' Now, because of Vivian, I can bring good news. She has strengthened my faith. She's come from so far away, with no blood relative here, and she has put her feet in our shoes. Vivian is not like our politicians."

In Uganda, corruption often seems to be the main growth industry. The Global Fund to Fight AIDS, Tuberculosis, and Malaria suspended funding to the country after discovering that grant money had been misappropriated. Ministry of Health officials were subsequently fired for embezzling millions meant for vaccines and immunization.

"Many donors are upset because they can't confirm that their money is being used properly," says Glyck, whose organization spends 85 percent of every dollar on services. "It's evil to take away the opportunity for health and education. This kind of corruption is murdering people."

Misuse of money outrages her when she thinks of the many child-headed households she's encountered. Matthias Ziiwa, who may now be seventeen or twenty—no one is sure—has been struggling to feed and clothe his five younger sisters since their parents died of AIDS in 2007. Behind their ramshackle house are seven graves in which he has buried his parents and other relatives. In addition to daily tending the family's vegetable plot, he hires himself out as a day laborer, earning $6 a week. "But a dress for one of the girls costs $3," he says. "And school uniforms and books are another $4.89 each." Matthias, who once dreamed of becoming a doctor, was forced to drop out of school in seventh grade.

Clearly, Glyck loves what she does. There's only one real downside. "It's excruciating to be away from Zak," she says. "The first time I left, I broke down and wailed. Now we have a tradition before I leave for a trip. We go to a 99-cent store and buy out all of their candy and pencils for the kids here. Zak really gets into it. When he's older, I'll take him with me."

Until her board approved a $40,000 salary in December 2007, the family was living primarily on her husband's income. "We've cut back on vacations, traveling, eating out," she says. "But it's more than worth it. It's so rewarding to see the same families every time I come; they're committed to improving their circumstances and beginning to gain a sense of trust in us, and they feel that we're all in this together."

When people tell her how impressed they are by what she has achieved in so short a time, she quips, "This is what a white Jewish mom and a black Catholic nun can do when they put their heads together." Then more seriously, she adds, "Working in Uganda has taught me that I don't want another child. I want ten thousand."

············· **Vivian's Key Questions to Ask Yourself** ·············

- Can you maintain a sustainable balance with your health and well-being, relationship, and parenting needs while following this passion?

- How can you learn the skill of "telling stories" so that you can naturally attract those who most resonate with your passion and who will become your undying supporters and promoters?
- Do you have a solid rock to stand on—can you be financially stable?
- Who are your fans?

Vivian's Success Strategy

"If you're starting out on your own little boat all by yourself, you may want to pull in and focus on building your platform and your support network. I've seen more than one little ship of passion sink because there wasn't enough support."

Her Artful Business Plan
Willa Shalit

Willa Shalit is rushing between appointments along a busy street in Manhattan when a passerby stops her and fingers Shalit's shoulder bag, a three-tone cotton sling patterned with Barack Obama faces. "I love this," the woman says. "Where did you get it?"

Shalit just happens to have the company's card, which specifies a website (obamabags.com) that sells not only this particular item but also a range of others made from Obama-print fabrics. "This is fantastic," the woman says. "You wouldn't have a few more of these cards, would you? I want to give them to my friends."

Shalit gives the woman a handful, then takes off, not once mentioning that she arranged for the bags' manufacture back during the presidential campaign, and that she imports them from

Rwanda. Her company, Fair Winds Trading (fairwindstrading.com), also imports non-Obama tote bags, baskets, place mats, tablecloths, ornaments, and jewelry, thus providing employment to thousands of women in Rwanda, Tanzania, Kenya, South Africa, Cambodia, Indonesia, and Haiti. Shalit came up with the idea for the Obama bags in February 2008, during one of her frequent trips to Rwanda. "I was there at the time of George Bush's visit to Africa, and I noticed fabric with his face printed on it everywhere. I thought, If they can do that with Bush's face, we can do it with Obama's."

Voilà: Obama handbags, shoulder bags, bandannas, table-cloths, and sarongs.

Voilà: Art meets business meets social activism, the driving force and inspiration behind Shalit's many enterprises.

Shalit, fifty-six, a thin woman with tight brown curls who often punctuates her conversation with a warm hand on her listener's knee or forearm, has spent the last three decades reinventing herself through four different careers. One of *Today* show film critic Gene Shalit's six children, she cut her entrepreneurial teeth at the age of nineteen with a vintage clothing store she owned and ran in the summertime on Martha's Vineyard. She would purchase her stock during the school year on trips through the Midwest. ("People have attics there, with a treasure trove of antique clothing.") After graduating from Oberlin College in 1978, she became a life-cast sculptor, making three-dimensional plaster likenesses of human faces and bodies. Living "very simply and frugally," she supported herself on her artist's income and money earned from seamstress work, with occasional help from her family. In 1989, she became an artist in residence at the College of Santa Fe, in New Mexico. By age thirty-seven, she'd made life castings of numerous celebrities, as well as five presidents— Nixon, Ford, Carter, Reagan, and the elder Bush—and she published a book about her sculptures. Two years later, in 1996, PBS aired a documentary about her work, titled *Willa: Behind the Mask.*

By the time she turned forty, Shalit was looking for a new mission. A writer friend introduced her to the emerging playwright Eve Ensler, who invited her to attend a reading of her latest project, *The Vagina Monologues*, then a work in progress. Shalit was bowled over by the play's message of spiritual and creative empowerment for women. "I thought Ensler was a genius, an incredible writer, and visionary," she says. "I resolved to help her get her voice out into the world." Despite daunting challenges, Shalit eventually guided production of Ensler's groundbreaking show into more than a hundred countries.

So many women who saw *The Vagina Monologues* approached the playwright afterward to talk about having been abused that Shalit and Ensler became "hyperaware of the pervasiveness of violence against women and knew we needed to do something about it," Shalit says. So in 1998, Ensler cocreated V-Day, a movement to fight violence against women, and appointed Shalit its founding executive director. Shalit had been raped at fifteen and was already "sensitive to others who have suffered physical, emotional, or sexual trauma," she says, but through her work for V-Day, Shalit realized that without money, women would never be able to extricate themselves from oppressive living situations.

So, at age forty-six, Shalit quit her position at V-Day and began searching for ways to help women become economically self-sufficient. In 2003, at the suggestion of a friend, she represented a group of businesswomen on a United Nations–sponsored trip to Rwanda, which was rebuilding itself after the 1994 genocide of more than eight hundred thousand people. The goal of the visit was to meet the widows and brainstorm ways to help them sell their handwoven baskets.

For Shalit, who is Jewish, the echoes of the Holocaust deepened her empathy for the victims. "When I met the women, they were shell-shocked," she says. "They had no money, food, or medicine, and only one *kitenge*—garment—to wear, but they had incredible dignity and great strength." She was also moved by how

Tutsi and Hutu weavers, formerly enemies, had sought reconcili-
ation by collaborating on the zigzag design of the Peace Basket,
which represents "the path of people walking up the hills of
Rwanda," Shalit says. "People walk in times of peace, so the pattern is a symbol of peaceful times."

After she returned to the United States, Shalit began import-
ing the Rwandan baskets on a small scale, while helping the weavers build up their capacity. The women's lives started to improve
almost immediately. "With the first money they received," Shalit
says, "they bought soap so they could clean themselves. You have
no idea what a difference it makes for a woman to walk down the
street if she's clean. Just a bar of soap is a huge thing."

Then, in 2005, Shalit met with Macy's CEO Terry Lundgren,
who was immediately enthusiastic about selling the baskets, but
Macy's purchasing procedures weren't set up to buy cottage
industry products from developing countries. "I said, 'No problem. I'll get the products here, and you can buy them from me."
She and her business partner Dean Ericson managed the new
endeavor, which Macy's titled the Path to Peace Collection
(macys.com/campaign/rwanda/index.jsp). Thus, Shalit's passions
converged into something beautiful to behold: a business model
that connected a recently devastated African country to the
global market, creating a real chance for economic and social
resurgence.

From the outset, Shalit was determined to sustain a steady
demand for the products. The hurdles, however, were consider-
able. Macy's required that the baskets be packed in plastic, but
Rwanda had banned plastic bags. So Shalit's in-country business
partners, Janet Nkubana and Joy Ndungutse, of a company called
Gahaya Links, obtained a government waiver allowing them to
bring in plastic bags from Kenya. When Macy's upped its order
from twelve hundred to thirty thousand baskets at the end of
2005, Ericson moved to Rwanda to help Gahaya Links increase
production.

By 2006, the project had grown so large that Shalit created Fair Winds Trading, investing $250,000 of the money she'd earned producing *The Vagina Monologues* and running V-Day. The company operates by partnering with about a dozen small, local artisanal workshops in Africa and Asia, which recruit, hire, and train weavers, beaders, sewers, cutters, and others. Today, Fair Winds has expanded to a staff of six in New York. In Rwanda, for instance, about three-quarters of the revenue ($1.6 million in 2007) that Fair Winds generates remains in the country, with weavers' incomes generally running between $725 and $1,450 per year or more (Rwandan per capita income is $370 a year). On most baskets, Shalit says, the weavers make $6.50 to $8 and Fair Winds 50 cents. Although it is common for men to dominate in African societies, women who trade with Fair Winds are opening bank accounts and retaining control of the money they've earned. They can now afford their children's school uniforms, and in some families, when the women leave home for training in basket-weaving, their husbands step in to cook and care for the children.

> ......
>
> ## The Most Important Thing I Learned
>
> "That everything will be all right. I worried a lot unnecessarily. It takes a lot of discipline not to worry."
>
> ......

Although Fair Winds is the focus of her work these days (her current salary: $120,000), Shalit has never entirely let go of her past endeavors. She still receives income from the foreign rights and licensing of *The Vagina Monologues* and makes life casts of friends. Her heart is very much in Rwanda, where she now spends about three weeks every year and where, in addition to her business projects, she has helped establish two orphanages and a bakery. The bakery, set up to feed the orphans and produce income, now employs twenty-nine people and has a monthly revenue of $2,000, an enormous sum for the country.

Shalit seems to be in perpetual motion, but she's had to learn to pace herself or suffer the consequences. After stepping down from V-Day in 2002, she became seriously depressed and suffered a rare physical reaction to an antidepressant that left her with third-degree burns over her body. "I shed my skin like a snake!" she recalls, still amazed at the aptness of the metaphor. "It was the most intense physical experience I've ever had."

Shalit now watches out for warning signs that she is working too hard, such as complaints from friends and family members that she is unreachable and not returning messages. "I tend toward workaholism, and that's not satisfying for me."

One way that Shalit stays grounded is by observing the Sabbath at her home in Santa Fe. For twenty-four hours, beginning Friday evenings, "I light candles, have friends over, and we have Shabbat dinner. I don't shop. I don't spend money. I don't write," she says. Shalit tries to live by the Jewish principle of *tikkun olam*—an injunction to repair a world that has been broken. On the Sabbath, however, her mandate is "to admire the perfection of the world" through gardening, music, books, and family. (Shalit, who has been separated from her husband for two years, has a twenty-two-year-old daughter, Natasha.)

Shalit has recently become more involved in projects in Haiti. In May 2010, at a meeting of the Clinton Foundation, she set a program in motion to jump-start the country's artisan sector so that its members could have work after the earthquake. "I took the challenge and partnered with an organization called Brand Aid, and during the next three months we designed a home décor line," she says. "It launched at Macy's department store on macys.com/Haiti. The Haitian people are creative, and they do beautiful metalwork and great papier-mâché. We have frames and trays and candleholders, and

· · · · · · · · · ·

The Most Important Thing I Did Right

"I have had unwavering determination to achieve a specific goal to provide employment for artisans. I could've gotten pulled in different directions, but I stayed with that specific purpose."

· · · · · · · · · ·

we also have some patchwork quilting that is turned into kitchen products. Haiti is a whole country of artists."

Is Shalit headed for yet another reinvention? She knows that her own "juice" comes from launching enterprises, so the reins of Fair Winds Trading may pass to another person while she moves on to the next chapter. Yet it's hard to imagine that her passions for helping others will ever ebb. Some time ago Aurea Kayiganwa, the leader of an organization of genocide widows, presented her with a Rwandan name she treasures: Uwacu (pronounced "oo-WAH-choo"). It means "ours."

Willa's Success Strategy

"If you find something that you are deeply passionate about, then you will have the energy to get through the hard times with the business. If you do something to try to make money that doesn't have a deep emotional or spiritual purpose, it's hard to continue to find the source of energy to get you through the difficult times that will come when you are switching careers."

She Saves Wild Cats
Kay McElroy

Kay McElroy was reading her local paper when she saw an ad: "Six-month-old cougar cub for sale. $1,000." The year was 1987, and the classifieds were a form of window-shopping for McElroy, who couldn't afford to buy anything. A divorced former school-teacher looking for a fresh start, she'd just moved from California to Mississippi and was unemployed.

"I'd never seen a cougar before and was curious," McElroy says. "So I called the owner to make an appointment." What she found stunned her. The starved cub, only knee-high, was confined to a tiny dog pen. His paws were so badly infected—from a botched declawing job—that he could barely stand.

Determined to rescue him, McElroy explained that she didn't have $1,000 but was willing to barter an ancient tractor that was on her property. The answer was no. Two weeks later, the owner showed up at her door with the sick animal. "If you want it, it's yours," he said. "I'll take the tractor."

After cobbling together a container for the cougar, McElroy spent days calling around the country trying to find it a home. "This was how I learned that people can't dump exotic pets on zoos," she says.

McElroy had two choices: build a proper enclosure and nurse the cat back to health or have him euthanized. She chose the former and tracked down an exotic cat breeder who told her what to feed a cougar (chicken, beef, and deer meat) and a veterinarian who prescribed antibiotics for his paws. Although Zack, as McElroy named him, had been severely malnourished, his body healed faster than his mind. "It took a lot to get him to trust me," she says. "I would take a book and sit next to him on the other side of his fence for hours. We eventually became very close." Whenever McElroy stopped by, Zack purred furiously to greet her; when he died three years ago, it was in McElroy's arms.

Shortly after taking in Zack, McElroy, then forty-three, launched a medical billing business with a partner who had accounting experience. They did extremely well; some years she earned more than $500,000. At the same time, McElroy began to educate herself about big cats. She learned that many states, including Mississippi, didn't have laws regulating the sale, breeding, and trade of exotic animals. "Reading about how badly these amazing creatures are treated, it broke my heart," she says.

Two years after the cougar arrived, someone phoned McElroy about two animals—Sparkles, a spotted leopard, and Big Al, a Siberian tiger—whose breeder was shutting down his business.

Siberians, which can grow to ten feet long and weigh as much as 700 pounds, are the world's largest cats; they're also critically endangered. Yet abandoned tigers are often sick and hard to handle; McElroy knew that a zoo wouldn't take either cat.

Big Al, who should have been a magnificent animal, was in appalling condition. He'd been confined to an underground cement bunker for three years without much daylight or exercise. He had such severe osteoporosis that his spine was bowed. McElroy brought him and Sparkles home. Then she began phasing out her billing business and started to build enclosures on the twenty acres she'd bought in Caledonia. That was the beginning of the Cedarhill Animal Sanctuary (cedrhill.org).

Over the years, McElroy has added a tiger compound, a cougar compound, plus an animal care center that includes a huge living area for the cats, a surgery room, an exotic food prep room, a domestic dog prep room (where food and medications are prepared), and a feral cat room. "That building is like the peak of my career," she says.

"Society's rejects have always challenged me," says McElroy. "When I taught kids from the Watts housing projects in Los Angeles, my students were young drug addicts, gang members, prostitutes, thieves: the outcasts whom no one had been able to reach. I taught them how to read. So I guess my transition to rejected and abused animals wasn't such a stretch."

. . . . . .

The Most Important Thing I Learned

"How much I was really capable of."

. . . . . .

Cedarhill obtained nonprofit status in 1992. As its reputation grew, more and more animals arrived, each with a history worse than the last. "You can't imagine what it is like to see one of these big cats feel the earth under its feet for the first time," says McElroy. "I remember Kimba, a Bengal tiger, coming here. He'd always been kept on a very short chain, standing on cement. When he touched grass, he jumped in surprise, then he ran and played. He's never stopped."

McElroy has also became an activist, lobbying for four years until Mississippi created laws to regulate the sale and trade of exotic animals. She's also working to end canned hunts, in which animals are kept in small enclosures, even in cages, so "sportsmen" in safari suits can stand on top of Land Rovers or swoop low in helicopters to shoot them. Tragically, hundreds of these hunts are still held across the country and are advertised extensively online. "These 'brave hunters' are photographed in macho style with their victims," McElroy says. "Someone comes back from a canned hunt with a stuffed head or a skin from an animal on the endangered list, and people think he went to Africa. Canned hunts are all about bragging rights. They have nothing to do with sport."

It's estimated that Texas holds about a thousand such hunts every year, with an additional five hundred taking place nationwide. "Exotic animals can be sold to breeders and so on, down the line, until they end up in canned hunts, illicit auctions, roadside zoos, research labs, or even in exotic food," she says.

McElroy, now sixty-eight, remains a tireless advocate. A typical day begins at dawn with the roar of five lions and twelve tigers: Bengal, Manchurian, Siberian, and Sumatran. They in turn rouse the rest of the sanctuary—four cougars; two bobcats; two shy wolves; two hundred abandoned domestic felines, many rescued after Hurricane Katrina; an assortment of dogs; two blind horses; potbellied pigs; and cockatoos and parrots, including one that perfectly mimics McElroy.

"They are all unadoptable," she says. "If they went to a shelter, they'd be killed. But once they come here, they're members of the Cedarhill family. They live out their days cared for, in comfort, and greatly loved."

Shortly after sunup, McElroy's mostly female crew sets out with each animal's customized breakfast. (She tends to hire women because many of the animals have been traumatized by men.) As the food arrives, the lions and the tigers race inside their enclosures, chuffing in pleasure.

As fond as she is of her rescued big cats, McElroy refuses to be photographed inside their enclosures or cuddling them. "To do so would project an image that these animals can be domesticated. They can't," she says. "A wild animal will never be 100 percent safe. I don't want to encourage people to view them as big, cuddly pussycats. They can maul and kill."

She rolls up her sleeve to show the scars on her right arm, saying, "This was my fault." In the early days of the sanctuary, she needed to relocate K.C., a cougar who'd apparently been abandoned by drug dealers without food, water, or shelter. His face, chest, and front legs looked like they had been deliberately lacerated with a weed eater. Amazingly, he survived and was brought to Cedarhill.

"I had to move him from one enclosure to another and asked a man to help me. He arrived with a shovel," McElroy says. "K.C. growled, thinking it was going to be used on him. He spun around in panic and tore my arm open." McElroy says she was rushed to the ER and required more than two hundred stitches and intravenous antibiotics. She recalls that when a sheriff told her, "Don't worry, we'll shoot the cougar," her response was, "Don't you touch that animal." It's the only time she or any of her employees have been attacked.

McElroy says K.C. eventually learned to believe her when she told him, "No one is going to hurt you ever again." Having dealt with so many cases of animal cruelty, she still cannot comprehend what causes people to be so brutal. "Animals have taught me, even wild ones, that their unconditional love is beyond our imagination. They are so forgiving of all the horrible things they've experienced."

McElroy has not opened the sanctuary to the public because "the animals have suffered enough at human hands," she says. Visiting donors, however, can see animals from a one-story guesthouse on the property that's decorated with animal print wallpaper and textiles.

"My biggest concern is fund-raising," says McElroy, who earns $33,000 a year. She continues to work seven days a week, despite ill health (she has renal disease and sleeps attached to a dialysis machine every night). Her savings were spent on Cedarhill years ago, and donations are down 50 percent since the economic crisis hit. "I stretch every dollar," she says. "But there are vet bills, utilities, food for the animals, for us. There have been times when I didn't have payroll for staff. But somehow, we always manage."

················· **Kay's Key Question to Ask Yourself** ·················
Can you let go of the past?

Shipping Help from America
Danielle Butin

A few days after the January 2010 earthquake that left Haiti in ruins, the warehouse of the Afya Foundation of America in Yonkers, New York, was buzzing with volunteers. Bundled against frigid temperatures, the workers, many of them students from local schools and scout troops, moved with a sense of urgency, loading shipping containers with crutches, syringes, IV starter kits, bandages, and more—much of the material recovered from hospitals that would otherwise have discarded it as waste, all of it collected by Afya and now destined for the island's stricken people.

At the center of the action, Afya's founder, Danielle Butin, forty-eight, a warmly forceful former health insurance company executive, fielded nonstop phone calls. A local nursing home had a hundred mattresses. Filmmaker Jonathan Demme and colleagues wanted to donate generators and lighting equipment. An anonymous benefactor from Dartmouth College offered to use his private plane to airlift supplies to Haiti; a local restaurateur suggested a fund-raising dinner to defray shipping costs—$6,000 to send one container to the island.

"The earthquake was so incomprehensible and intolerable that giving a check wasn't enough," Butin says. "People needed a way to act." Afya (the word is Swahili for "health") offered them a way. By the end of January, donor institutions and individuals had committed to more than a million dollars' worth of relief supplies. More than a thousand volunteers had helped fill seven jam-packed forty-foot containers headed for one of the clinics in Haiti run by Partners in Health (PIH), a U.S.-based nonprofit that provides health care to poor communities in twelve countries around the world.

Afya's prompt and effective response to the devastating earthquake put the fledgling foundation, barely two years old at the time, "on the world health map overnight," Butin says. PIH, which coordinated medical relief in Haiti, began referring institutions, individuals, and charities to Afya. "Until then," Butin says, "we'd been a mom-and-pop organization with slim exposure nationally." The referrals brought in more materials and more funds for shipping them. "We started getting calls from hospitals around the country that had supplies to donate," she says.

Butin, who trained as an occupational therapist and still occasionally lectures on the subject at Columbia University, launched Afya (afyafoundation.org) after a trip to Tanzania in 2007. She'd just been downsized from the Fortune 500 health insurance company where she'd created and run wellness programs focusing

. . . .

The Most Important Thing I've Learned

"I came from a high-level, executive, strategic-planning job, and something I've learned is that you don't need a perfectly boxed-in plan in order to be successful. What you do have to have: faith in the vision and the process. And you must remain awake and alert to all of the people around you."

. . . .

on elder- and end-of-life care. Instead of moping or plunging into a job search, Butin decided to spend part of her severance package on a long-held dream: a trip to Africa. "For ten years, I'd been taking African dance classes that were accompanied by six to twelve African drummers," she says. "That drumming became my heartbeat."

During her sojourn, she visited Masai healers, hiked through Tanzanian forests, and got unexpected glimpses of the challenges faced by health-care providers in rural Africa. At a tented camp, she met an English doctor, on leave from her work at a Ugandan hospital, who wept in frustration as she recounted how donated supplies too often didn't match the clinic's needs. There would be ECG leads but no ECG machine, let alone electricity to run one.

······················**The Biggest Mistake I Made**·······················

"Not paying enough attention to the people I love most in my personal life. I was so completely consumed with the Herculean task of birthing this foundation. I knew nothing about warehouses, trucking, international customs, so for the first year and a half I was totally preoccupied, not conscious enough of the needs of people I love. And I regret that. It is precious time that doesn't return to us. Thankfully, I realized that this was a mistake I could repair. I talked about this at length with my significant other and my children, apologizing deeply for my lack of availability. I made a serious commitment to 'coming back.' Today, when eating out at a restaurant with my significant other, I am grateful that my BlackBerry is unglued from my hand and buried in my bag. When I'm with my children and they are hanging out with me in the kitchen, my laptop isn't open on the counter, I'm back to baking and being present and in the moment . . . this is precious time, and these are precious relationships, and they need to be honored and cared for."

American nurses working at an HIV clinic in rural Tanzania told her they lacked the equipment needed to start IV lines. "I couldn't understand it," Butin says. "I knew the stuff was out there, and I knew there was this huge need. I thought, This is insanity! I'm going to do something. As an occupational therapist, I'm trained to assess specific health care challenges and meet them. To me, getting surplus supplies to where they were needed was just another challenge, on a larger scale."

Butin's resolve crystallized on the return flight as she read Tracy Kidder's best-selling book *Mountains beyond Mountains*, about acclaimed Harvard physician-anthropologist Paul Farmer, who founded PIH in rural Haiti. She was deeply moved by Farmer's dedication. "I thought, I can do this. I have the training and experience. This is what I'm supposed to do."

Back home in the riverside village of Hastings-on-Hudson, a half-hour train ride from New York City, Butin, a divorced mother of three, felt the sting of financial doubt. As an executive, she'd earned $150,000 a year and also had income from teaching and consulting. "We didn't lead an extravagant lifestyle," she says. Still, she knew that pursuing her mission meant the family would be living on less. She worried that the change wouldn't be fair to her son and two daughters, then ages fifteen, thirteen, and nine. So, for a month and a half, she went on interviews for executive health-care positions at large corporations. But every time, she says, "I felt nauseous. My head was saying one thing, and my gut was saying another. I went out to dinner with close friends, had a glass of wine, and bawled my eyes out. Finally my friends said, 'You gotta do it.' And the next morning I woke up and knew they were right." One of the people urging Butin on, she says, was her significant other, Tracy Allan, a photographer and a filmmaker. Allan pitched in from the start, picking up donated supplies in a rented truck, helping Butin set up a warehouse, and designing Afya's website; now he documents the foundation's work on video.

Armed with a renewed sense of purpose, Butin began by doing something radical in its simplicity: cold-calling. Her old insurance-job contacts weren't appropriate for this new enterprise, she says, so she had to build a network from scratch. She cold-called people at New York hospitals and asked if they had equipment to donate; she cold-called PIH to ask how she could become involved. She cold-called landlords to find a warehouse and was offered a 4,000-square-foot space in Yonkers. In September 2009, Afya moved to a sprawling place almost three times the size of her original location. "That was a stroke of luck," says Butin, "because we would never have had room for all of the supplies we collected in January for Haiti if we hadn't moved then." Now they have moved a third time, to slightly larger quarters.

The response to her calls was overwhelmingly positive. "You really want to go the extra mile for her," says Kathy Smith-Bernier, the director of environmental services at St. John's Riverside Hospital in Yonkers and one of the first to be swayed by Butin. "Her passion and dedication come through almost immediately."

. . . .

The Most Important Thing I Did Right

"I believed—and continue to believe—in the underdog. Every morning, our warehouse is filled with volunteers who are considered populations at risk—children with Asperger's syndrome, adults with developmental disabilities, folks with chronic mental illness, kids living in residential facilities, people recovering from substance abuse. We have opened our doors to therapeutic treatment centers for two reasons: These folks are rarely offered an opportunity to give back, but they have huge hearts and they 'get it'—they have enormous compassion for the underserved abroad. At Afya, they can learn work-related skills and practice them through altruism. A number of our volunteers (who practiced working with us) have graduated to full-time employment in the community."

. . . .

St. John's has since donated operating-room tools, their boxes still unopened; four dialysis machines; six CPR mannequins; and roughly thirty wheelchairs, among other supplies. All of the equipment is in good condition, but it's no longer state of the art—which in the competitive American health-care market means it gets replaced. "Think of buying a computer that's outdated as soon as you get it," says Smith-Bernier. If the equipment isn't donated, it will either be medically incinerated or sent to landfills. So far, Afya has spared two million pounds of medical supplies and equipment from what Butin calls premature burial.

Gradually, her plans for Afya took shape. Butin would collect donated supplies in her warehouse. She'd identify needy institutions with input from PIH and other nonprofit organizations that would arrange to distribute the supplies in impoverished regions. Eventually, Butin secured the help of more global-aid groups, such as U.S. Doctors for Africa and government health agencies in specific countries. Aid groups or sponsors pay freight costs and a per-shipment recovery fee to Afya to offset operating expenses. Community organizations and schools looking for class projects also help by raising funds to cover specific shipments. The foundation avoids the problem of theft that sometimes besets aid organizations by choosing recipients very carefully. "We work only with clinics that have credible oversight and a strong infrastructure," says Butin.

She estimates that as of March 2011, each of the fifty-seven containers Afya has shipped during its nearly three years of existence—to hospitals, clinics, and schools in Malawi, Rwanda, Ethiopia, Tanzania, Nigeria, Ghana, Cape Verde, Sierra Leone, and Haiti—carried at least $150,000 worth of goods, which puts their total value somewhere north of $6.6 million. Of course, on a human level, the benefits to communities Afya has served are immeasurable. "Her supplies really allowed the district hospital where we work to begin functioning," says Keith Joseph, MD, of

PIH, who oversees the organization's work in rural Malawi. "Thousands of people here have been directly helped by her efforts."

Afya isn't the only medical-supply-recovery organization sending goods overseas, although it is the only major group operating in the New York metro area. What sets Afya apart is its founder's occupational therapy training and her personal contact with needy institutions. Butin is attuned to how products can improve patients' outcome, and she frequently visits clinics and other client organizations overseas—she's in Haiti every six weeks, Africa twice a year—so she can understand exactly what supplies will make a difference. For example, in Haiti, women whose breasts were injured during the earthquake are getting sports bras ("Compression relieves the pain"); those who had amputations and live in tented camps are especially vulnerable to assault when they go out at night to find a portable toilet, "so we're sending them commodes," she says.

Butin's huge network of young, enthusiastic volunteers also sets her team apart. Last year she received an award from her alma mater, Scarsdale High School, not far from her warehouse, and after the Haiti earthquake the principal sent an e-mail message to all of the students, saying that Butin could use their support. Since then, hundreds of kids have contacted Afya, offering their help. One of the teen volunteers took over when a doctor in Malawi who's also a rock musician asked Afya for musical instruments, thinking his HIV-infected adolescent patients might be inspired to stay on their medications if they learned to play. "This high school kid got a whole community to donate instruments," Butin says. Another teen volunteering for Afya as part of a community-service project ended up collecting enough supplies to start three soccer leagues in rural Malawi. One group of students raised funds by making bracelets, another by holding a fashion show. High school seniors who went to Afya in response to President Obama's call for national service on Martin Luther King Jr. Day are forming Afya clubs on their college campuses to collect supplies and raise money for shipping.

"It makes people feel good to know they can give back," Butin says. "I'm just helping them do it."

Despite Afya's successes during the last three years, some hospitals Butin has contacted have declined to participate and still consign usable equipment to the dump. "Some collect supplies only for their own medical staff's mission trips," she explains. "Others don't fully understand the benefits of our recovery program." Afya is also constantly scrounging for sponsors to pick up shipping costs. Butin is unfazed by these challenges. "I am wired to jump over hurdles," she says.

Besides Butin, Afya's paid staff consists of four part-timers and only one other full-time person, Sarah Schuyler. "She does everything from loading thousands of pounds of materials into containers to organizing complicated customs clearance with officials in foreign countries," says Butin. For a year and a half after she launched Afya, Butin took no paycheck, living instead on her severance pay; the second year, thanks to her board of directors—drawn from the health-care, education, nonprofit, and business communities—she was paid $60,000, less than half of what she'd earned in her previous career. "Yes, our lives changed," she says. "The kids became very good at preparing their own meals." They also pitched in at Afya. "My son, now in film school, shot video and stills for us, and the girls did all of the box labeling in the beginning and still bring in friends to help."

Butin yearns for funding to expand the foundation's infrastructure. "Sarah and I are blessed with enormous energy, but we can't get everything done," she says.

Butin's goals for Afya continually evolve. Thanks to a grant from the American Jewish Joint Distribution Committee, she's started a program in Haiti to train rehab technicians to make products, such as special shoes, that will help people with disabilities. Stateside, she supervises a prevocational training program with occupational therapy graduate students from Columbia University and New York University. People with mental illness go to the Yonkers warehouse to learn how to function in a work environment as they sort donated goods for Afya.

Reflecting on Afya's success and her midlife career change, Butin adds, "I never would have been able to do this when I was in my twenties. I didn't have the range of interpersonal experience or the understanding of how to get things done, not to mention the confidence in my own decision making." Is she ever discouraged by the magnitude of the problems she is addressing? Butin looks baffled, as if such a thought had never entered her mind. "No," she says firmly. "I am inspired every day by what I do.

"But what would make me cry now"—and she tears up as she says this—"is the realization that there is no bigger blessing than to be able to do this work. We've sent these supplies that have changed people's lives. But we've also built a place where people can come and make a real difference."

. . . .

The Most Surprising Thing about My Reinvention

"Discovering the capacity and boundlessness of the human heart. I remember a five-year-old boy who approached me after the Haitian earthquake. He had a Ziploc bag with ten dimes inside. He got an allowance of ten cents every week, and he donated ten weeks' allowance to the earthquake victims. This is just one child's story. The response to Afya has been bigger and broader and more magnified than I ever anticipated. People need a 'home' where they can help, in any and every way possible. It's an incredibly beautiful thing."

. . . .

. . . . **Danielle's Questions to Ask Yourself** . . . .

- What are you passionate about? I knew I was passionate about Africa. Years ago, out of the blue, I started taking West African dancing and drumming classes; this graduated to wanting a home filled with African art and spiritual artifacts. This was the intro that informed my work . . . my passion for Africa was obvious to me.

- What voice will you listen to? A long time ago, my significant other taught me the power that faith has in how we live and function. Doubting, living in fear, disables us. One day in the warehouse, early on, the negative voice took hold, and I stood there, with tears rolling down my face, overwhelmed by the task ahead of me. I chose to quiet that voice and quietly shift to a place of faith, trusting it would all be okay. After all, this work had been delivered to me in the heart of the Serengeti. . . . it had to be okay! Choose the voice you will listen to carefully. One voice can harm you or undermine your confidence, but another can catapult you forward.

- Who will offer you support? Find people—family or friends—who appreciate your courage and want to help you build. I will never forget an amazing friend who showed up with trays of burritos and tacos to feed everyone when we packed our first container. Every expression of support is huge and keeps you moving forward.

- How will you manage financially while you are launching? Create an interim financial plan. I continued to teach, consult, and offer workshops on aging (my other passion!) while launching Afya. Doing all of that during the launch was an incredible amount of work, but I needed to make sure that I could survive during this interim period.

5

Discovering Your Business Sense

The upside of being an entrepreneur is creating a company on your own without anyone else's signoff or interference. The downside is having to do *everything* on your own, without anyone else's backup or commitment. So how do you maximize the upside and minimize the downside? Find out from these women, who reinvented their lives by coming up with a product or business that fills a real need.

She's a Wrap Star
Jill Boehler

Jill Boehler felt like a celebrity. Seated in the spotlight in one of CNBC's studios, with the cameras rolling, she was being interviewed by the charismatic host of a talk show about entrepreneurs,

The Big Idea with Donny Deutsch. Earlier that day, she'd left her home in Baltimore and flown to New York, where a black stretch limo met her at the airport and chauffeured her to the studio in New Jersey. A stylist there had curled her eyelashes and sprayed her hair. Now she was recounting for a national television audience how she had started a business selling silky, warm, microfiber wraps that fold into pouches small enough to stash in purses. Deutsch, who is a legend in the advertising business, leaned over to stroke the wrap draped around her neck. "I love it. What a great idea!" he cooed.

What Boehler didn't reveal that June day in 2007 was how much she needed the publicity. Creating the company had dragged her deep into debt, and she didn't know whether she'd be able to stay in business. Still, she carried off the interview with aplomb, thrilled with all of the attention. Making her TV debut, she says, "was like entering a different world." Even more amazing was how the appearance boosted her business. The evening her segment aired, Boehler was stunned to find hundreds of orders in her e-mail inbox. "Donny Deutsch catapulted my company to another level," she says.

Just two and a half years earlier, the idea for the wraps hadn't even entered her head. Boehler, then fifty-two, was working long hours as a speech pathologist at charter schools in Lawrence, Massachusetts, and planned to wind down her thirty-two-year career in the field. "I would sit on the floor with kids and then find it hard to get up," she recalls. "I felt old. That's the first time I knew I was past it." Besides teaching for three decades, she'd published a textbook for speech therapists and run a private practice. She and her husband, Rich, a physician, had raised three children, the youngest of whom, Jordan, would soon be entering college. By spring 2005, she was ready to retire.

While vacationing that summer, though, Boehler found a new direction. On a sweltering July evening, as she sat shivering in an air-conditioned restaurant, she watched Rich pull out his reading

· · · · · · · · · ·

The Most Important Thing I Learned

"How many hours a day are involved in learning your own business and starting over. It really turns into 24/7, almost like having another child."

· · · · · · · · · ·

glasses and thought, Wouldn't it be great if I had a wrap that was small enough to fit into my purse, like a pair of spectacles? All of her life, she'd had ideas for inventions (a board game to help people with aphasia remember words had earned her $15,000 in royalties), but most of her thoughts went no further than the journal where she jotted them down.

The wrap was different. She mentioned the concept to her oldest son, Adam, then twenty-six, who was in France visiting a friend whose family owned a pajama factory there. The family offered to introduce Boehler to some French designers and fabric suppliers in the area. Three months later, she was sitting at a conference table in the city of Lyons, surrounded by mannequins and young, hip designers. "They were drawing sketches and asking my opinion. I had no idea what I was doing," she says. "The whole thing was hilarious." On the third day of her visit, she scoured Lyons' textile district for materials, but they were all either too bulky or too flimsy. When she sat down in a street café for a break, a cyclist rolled up wearing biker shorts. Boehler took one look at the shiny, stretchy microfiber and knew she'd found her fabric. It was light enough to fold into a small purse, warmer than silk, shiny enough to dress up an outfit, and, best of all, it was wrinkle-resistant.

Boehler returned to the United States with a design, a prototype, and a name for her wrap: the Chilly Jilly. Then she began trawling the Internet for a manufacturer close enough to her home in Baltimore (where her husband had taken a new job) that she could build a personal relationship with the owner and make last-minute changes, if the need arose.

To her surprise, producing the wrap was not her biggest expense. The first batch of two hundred, each folded into a small matching pouch, came to $1,400. Yet legal and marketing costs soon added up: $25,000 to pay a lawyer to file the patent; $20,000 to a Web designer to create her site, chillyjilly.com. Boehler borrowed $25,000 on credit cards and withdrew $45,000 from her son Jordan's college fund. (Later she took out a loan to cover his tuition.) Even though her family was supportive, Boehler didn't like using their money in this way. "We aren't far from retirement," she says. "I knew my failure could change our lives."

Once Boehler had her first order in hand, it was time to start selling. Most entrepreneurs with new products hire sales representatives or pitch their products to store owners after making an appointment. She didn't know this, however, so for the first few weeks, she made cold calls to thirty boutiques in ten towns, emphasizing the wrap's versatility. ("You can wear it around your bathing suit as a sarong and then in the evening as a wrap—from the pool to the restaurant!") Boehler sold all two hundred and went back to the factory for nine hundred more, at a cost of $6,300.

The Most Important Thing I Did Right

"I believed in the product and didn't listen to people who said launching a business would be too difficult. People are naysayers. 'This is a problem, it will never happen'—I just tuned that out."

Some boutique owners bought a dozen to resell at $30 each. Others politely sent her on her way. The rejections, although infrequent, hurt. "Once, before I even finished my pitch, the store owner snapped, 'We're not interested,'" Boehler recalls. She fled to her car and wept, wondering whether she should cut her losses and fold the business. The financial pressure was driving her crazy and costing her sleep. She eventually sought help from her doctor, who prescribed Ambien for the insomnia and later Xanax to relieve her anxiety.

Pinning her hopes on a mention from Oprah Winfrey, Boehler e-mailed and called staff on the show and at O magazine every single day for six months straight. She pitched to other media outlets as well, finally landing a mention in *Self* magazine and on iVillage.com. One day, in the summer of 2007, a customer suggested that she contact the producers of *The Big Idea with Donny Deutsch*, because of its focus on innovative entrepreneurs. After the show aired and orders poured in, Boehler hired a part-time assistant and sales representatives around the country.

Then, in January 2008, she got her second big break. At a weekend accessories trade show, a QVC buyer stumbled on the Chilly Jilly display and left a message asking Boehler to call back. Boehler did—and two days later, she was sitting at QVC headquarters being quizzed by three buyers. "I started doing my spiel, but then I realized it wasn't a matter of *if* they would have me on but *when*. They just wanted to see if I would agree to their terms."

Boehler has since appeared on QVC twenty-five times, and her success as an inventor and an entrepreneur has earned her the admiration of QVC's largely female audience, says Rich Yoegel, QVC's director of merchandising. Last year, her company made more than $250,000 in profits, which enabled her to pay off her credit card debt and begin to save.

These days, her business is almost a family enterprise. Rich helps carry heavy boxes when he's home; Jordan, now twenty-three, designed the artwork for the first Chilly Jilly bag; daughter Kim, twenty-eight, models the wraps for chillyjilly.com and other promotional materials; and oldest son Adam, thirty-two, a venture capitalist, gives her business advice. "Adam listened to every challenge, reasoned away every failure, and cheered every success," she says.

Sometimes Boehler thinks about retiring (no more weekends attending trade shows)—but not yet. "Besides wraps of various sizes, we now have gloves and wrapper blankets, which are great for travel," she says. "And I have new products to launch. I don't feel as if I'm done yet. I feel like I'm in a movie, and I want to see what happens next."

The Egg Banker
Diana Thomas

In a Lexington, Kentucky, fertility clinic, in a lab not much bigger than a walk-in closet, three hundred eggs sit in liquid nitrogen, waiting to be chosen for fertilization. They belong to, among others, nineteen-year-old Victoria, a brown-eyed college student whose special talents include lacrosse and tennis; Kymberly, a twenty-four-year-old Korean American with a passion for hunting; and Priyanka, a twenty-seven-year-old Indian who speaks fluent Hindi. Plucked from the ovaries of healthy women under age thirty, the eggs will almost certainly find their way into the uterus of a woman over forty.

Diana Thomas's company, the World Egg Bank, may well be making the match. In the next few years, her agency hopes to corner 10 percent of the egg donor market in the United States. Thomas, fifty-five, started her company in 1996 as X and Y Consulting, to provide her clients—99 percent of whom are over forty—with viable eggs. Eight years later, she launched a division, Cryo Eggs International (CEI), to offer the option of using the latest frozen-egg technology. Then, in 2009, she merged the two companies to create the World Egg Bank. "The World Egg Bank provides all technologies for women who need donor eggs to conceive, under one umbrella," says Thomas. "We are a one-stop service provider for infertile women."

For Thomas's clients, having the choice—and the chance—to become pregnant with a donor egg is the ultimate gift. It comes with a price tag, though: typically, $25,000 to $40,000 for each pregnancy attempt that uses fresh eggs. The fee covers recruiting, compensating, and insuring the donor; screening tests (donors have to take genetic and psychological

. . . .

The Most Important Thing I Learned

"I had no idea of the worldwide impact I could have on so many lives, in such a meaningful way."

. . . .

exams); and transportation. Using frozen-egg technology elimi-nates the donor's need to travel and costs less: from $15,000 to $18,000 per attempt.

The probability of getting pregnant with your own eggs is about 10 percent at age forty. By that time, the eggs that remain often have abnormal chromosomes, and about one-third of the conceptions that do occur end in miscarriage. Although birthrates for women ages forty to forty-four have increased dramatically in recent years, the rise is linked mostly to advances in technology and the advent of many fertility-enhancing therapies. "Beyond forty-five, it's rare to get pregnant. We're talking almost lottery odds," says Jamie Akin, MD, the medical director of the Bluegrass Fertility Center and an early partner in CEI. "The Hollywood actresses who become pregnant in their mid-forties have almost certainly done it with donor eggs."

The struggle to get pregnant is one that Thomas knows per-sonally. She first attempted to conceive at twenty-five, when she was newly married to her college sweetheart. They had settled in Edmonton, Alberta, where Thomas worked as head of architec-tural history and preservation for the province. Unable to get pregnant after trying for a year, Thomas and her husband were tested. He checked out fine. Doctors performed laparoscopies on Thomas, in search of fibroids or endometriosis or anything that might inhibit implantation of an egg, and when they found noth-ing, they began a series of fertility treatments. "I questioned myself all the time," Thomas says now. "I would wonder, Should I stand on my head after sex? Did I contract a disease while traveling?" None of the treatments worked, and after three years, her mar-riage failed. Thomas moved to Phoenix and took a job preserving historic structures for the state.

Yet the desire to become pregnant never faded. She married her second husband, Andre Best, an environmental compliance officer for the city, when she was thirty-three. Within a year she was back in the baby-making game.

This time around, Thomas was better prepared for the doctor visits—and their inevitable emotional toll. Sitting in waiting rooms, she could easily pick out the angry, the grieving, and the women like her, many of whom were eager to share their stories. Thomas signed up for intrauterine insemination (commonly known as artificial insemination), and when that failed, in vitro fertilization (IVF), in which eggs are fertilized by sperm outside of the womb. She and her husband drained their savings and relied on their combined salaries—under $100,000—to help fund treatments, which eventually totaled $60,000. When a sick neighbor whom Thomas had cared for in Canada left her $7,000 in his will, she used the money for her third and final chance at an IVF pregnancy with her own eggs.

The day after the procedure, the phone rang in her kitchen. It was the embryologist, breaking the news that the eggs had not proved viable. "I was home alone, and I remember not being able to breathe," Thomas says. "It's so overwhelming to hear that all of the money you spent and the effort you put into it and the hopes you had have just vanished." She was thirty-nine; it was time to move on. Thomas flirted with the idea of adoption but soon realized it wasn't for her. "I had a strong biological drive to carry a child," she says. For that reason, and because she wanted her husband to have the opportunity to pass his genes on to the next generation, she began to consider using donor eggs. "I had to let go of the idea that my child would have a nose like my mother's or that he would be three-quarters Irish," she says. "I decided to use another woman's eggs because I felt very strongly that I would love the child no matter what."

It was 1995, when there was little choice with donor eggs. "The clinics were handing you two profiles to choose from," Thomas says. "The process didn't acknowledge the emotional side of using an egg donor." That's when she got the go-ahead from her doctors to search for a donor herself. She placed an ad in Arizona State University's student newspaper that read: "Would you like to help a couple have a child? I'm looking for an egg donor. Can we meet?" Six young women responded. Armed with literature from the American Society for Reproductive Medicine, Thomas met each of the potential donors at an espresso bar on ASU's main drag.

Thomas instantly connected with Nicole Leach, a twenty-year-old student who shared Thomas's coloring and also asked smart, serious questions. Thomas agreed to pay Leach $500. Leach spent a month wearing estrogen and progesterone patches and then took the Pill to synchronize her cycle with Thomas's. When Leach's eggs matured, they were removed by needle from her ovaries.

· · · · · ·

The Most Important Thing I Did Right

"Making sure that I maintained the highest standard of integrity and expertise in a business model. At every level of the business structure, the focus was on making sure that a woman went home with a baby."

· · · · · ·

Thomas drove Leach to the specialist's office and sat in on the procedure so that she could hold the younger woman's hand. "I felt like her mother," Thomas says. "I was very protective of her."

The eggs were mixed with Best's sperm that same day. Three days later, Thomas stared at the eight-cell embryos under a microscope moments before they were transferred to her uterus, a privilege not available in today's era of malpractice concerns and strict privacy laws. "Imagine knowing the moment of conception," she says. "I felt like I was in a sci-fi movie."

Thomas waited nervously for an embryo to attach to her uterine wall. The stakes were high: the donor cycle cost $40,000, which she and Best had financed by taking out a second mortgage. To their profound relief, it worked. Their son August was born in 1996, the same year that Thomas turned forty.

A few months later, Thomas got a call from her fertility specialist. It wasn't about hormone levels or follicle growth. Instead, the doctor had another couple desperate to choose their own egg donor, and they hoped Thomas would help them find someone.

"It began to resonate with me that there was something in this," says Thomas, who had transitioned to a job share at the historical registry so that she could spend more time with her son. "I realized I could control my own hours and do something that was immensely gratifying." She named her company X and Y Consulting and invested $10,000 in ads, computers, and attorney fees for drafting contracts.

In the next four years the business grew, and so did Thomas's family. In 2000, she managed the construction of a home office from her hospital bed, where she was in preterm labor with her twin sons, Emerson and Nolan, a "gift" from Tiffany Bates, a donor whom Thomas had recruited to X and Y the year before. By this time, she was experienced at brokering relationships between donors and clients and well understood the pitfalls. "Everyone in this business faces legal situations," Thomas says. "Your clients may have spent thousands of dollars vetting a donor, and then the donor says, 'Gee, my boyfriend doesn't like this.' I've had to learn how to negotiate those situations over the years."

Also in 2000, Thomas decided to go national. She took her business to the web (eggdonorsnow.com), where she posts photos of donors alongside lists of their talents and interests—a sort of match.com for the childless. "I'd get the fallout from these fly-by-night operations that were started by donors who thought, This looks like an easy way to make money," Thomas says. "My resolve was to be as good and ethical and knowledgeable about my business as anyone can be." She says her biggest challenge was charging for her services: "It probably sounds odd, but I knew from a recipient's perspective how unbearably expensive the whole process was. My goal wasn't to create another barrier for anyone."

Two years later, she attended a conference on reproductive technology and heard about a theoretical method called cryopreservation. Embryos had been successfully frozen since 1986; this would extend the technology to freezing donor eggs, which would make the need to synchronize cycles obsolete. Instead of flying donors around the country to meet a recipient for egg retrieval, Thomas would only need to ship the eggs, dramatically reducing costs. "I knew it would be the future of the industry," she says.

The following year, Jeffrey Boldt, PhD, the scientific director for assisted fertility services at the Community Health Network in Indianapolis, published a research paper in which he demonstrated a 46 percent pregnancy success rate using cryopreservation. Thomas and Akin, from the Bluegrass Fertility Center, met with Boldt to discuss starting a commercial egg bank, and the trio formed CEI. They enlisted six physicians to invest; Thomas, who owns 60 percent of the business, contributed $60,000. Akin would act as medical director, and Boldt would supervise the lab as scientific director.

For the first frozen-egg retrieval, Thomas boarded a plane with fifteen recruits and met Akin at the lab in Lexington. "I felt like a den mother," says Thomas, who regularly traveled with her young donors (now chaperones go in her place). The experience convinced her that frozen-egg banks would soon become as ubiquitous as their sperm counterparts.

Yet as CEI came together, Thomas's marriage fell apart. She and Best legally separated in 2005, and their divorce became official two years later. Thomas attributes the split, in large part, to their protracted experience with infertility. "Having children became both a mutual goal and a consuming focus in our lives," she says of the ten-year stretch. "Once we completed our family,

· ·

The Most Surprising Thing about My Reinvention

"I thought it would be a pretty wild ride, because I knew I didn't have anyone to model myself after. On a personal level, though, I really didn't expect to experience the freedom I did after finding out that my challenges were actually opportunities in disguise."

· ·

we realized that without a joint goal to focus on, we had little in common."

Today, with her sons ensconced in their routines (August is now fifteen, and the twins are eleven), Thomas says she couldn't be happier. "I love being an older mother," she says. "The travel through that dark and lonely tunnel from recognizing my own infertility to three almost-teenage boys is something I would do all over again. I reinvented myself to help other women, and later, my children reinvented me by providing a whole new dimension to my life. They remind me every day why I love what I do and the rewards of enduring obstacle after obstacle to try to conceive. It's also rewarding to know that I have cut the learning curve in half for other women like me, who had to figure out how to have a baby when our biology says it's too late."

·············· Diana's Key Questions to Ask Yourself ··············

- Will you be able to keep your sights on the goal when you face challenges that will try to drive you away from that goal?

- Are you prepared to be flexible and creative when you didn't think you'd have to be?

- Do you have a good sense of humor?

She De-stressed in a New Career
Mary Robbins

In 2004, Mary Robbins, forty-seven, a clinical social worker in Orange, Connecticut, who specializes in emergency counseling for suicidal and homicidal children, felt weighed down by the ongoing responsibility of making life-and-death decisions about such troubled kids. "Just when I thought nothing could be worse than what I'd heard a day earlier, it would be topped by something more horrific," she says.

Then one afternoon, while watching her seven-year-old daughter in a gymnastics class, Robbins chatted with a mom who mentioned that she sold Mary Kay cosmetics for a living. Robbins blurted out, "Oh, *I* want to do that!" She thought the job sounded like fun and could balance out her other one: "Nobody dies if you're wrong about lipstick."

Robbins signed a Mary Kay contract on the spot (the woman had extras in her car). During the next three weeks, she invested $1,800 in a company sales kit and a supply of cosmetics and sold $700 worth of makeup. She loved the products and spent around fifteen hours a week—pleasurable and stress-free—selling Mary Kay. "It was so easy and fun," she says.

Even her young daughter was into the cosmetics gig. She wanted to play with the products, but Robbins was careful to

· · · · · · · · · ·

The Most Important Thing I Did Right

"Just jumping into it. You can research and research and research, but you can't predict everything you don't know, and once you discover the mistake, you can change."

· · · · · · · · · ·

· ·

The Most Important Thing I Learned

"I feel like I got a master's degree in business education. I went into this thinking, I can do it! No problem! Then I realized it was huge. It takes a lot of effort and time. I've had other women volunteers who help. We're all learning new stuff all the time, and there is so much more to learn."

· ·

· · · · · · · · · · · · **My Biggest Mistake** · · · · · · · · · · · ·

"I made ten thousand big mistakes."

keep her away from the antiaging lotions, which she feared might not be good for young skin. About a year later, this concern gave her an idea: Why not make skin care products especially for young girls? In what she now describes as a fit of naïveté, she thought, If Mary Kay can create a business, so can I. She put together a plan, got her daughter's friends to vote on their favorite name (Sassy), and hired a manufacturer to make shampoos and facial washes from organic honey, olive oil, and chamomile extract. The copy on her recyclable bottles is designed to boost girls' self-esteem: "If you believe you are beautiful, so will others! Look in the mirror, focus on the positive, and repeat, 'I am beautiful!'"

"Some of the girls I treat as a social worker can't see their inner beauty, so they make terrible cuts on their arms," says Robbins, who regards her enterprise (sassyshampoo.com) as a natural extension of the therapeutic work she still does with teenagers. "My hope is that I will help young girls by showing them they have both external and internal beauty."

· · · · · ·

The Most Important Thing to Have as You Consider Reinventing Your Life

"Definitely, definitely, have a business plan. And a lot of courage."

· · · · · ·

· ·

The Most Surprising Thing about My Reinvention

"Finding that when you need something, sometimes it just appears. I needed a logo, and nothing the illustrator came up with looked right. I met with a woman from Wisconsin for a totally different reason and showed her the logo, and she reworked it and gave it to me. It was so much better looking. When I wanted to go in another direction with the logo, the mother of a friend of my daughter's said she'd redo it for free."

· ·

Furnishing Her Life with Meaning
Shelly Leer

One summer evening in Carmel, Indiana, Shelly Leer spotted her neighbor, an upholsterer, working in her garage studio. Leer's kids were already in bed, so she strolled over to check out her friend's project—and to vent her frustration that she couldn't find enough freelance work as a paralegal. Grateful for someone to talk to, Leer started dropping in nearly every night as her friend worked. After a few weeks, she casually picked up a staple remover and began to help, yanking huge upholstery staples out of an old chair.

"It felt gratifying to pull something apart and have a clean slate," she says. She continued helping her neighbor and liked the work so much that she ended up taking a $100 class at a local vocational school to get training in upholstery. It was transformative. She discovered she had a knack for redesigning furniture.

During the next twelve years, Leer worked out of a shop in her garage. She quit her legal work and became adept at a complex upholstery maneuver called button tufting. She reupholstered, or designed and built, around three hundred pieces of furniture, such as ottomans and children's

· · · · · · · · · ·

The Most Important Thing I Learned

"You can't just act confident, you need to *have* the confidence. When you get to a level where you feel deserving of new things, the doors open up for you so much more."

· · · · · · · · · ·

· · · · · · · · · · · · **My Biggest Mistake** · · · · · · · · · · · · · ·

"I'm too friendly with the people who are my students. They may say that's what makes it fun, but you lose that little bit of authority. I need to have more of a professional air about me, while still being approachable."

· ·

rocking chairs, netting $15,000 a year, enough to supplement the household income. It was lonely work, though, and she wanted to earn more.

Craving companionship, Leer began to give free sewing classes at a women's shelter. She taught the residents how to turn donated jeans into denim skirts and embellish clothes with gold lamé braid and feathers. "I loved how helping them learn one little thing boosted their confidence so much," she says. "That's when I knew that teaching my skills was more important than using them." Now Leer holds classes—showing students how to craft upholstery, sew for the home, and build furniture from reclaimed items—in a studio space she has leased. She also writes a design blog (modhomeec.com) and a do-it-yourself column for an Indianapolis newspaper. She earned $30,000 in 2010.

"I realized I could teach people something that seems simple to me but is exciting to them. I value that," says Leer, fifty-five. "Giving up office work was the best thing I ever did. You should never think that the place you're in is the end, because it always leads to something else."

. . . .

The Most Important Thing I Did Right

"I connected with a group of people around Indiana who are into mid-century design. There were so many artsy people. I went to some of the parties they had, and I felt very uncomfortable. Yet I did it, and I made friends. And I've used Facebook that way."

. . . .

Shelly's Success Strategy

"When you're successful, people think it happened suddenly—but it's because you've been preparing."

Wife for Hire
Kay Morrison

The mansion on an oak-lined street in New Orleans is one of those drop-dead gorgeous homes that gives visitors serious real estate envy. It's not merely the furnishings that impress or the original artwork. It's the serenity. The owners, an empty-nest couple, entertain every weekend, host fund-raising parties, and welcome houseguests monthly, yet there's zero clutter: no stray bills, keys, or to-do lists lying around. It's as if a good witch had cast a declutter spell.

"Believe your crazy ideas. First of all, they're probably not that crazy. And no matter how crazy they are, they might just work."

This picture-perfect tidiness is the work of Kay Morrison, who four and a half years ago created a business out of the fact that too many people have too little time to manage their domestic lives. Through her company, the Occasional Wife (theoccasionalwife.com), New Orleans residents can hire a helper who, for $40 an hour, will shop for groceries, plan a birthday party, organize closets, hold an estate sale, prepare a house to go on the market, manage a move, buy presents, or research housing options—pretty much anything except clean house ("That's the one service we don't offer," Morrison says).

The mansion's owners are regular clients who pay for a spectrum of services, including sorting their mail and paying bills when they're out of town. Today Morrison has brought over a team to install shelving in the couple's home office. Wearing a retro-style sundress—wide belt, full skirt—Morrison looks every bit the classic 1950s housewife as she directs a "wife" (a recent college grad who majored in chemistry and is good with a hammer) and her handyman helper.

Morrison came up with the wife idea one particularly harried morning in 2004 when she was working about seventy hours a week as an executive at Starwood Hotels and Resorts. She was frantically packing for a business trip while trying to help her husband, Camp Morrison, manage breakfast with their kids (Flynn, then four, and Annabel, two). Exhausted, she suddenly stopped and sighed.

"What this family needs is a wife," Camp said. A private detective, he already knew the difficulty of juggling half of the child-care load.

"Hey," Morrison shot back, "give me a little credit here. For a woman who's traveling all the time, I think I'm doing a good job."

"You're right," Camp said. "We need an *occasional* wife." He explained that this was the title of a 1960s sitcom about a single "gal" who lived in an apartment complex and sometimes pretended to be married to her executive neighbor. What the family could use, he went on, was "someone to fill in now and then when too many balls are dropping."

Morrison began to fantasize about the possibilities. For twenty-one years, she'd worked her way up in the hospitality industry to become a global accounts director with Starwood. She drove a Jaguar and earned a healthy salary, plus fabulous bonuses. She hated the travel, though: she was on the road at least two weeks a month and often went overseas. Why don't I start a wife business myself? she thought. Soon she was doodling logo designs on airplane napkins and brainstorming possible services to offer.

························· **My Biggest Mistake** ·························

"I probably moved too quickly on certain things in the business. I wanted to grow fast, but I should have slowed down some to ensure that my growth would be beneficial. I should have built a better inner structure while I was growing so that it would've been easier to move the business into the national arena. (I'm entirely based in New Orleans at this point, but I have always had the idea of franchising.)"

Then Hurricane Katrina hit New Orleans. In August 2005, the Morrisons fled to Alabama, continued on to New Hampshire, and finally settled into a colleague's vacation home in Massachusetts. Back in Louisiana, four feet of water flooded the family's 1920s bungalow. Throughout the chaos, however, Morrison never stopped working, fielding phone calls from Starwood clients on her cell. To cope with the anxiety, "I baked a cake every night and washed it down with a six-pack of beer," she says.

The Most Important Thing I Did Right

"Almost exactly what I did wrong: I didn't think too hard. I just went with it. I chose something I loved and was passionate about it."

When the family returned home in February 2006, Morrison threw all of her energy into her kids, her house, and her job—Starwood named her its Outstanding Salesperson that year—but inside she resented the time away from home that her work required. Her lowest point came when a business trip caused her to miss Flynn's first day of kindergarten. "I thought, Why? So I can drive a Jag and carry my laptop in a $500 Coach case? That's crazy."

Morrison gave notice the next day and left Starwood in December. She cashed in $35,000 from her 401(k) to start the company and four months later ran an ad in a local weekly, using the whimsical logo she'd conceptualized: a cartoon image of a 1950s housewife, svelte, smiling, wearing a white apron, and holding up a sparkling martini glass. Morrison named her Olive, and in April 2007, the Occasional Wife opened for business.

At first, Morrison received a mere five calls a week. "I worried that the idea wasn't taking off, that my look wasn't right," she says. Much as she loved the freedom to drop off and pick up her kids at school every day, Morrison knew she needed to ramp up her work efforts. Over the years, she says, she had learned that "offering free services is an excellent way to get exposure." So when her

neighbor, who headed the nonprofit Alliance for Affordable
Energy, contacted her, Morrison agreed to organize a press event
and fund-raiser at the company's new headquarters. Her efforts
brought in $2,000, and the group's officers were so delighted,
they nominated her for *City Business* magazine's Innovator of the
Year award. She was one of the winners. Thanks to the publicity
and a few more ads, requests for "wives" increased to about five a
day. By the end of 2008, she'd spruced up more than a hundred
homes and added two services: gardening and packing for cross-
country moves.

Next on her agenda was opening a retail store to sell organizational products (there wasn't a single Container Store in Louisiana). She needed funds, of course, about $100,000, and figured
she'd get the money by bringing in a partner. So Morrison
recruited a lawyer—the wife of a friend of Camp's—to help with
legal issues. The joint venture didn't work out, and the woman
eventually quit. A year later, Morrison invited her best friend,
Ginger Ellis, to head up the retail part of the business. Ellis, who
invested the necessary capital, stayed on, but it took the pair a
while to figure out how to work together harmoniously.

Meanwhile, a community of feminist bloggers started to criti-
cize the corporate logo. "What the . . . ?!!" wrote someone on the
Gender Bender Blog. "Observe this wife's super thinness. And her
maid costume. With the high heels." The vitriol was picked up by
Jezebel.com, which asked, "Do we really want to keep perpetuat-
ing the idea that a wife is someone who does 'anything you do not
have time for'?" Still, many of Jezebel's readers got the joke, and
Morrison, who regards herself as "the consummate feminist," jus-
tifies the name by saying it "puts a price tag on women's work." In
the end, the controversy boosted the Occasional Wife's visibility.

Two years ago, she launched a new service she calls twirling.
"People hire us instead of an interior decorator," says "wife" Court-
ney Abercrombie, who runs the service. "It's redecorating, but we

use what they already own. We take what people have and make it work better for them." Twirling and the retail store, which sells file folders with labels reading BLAH, MORE BLAH, and CRAP, now constitute the bedrock of the business.

As she heads into her fifth year, Morrison doubles as an efficiency expert, with paid speaking gigs for corporations, women's clubs, real estate companies, and non-profits. She has recouped her initial $35,000 investment and funneled it, along with most of the earnings, back into the business, paying herself about $2,000 a month.

The Most Surprising Thing about My Reinvention

"The impact my reinvention would have on other peoples' lives. I looked at this as a monetary business, but the service component has touched me and changed my life in the process. My family has been reinvented. My relationships with people have been reinvented. Everything has been reinvented."

Her own house is as organized and well twirled as any client's. Baskets of ferns hang from the porch ceiling, and a vase of long-stemmed pink roses in the living room complements the retro decor. It does get cluttered, she says, but everything has a place, and these days she has time to put it all back together. In the entrance hall, a black-and-white portrait of her mother shows an attractive woman of the 1950s who could have passed for June Cleaver. "She taught me to manage my time," Morrison says. "She would have been a powerhouse today."

Kay's Key Questions to Ask Yourself

- How can you best prepare yourself financially to make this easiest on your family?
- What is driving you—to own or start your own business or to take a less important role in a company?

From Flight Attendant
to Fashionista
Sandy Stein

Sandy Stein, of West Hills, California, had been a flight attendant for more than thirty years when the airline business tanked in 2001 and her income fell as she was forced to work fewer hours. Three years later, she says, her husband lost his consulting job, and Stein, then fifty-three, realized that it was up to her to provide a stable home for their ten-year-old son. Inspiration arrived one night as she slept: in a dream she saw a decorative key chain that attached to the side of a woman's purse so that she could always find her keys.

The next morning, Stein fashioned a rough model of the gadget, using a wire memo holder. This is going to sell like crazy, she thought. How many times are your keys at the bottom of your bag? She named her device the Finders Key Purse, a play on "finders keepers," and had a prototype made, but when she approached gift companies about distribution, they turned her down because it wasn't part of a bigger line.

Her friends were enthusiastic, however, so Stein asked them to help sell the Finders Key Purse around the country and offered each person a percentage of her own sales, as well as other financial incentives. Stein stashed her inventory of 180,000 key chains, priced at $7 to $10 apiece, in a rented office and handled the shipping herself. Within a year, her sales team had grown from twenty to two thousand, and they had

· · · · · · · · · ·

The Most Important Thing I Learned

"If I have to be mean, so be it. When I was a flight attendant, I was there to make everybody happy. Now I'm here to conduct business. If I have to tell people I don't want to work with them because I don't feel comfortable, so be it. This is very different from what I anticipated."

· · · · · · · · · ·

· · · · · · · · · ·

The Most Important Thing I Did Right

"Hired people who are smarter than me. I'm a strong leader, but I'm not well versed in a lot of the fields that are necessary to have a successful business, so I hired smart people in those fields. We work together as a team, and I don't micromanage. If we're a team, it works. If I'm by myself, nothing happens."

· · · · · · · · · ·

sold one million key chains. Stein kept her airline job for the first year as a safety net, but she busily pitched her product to everyone she met: waitresses, janitors, men on the street. "I lived, breathed, and became a key chain," she says, laughing. "My son was like, 'Mom, do you have to talk about it *all* the time?'"

Stein had earned about $40,000 a year as a flight attendant; now she can pay herself a salary of more than $300,000. Her company, Alexx Inc. (isnthisclever.com), has grown to sell a range of gift items. And, despite the economic downturn, the business grossed more than $6 million in 2010.

Recently, Alexx Inc. got licensed with the NBA, and, says Stein, good things keep happening, such as the publicity she's received. "I don't have a press or publicity company seeking this out. It just comes," she says. So, what's the secret to her success? "A lot of people try to do this, and they give up," she says.

"I never gave up."

·············· **Sandy's Key Questions to Ask Yourself** ··············

- Are you ready to fully commit yourself?
- Are you willing to put up with naysayers who will say, "You absolutely cannot do this"?
- Do you have enough money to weather the bad times?
- Are you surrounded by people who care, who will have your back, and who are smarter than you in their fields?
- Do you have an honest bookkeeper?

The Million-Dollar Coupon Clipper
Teri Gault

Twelve years ago Teri Gault, of Santa Clarita, California, was singing background vocals, teaching music, performing, and dreaming of winning a Grammy. At thirty-nine, she was also, she says, "running my tail off for very little." To stretch her tiny income, she spent hours clipping coupons and scouring ads for sales, saving about $100 on each shopping trip. But the penny-pinching was tedious and time consuming. One day, she realized that if she had the money, she'd gladly pay someone to do the job for her. Her next thought was, What if people paid *me? Ka-ching*: the Grocery Game (the grocerygame.com) was born.

Gault envisioned the Grocery Game as a website that would offer regional lists of supermarket deals, coupons in local papers, and special offers. Members would save hundreds of dollars on groceries by paying a $10 to $20 fee every eight weeks to gain access to their local lists. The day she turned forty, Gault bought herself a business license with $65 she'd saved from spare change. She found a company that offered free Web hosting services for three months and, with help from its tech support team, taught herself to build a site. "From midnight to 4 AM they were bored, and they'd teach

---

My Biggest Mistake

"Hiring people because they were friends and they needed a job. In the early days friends would come to me and ask for work, and, of course, I'd want to help them, even though they didn't seem quite qualified. I'd go ahead and hire them, but it backfired every time. Employees need to have the skills to do what you need them to do. I'm not against hiring friends or relatives if they're qualified. My general manager is my sister. But the company has to come first. You're either qualified or you aren't."

me how to do it," Gault says. "That was my schedule for about two weeks." She took out an ad in a local paper for three weeks, and after that, word of mouth took over. "Soon after I launched the site, I'd heard from shoppers in almost every state in the country, wondering whether I had lists for their area," she says.

"The first year, I made 87 cents an hour for my work. I had three part-time jobs to compensate," says Gault. "To start a new business, especially on a shoestring—and to be working the way that I was—will take a toll on your body. My husband says he doesn't know if I ever slept because my computer was in our bedroom. I would be working until one in the morning and would get up again at four, seven days a week."

· · · · · ·

The Most Important Thing I Learned

"Just because I didn't do something before doesn't mean I can't do it now. I have a brain. And it's pretty pliable."

· · · · · ·

The work paid off. She began the process of franchising her business, and in three years the Grocery Game was available in every state. These days it's especially active. "We are the kind of business that does well in a recession," she understates. As the CEO of a company that grosses more than $12 million a year, Gault pays herself a salary that's more than 10 times what she made as a musician. "It's wonderful to be able to call a plumber and not cry if the bill comes to $350," she says.

· ·

The Most Surprising Thing about My Reinvention

"I thought I was going to feel that I had been neutered, in a sense, by being the Coupon Queen. But all of these years I've just had a blast. I thought I would be grieving, not being able to do my music, but you know what I do? I go to the Hollywood Bowl. I go to Disney Hall. I hire carolers to come to my company parties, and I jump in and I sing with them. I go to concerts. And I can totally enjoy that."

· ·

Gault still performs but only takes gigs she loves. Although the Grammy dream is history, she says, "That's okay, I'm enjoying life in a totally different way now."

Teri's Success Strategy

"I don't throw up my hands at a challenge. My first thought is: how can we do it?"

Cancer Wigged Her Out
Sheril Cohen

Sheril Cohen, forty-six, describes her first wig-shopping experience as harried and demoralizing. A month later, she would start an aggressive course of chemotherapy to fight the cancer that had spread to her lymph nodes. She knew that her hair would fall out soon afterward. "I was adamantly private about my cancer," Cohen says. "But when you lose your hair, you're outed."

The salesman at the upscale New York City wig store showed her its stock, told her she'd never find a wig to match her own long black hair, then ushered her out—he had another customer. Even at stores where the salespeople weren't so abrupt, Cohen says, "It was like trying on bathing suits in a parking lot."

She eventually bought three wigs and even sewed one hairpiece into a baseball cap to wear while running. Yet the memories of her humiliating shopping experiences stayed with Cohen and, ultimately, inspired her to start her own business. Girl on the Go (girlonthego.biz), launched in December 2003, offers at-home wig consultation, fitting, and styling.

Cohen, who runs the business from her home in Clifton Park, New York, once earned big money as a marketing executive. Life was all about work: "I'd wake up at six o'clock," she says, "go running, get to the office at 9:30, work for twelve hours, and eat dinner on the way back to my Manhattan apartment." She'd been at a new job for only a month when she realized that the hard lumps she'd felt on her torso two months earlier had grown.

"I panicked, of course, but I was also kind of stoic," Cohen says. "I intuitively knew I had cancer." Her mother had died seven years earlier of pancreatic cancer, and Cohen had spent her first year out of grad school taking care of her. "The week before I found the lumps, I woke up in the middle of the night, alone, and felt a kiss on the cheek," she says. "I hadn't felt those lips in so long, but I knew they were my mom's. She was coming to protect me from the bad news I was about to hear."

Doctors struggled for six weeks to target the disease's primary location, then finally decided to treat Cohen as a breast cancer patient. She started chemo and threw herself into work. "I was sick but insane about getting things done," she says. "I'd gotten so far in my career, and I didn't want all of my accomplishments to just go away."

At first, her hair shed on her pillow; then the curls began to fall out more easily—she'd find them on her computer keyboard. Eventually, the hair started coming out in fistfuls. "My three-year-old nephew touched my ponytail, and it felt like the whole thing was going to fall off. So my sister and I just cut it," she says. "I hated that moment in my life."

For more than two months, Cohen wore a wig to work. "One or two people said they liked it," she recalls. "Maybe they were trying to be supportive, but pointing out my wig just made me feel belittled. I was grabbing every single cell of courage I had to go to work and feel normal."

Finally, in March 2001, four months after her diagnosis, she went on disability leave. "I was trying to arrange chemo around traveling," she says. "Then my oncologist told me, 'Work or live.'"

Cohen underwent fifteen months of treatments, including a bone marrow transplant. Declared cancer-free in January 2002, she then started immunology treatments. In March she returned to work, assuming that she'd settle into her old life without a hitch, but her experience had changed her. "I just didn't care whose team got the budget and who was sitting to the left of the senior vice president," she says. The upside of returning to the office: coworkers confided in Cohen about their own sick friends and family and their trouble finding wigs. Cohen guided some of the women through the process.

"It dawned on me that cancer patients were desperate for help," Cohen says. "There's no shortage of wig shops around the country, many offering famous brands at prices that range from $70 for basic acrylic to $7,000 for human hair. But some are trying to sell you what they have instead of what you need." So she developed what she calls the house-call Mary Kay model: a client requests a wig, and a Girl on the Go representative visits her home to fit her with it—no fluorescent lights, no crowds, no rushed salesmen. "People turn to us because we understand what they're going through," she says. "Plus, they connect with my story."

Before launching her company, Cohen spent almost a year researching the wig industry and looking for a manufacturer that sold good-quality products. "There are all kinds of cheap, horrible wigs in stores," she says. "Those might be fine for making a Friday night fashion statement, but they won't last a year." Cohen sampled hundreds of pieces from China, Korea, Belgium, Poland, New York, and Florida—spending about $6,000 along the way— and finally chose a Brooklyn-based manufacturer and wholesaler. Today she has two additional vendors that supply only what she needs. "I don't want to buy in bulk," she says, "because I don't want to be stuck having twenty blond wigs to unload." She also has two freelancers who handcraft wigs for her. A wig knotted with human hair starts at $1,000 and goes up to $3,600; synthetic wigs start around $500. With a manufacturer on board, Cohen had brochures printed by the thousands and mailed them to about a hundred medical offices, hoping that doctors would display them in their waiting rooms. "The response was pretty much zero," she says. Some doctors didn't want to be seen as endorsing Cohen's products or be held responsible for any defects in them; others objected to her prices. One director of a not-for-profit cancer center in Boston was especially discouraging. "She thought displaying our brochure in her lobby would be damaging to a woman's soul because it's not about what you look like on the outside, it's about the strength you have on the inside," Cohen remembers.

She finally got a break when her own oncologist, Linda Vahdat, MD, of Weill Cornell Medical College, agreed to place Girl on the Go brochures in her office. "We handed them out gingerly at first to see if the business got good feedback," Vahdat says. "We were amazed by the response."

Cohen stayed at her job for a little more than a year after starting her business. She'd whittled twelve-hour days down to eight and spent her free time tending to her start-up. The sales that year—almost $20,000—would not even cover her monthly rent, which was more than $2,000. Nonetheless, Cohen quit her job, moved out of her apartment, and shuttled for two years from her sister's house in New Jersey to her dad's house in Albany, New York, and to her then boyfriend's house in Boston. She lived on her savings.

In year two, sales more than quadrupled and are projected to hit $300,000 this year. Girl on the Go now has representatives in

. . . .

The Most Important Thing I Did Right

"Providing a personal touch. I don't sell cheap wigs; I sell great wigs. There are lots of places to get great wigs and more places to get horrible ones. I provide people with care, whether it's from me or my stylist."

. . . .

nine states, from New York to North Carolina to Wisconsin. For clients in areas without reps, Cohen offers a service called Look Just Like You. Women send in a hair swatch and a few pictures; Cohen sends them a wig to match their look. One woman, diagnosed with cancer for the third time, used the service before going to a friend's wedding. "She felt fat and ugly from her medication and didn't want to go wig shopping in public," Cohen says. As a thank-you, the client sent Cohen pictures of herself beaming at the reception.

Another client, Joan Kaplan, a global marketer for Pfizer pharmaceuticals, requested Cohen's standard service around five years ago, after being diagnosed with breast cancer for the second time. "I travel for business and constantly meet people. I have to look normal," Kaplan says. Cohen even held Kaplan's hand when the last of her hair was shaved from her head.

These days, Cohen rarely goes on consultations (stylists and representatives do that job), and she has hired a phone center to field her calls—"a level of success in itself," she says. Still, Cohen spends a large part of her day on the phone, speaking with customers. "I'm part therapist, part wig saleswoman, " she says.

Although Cohen keeps a sketch of Wall Street in the foyer of her house, she has left her old life behind. She hopes to turn her company into a multimillion-dollar business. "I want to let people know that wearing a wig isn't a death sentence," she says. "I want my name to mean something to people."

·········· **Sheril's Key Questions to Ask Yourself** ··········

- Are you willing to work 100 percent of the time? You need to understand that you aren't only reinventing your job, you're reinventing your life.

- Are you okay with not knowing what you're going to make and making less than you thought you would?

Sheril's Success Strategy

"You have to judge success in different ways. I don't make a six-figure salary. I don't have a 401(k) or a pension. That's a huge concern for me, but success is that I pay all of my own bills, and I get paid in thank-you notes. Most days, I'm appreciative of how far I've come. "

She Found Her Inner Publicist
Carrol Van Stone

Carrol Van Stone, fifty-two, of Shepherdstown, West Virginia, was an executive secretary for nearly two decades, but her passion was tracking the news. Sometimes she'd even take a sick day so that she could watch events unfold on TV. Still, she was the opposite of a bad employee. She often noticed how the news tied in with what her bosses were working on, and she began to come up with creative ways to generate press. In other words, she was thinking like a publicist.

Once, when Van Stone worked for a nonprofit think tank and the news was filled with stories about troubled schools, she

· ·

The Most Important Thing I Learned

"Once you successfully reinvent yourself, going backward is not an option. Obviously, the economy shook things up for everybody, but I'm not lying in bed thinking that I can go back to typing ninety words per minute. I'm thinking about how I can put a twist in my PR business. Who the heck would want me as an executive secretary after I've been doing what I've been doing for eleven years? I would be out of place. No, if it fails now, I can only go forward."

· ·

pitched her boss to the local TV and radio shows as an expert they could interview. Van Stone's success at winning him visibility made her realize that she was "maxed out as a secretary" and could be earning much more money as a publicist.

At forty-one, Van Stone revamped her résumé and aimed for a PR job. Calling herself an executive secretary/scheduler ("Being a scheduler means your external contacts are significant," she says), she moved her publicity achievements to the top of the job description. "Even though it was the smallest part of my twenty years of experience," she says, "it was the most important part for the transition." Then she applied to a one-man firm that could only afford to hire someone who was trying to break in. It was a perfect match. When she became so successful that her boss couldn't continue to pay her bonuses, she found a position with a company that allowed her to take on freelance contracts. In 2002, she went entirely freelance (visibilitybookings.com). Her reinvention took all of two years.

The Most Important Thing I Did Right

"Treating people well and insisting that my clients do the same. Treating people well involves several things: running on time, being respectful when they're working, and then thanking them, not in an e-mail but in a handwritten note. I can't tell you how many e-mails I get from people thanking me for my handwritten notes."

My Biggest Mistake

"Not following my instincts. When I knew a particular personality or business wasn't a good fit, I still pursued it, believing that any business was better than no business. Not true. Growth can't be sustained unless all of the parts are positive."

Van Stone believes the shrewdness she developed as an executive secretary helped her market herself. She lands clients at networking meetings, through Craigslist, from referrals, and by plain old cold-calling. "I'm not afraid of picking up the Yellow Pages and just phoning people," she says, "and I don't fear rejection."

In 2010, she made over $200,000, more than four times her executive secretary salary. This year, she expects to do even better. "I'm flexible and a bargain compared with a full-service PR firm," she says. "Money doesn't buy happiness, but it allows you to go out and buy a Cadillac, so you can drive around and look for happiness."

.... **Carrol's Key Questions to Ask Yourself** ....

- Do you believe in yourself enough to withstand sarcasm, criticism, and even putdowns and naysayers?
- What about your earlier life/career did you like?
- Are you prepared to make mistakes as the new you?

Carrol's Success Strategy

"I'm not afraid of cold-calling. I don't fear rejection."

Discovering the Art of Instruction
Patty Palmer

In her life before motherhood, Patty Palmer, forty-seven, worked as a clothing designer and ran her own company. A year after she had her first child, at age twenty-nine, she quit the fashion industry to be at home full time. As her three kids reached school age, she enthusiastically volunteered for jobs that ranged from PTA president to fund-raising chair to district advisory committee chairman for the school district.

As her youngest child entered kindergarten ten years later, Palmer felt ready to go back to work for pay. She had no interest in returning to fashion, but she didn't know what else to do. "It was a painful process of asking myself, 'What am I qualified for?'" she recalls.

When Palmer put out feelers, a friend said that her child's elementary school needed an art teacher. Palmer thought it was a long shot because she didn't have teaching credentials. Yet she *had* graduated from art school, and she'd had a passion for drawing since she was a young girl. Before motherhood, she had sketched nearly every day of her life. She put together a portfolio of art projects that she'd done while volunteering at her kids' school and created some sample lessons. "Within a week, I was setting up my classroom for my first-ever teaching job," she says. The salary wasn't high, but the nine hours a week were a perfect fit for her life as a mom.

Palmer had no idea how to come up with an entire year's worth of art lessons for three hundred children in grades K through 6. She bought whatever books she could find and scoured the Internet for ideas, but she found little help. She managed to eke out acceptable lessons her first year, but she knew she could do better. The more she taught, the more inspired she became. She turned children's books, greeting cards, and nature into lesson plans. She was in a groove. "It was like, here I am again," she says. "The artist is back."

She was so proud of her students that in 2007 she created a blog, interspersing her writing with pictures drawn by her students, to share the kids' work with their parents. The blog didn't seem to catch on with moms and dads, but art teachers from all over started posting comments and asking Palmer for more step-by-step specifics. She realized that the blog was the perfect platform to create the very thing that she had been seeking when she started out: support, guidance, and projects to get excited about. She began to post photo-tutorials, tips, and student examples. Within months, she had a following of art instructors, school teachers, and home-schooling parents. She named her blog Deep Space Sparkle (deepspacesparkle.com) after her favorite Crayola crayon color. It became a space for others to get ideas and to weigh in on different challenges that they experienced in the art room.

. . . .

The Most Important Thing I Did Right

"Deciding to eliminate small ads on my blog. A little creative thinking led me to the idea of developing lesson plans. My price point was low, and as I sold more, people suggested that I raise my price. I wanted to stay true to my mission of providing a 'bundle-your-own' art booklet, so I kept the price low. Price is rarely a hurdle for my customers."

. . . .

In 2009, Palmer and her husband were celebrating their anniversary with champagne at a French restaurant and talking about the evolution of her blog into a community of two hundred daily visitors. Although she still primarily wanted to support art teachers, she also wished she could find a way to capitalize on the traffic. Palmer's husband, a computer engineer, had an idea: instead of cluttering the site with ads, why not create helpful content that visitors could download and buy? During the next few months, Palmer put together detailed, theme-based art lessons, including student handouts, that could be inexpensively downloaded as PDF files. Her goal was to add one a month. "Sales and requests for more piled in," she says. "I filled a need." By the following year, she was making more from the sale of art booklets than from her teaching salary.

That growth has only continued. Palmer now gets around three thousand visitors a day and sells about nine hundred booklets a month. "I have customers in Australia, Africa, Brazil, China, the UK, and France," she says. "Every month just gets better." She spends two days a week in the classroom—she loves working with the children too much to stop—and the rest of her time she develops art lessons and expands her blog. "Nothing about my day feels like work," she says. "All of the things I've done during my life—working in a creative field, owning a business, volunteering in the schools—have joined together to resurface in a whole new life. When you do something that truly stems from your heart, it's amazing how good things can just happen."

······· **Patty's Key Question to Ask Yourself** ·······

What do you enjoy doing? So often women get bogged down with the pressure to commit themselves to tasks that they're really good at but hate. Sometimes you can go decades doing something really well before you realize that you never actually liked doing it.

Patty's Success Strategy

"Nothing is as important as finding your passion. It's what will feed you through the rough patches."

Miracle in the Ladies' Room
Stefanie Ziev

In her fifteen years as a television executive, Stefanie Ziev made TV movies, hobnobbed with celebrities, and walked the red carpet at the Emmys. In 2006, a friend recommended her for an even bigger job at one of the top networks.

Preparing for the interview, Ziev went to a career counselor.

It was during one of those sessions that Ziev, then thirty-six, began to question her life's autopilot trajectory. At work, she was distressed by her boss and by the fear-driven nature of the entertainment industry. In her personal life, she was on the verge of getting engaged but knew deep down that the guy wasn't right for her. "I was having an inner battle," she says.

Before Ziev could spend too much time reflecting on her next move—and before she had a chance to interview for the new job—the position disappeared. She still had a few sessions left with the career counselor, though, and one day she heard herself blurt out, "You know what I would do if I could do anything?" When the counselor asked, "What?" Ziev replied, "I'd like to run personal growth workshops." She had attended self-help and personal development workshops during her twenties and thirties and loved to explore psychological complexities with her friends and coworkers. "Growing up, I was the quintessential Dear Abby," she says. "I was always a really good listener, I asked a lot of questions, and I liked to get deep." Instead of laughing at her out-of-the-blue exclamation, the counselor suggested that Ziev pursue a career as a life coach. And Ziev listened. "It wasn't as if I hated my job," she says. "I just felt that something inside me was waiting to emerge."

Five months later, having broken up with her boyfriend, Ziev signed up for a coaching certification program that held classes in the evenings. She figured she'd get certified during the course of the next nine months and then quietly build her business for another year before she made a complete break from TV. "Only a handful of people knew about my secret plan," she says. "At times, I admit, it was hard to contain my excitement."

On the day Ziev got certified, she rushed to the restroom with a coworker to spill her big news. She was explaining her new business and doing a happy dance when one of the bathroom stall doors swung open. "I froze mid-dance and tried to wish the moment away," she says. But then the unexpected intruder, someone Ziev had never worked with, smiled and said that she was looking for a life coach. It turned out that she was a writer/director who was eager to leave her day job and find more time to create. She took Ziev's phone number and within the week became her first client.

Later that month, Ziev found herself in the office of her company's COO. It wasn't a moment that she had planned out, but she explained to her supportive manager that she felt driven to move on. She asked to opt out of her contract. "There were people who told me I was out of my mind," she says. "It was a huge risk, but there was this intuition, this higher voice, that pushed me on. It was a profound moment of choice." She negotiated a package and made sure she had enough savings to support herself for a year, giving herself time to get her business off the ground.

As she built Ziev Coaching (ZievCoaching.com), her niche became helping women transition into new careers grounded in purpose and passion. Prospective clients came to her through word of mouth. "When a client had a dramatic external shift, all of a sudden her friends were like, 'I want some of that,'" she says. She also held workshops, teleconferences, and retreats.

Ziev has found that she loves her new role as a "cheerleader for personal growth" as much as she thought she would. "What brings me joy is holding the vision my clients have for themselves

. . . .

The Most Important Thing I Learned

"I knew nothing about business when I started. I genuinely believed that my ability and desire to serve as a life coach and my extensive contact list would magically generate clients. While that happened to some extent, it didn't build my business to any sustainable level. I now know that the business is as important as the service that I am providing. It's a living, breathing thing that needs to be marketed, publicized, and socially networked in order to grow."

. . . .

**The Most Important
Thing I Did Right**

"I left my full-time job when
I had enough money in the
bank to last me twelve to fifteen months. This allowed me
to build the business without
feeling the pressure, because
the business didn't have to
support me right away."

before they can fully own it," she says.
"I get excited knowing that I am helping people emerge into the bigness of
who they're here to become."

Ziev's transformation into a life
coach has proved challenging, at
times exhilarating and at other times
frightening. "Reinvention can sound
romantic, but it's important not to be
Pollyanna about it," says Ziev. "It's not
black and white. It's messy." Although
Ziev is a natural at the coaching part
of the equation, being an entrepre-
neur was harder. "I am still learning and figuring it out," she says.

More than three years since she launched the business, the
client she picked up in the ladies' room is still with her. Now that
Ziev has helped hundreds of other women and men find their
way, she is in the midst of her own personal shift, figuring out
where she wants to go from here. "As much as I love my individual
coaching clients, I believe I'm here to do it on a bigger scale," she
says. "The truth is, I have always wanted to be my version of Phil
Donahue." She's thinking about a book or a TV show or both.
"When you consciously choose to make changes in your life, you
have to embrace all that it brings forward," she says. "Right now
I'm in the process of saying yes to the mess!"

Reinventing via Inventions
Holly Tucker

Holly Tucker, a longtime travel agent, was a huge fan of reality TV.
Survivor, Big Brother, Project Runway, Top Chef, you name it. Yet
her fascination with the genre reached new levels when the show

American Inventor premiered on NBC in 2006 at a time when Tucker, then forty-six, was facing difficult health issues. She was in the middle of radiation treatments after having a malignant carotid body tumor removed from her neck. The side effects were excruciating. "It was like I was swallowing razor blades," she says. "I had to take pain pills in order to eat or sleep."

Tucker was so excited by the concept of the show that it diverted her attention from her illness. She had always considered herself a problem solver but never an inventor. "I thought inventing was for people who are technical," she says. "But it was clear on this show that any new products, not only cell phones or microwaves, were considered inventions. It was liberating for me." Instead of dwelling on her medical problems, Tucker talked to friends and family about how she was going to audition for the program's next season. She even had an invention ready. She had come up with it the previous year during a trip to Thailand, after suffering from heat stroke. She'd designed an ice hat—a hat that held a bag of ice on top of her head—to keep her cool in the blazing heat.

· · · · · ·

The Most Important Thing I Learned

"I never realized how something could completely consume my every thought and give me so much joy! My husband, Chris, is passionate about golf, and if he isn't golfing, he's watching it or reading about it. I never really understood that feeling until now."

· · · · · ·

When the network announced audition dates for *American Inventor* the next fall, Tucker signed herself up, along with her sister, whom she'd talked into going with her. She promised to come up with an invention for her sister, too. A few months later, after lying down for a nap, Tucker came up with the idea. She had lost one of her sandals in her closet and was too exhausted to dig through the clutter to find it. Sick of the mess of shoes, she decided that the perfect place to store footwear would be in a storage system hidden underneath her bed, behind a bed skirt. The next day she went to WalMart, bought a clear plastic shower curtain, and made a prototype of the Shoe Skirt. She pulled her shoes out of the closet and tried it out. It worked fabulously. "What's so ironic is that I had been too tired to go into the closet to look for the lost sandal, and now I was dragging shoes out of my closet to put in the skirt," says Tucker. "I got so excited that it gave me energy."

Tucker knew she was on to something (and she wasn't going to hand it over to her sister!). She ordered books and searched inventor websites to find out what steps to take. She started an inventor's book, logging each development, so that she could later apply for a patent. She became consumed with brainstorming—and with talking about all of her ideas, the good, the bad, and the ugly. "It got really old for my sister," she says. "I'd have to get her permission: 'Can I talk about some inventions now?'"

That spring, Tucker auditioned for *American Inventor* with her ice hat. She didn't make it past the first round, but she was hooked. "I wasn't looking for fame and fortune," she says. "I just wanted to go through the process." What had started as simply seeking a reality TV adventure had morphed into a newfound passion for inventing. It was fun, and it filled a void. "Because I was still struggling with my health," she says, "I was tired and couldn't do as much as I used to. Inventing filled me with so much joy."

* *

The Most Important Thing I Did Right

"I read, searched, and learned as much as I could, finding websites, making friends on the bulletin boards, buying books and reading them from cover to cover, and just throwing myself into it 100 percent. My goal wasn't only to get a product to market, it was to learn about the whole process and how to enjoy the adventure."

* *

The following year, Tucker took her Shoe Skirt and auditioned for *Everyday Edisons*, an invention show on PBS that aired in 2009. Out of thirteen thousand applicants, Tucker became one of nine people chosen to take her invention from idea to store shelf. The Shoe Skirt started selling at Bed Bath & Beyond in 2010. Tucker signed a contract so she no longer owns the product rights, but she'll get royalties on sales for twenty years. "Being chosen for the show changed my life," she says. "It validated that I really *am* an inventor. Once I accepted the fact that I was good at thinking of simple and useful products, there was no going back."

Today, Tucker has dozens of ideas in her invention book and five patents on products. She regularly enters product searches that she finds online. She has had a nationally televised infomercial and a licensing contract with WestPoint Home. She still watches reality TV but has no interest in becoming a contestant again.

"No matter what happens on this entrepreneurial journey, I'm already a winner," she says. "I will always know that instead of giving in to pain and fear, I chose a new path and found joy, imagination, and creativity by reinventing myself as an inventor. I'm coming up with new ideas, trying different avenues, exploring that whole world, and knowing I fit in. You can't stop me now!"

·············· **My Biggest Mistake** ··············

"Talking about inventions all the time! It was all I could think about."

The DNA Detective
Colleen Fitzpatrick

Lashed by frigid rain, two hikers, wrapped in thick parkas and carrying heavy packs, stopped abruptly on their trek across the glacial ice of Mount Sanford, Alaska. "Oh, my God," the first man said, looking down at the rock-strewn ice before him. His friend caught up, then stared in horror, too. A perfectly preserved human arm poked out of the ice, the alabaster hand pointing north by northwest.

It was July 1999, and the hikers were pilots who had made several trips to the icy Alaskan mountainside in an attempt to solve the puzzle of Northwest Airlines Flight 4422, one of the most mysterious crashes in commercial-aviation history. After taking off from Anchorage on a clear night in March 1948, the chartered DC-4 had slammed into the western face of a 16,000-foot peak, burst into flames, and plummeted down the mountain's icy flank, then broke into pieces on the glacier. The twenty-four passengers—merchant mariners who had sailed an oil tanker from the United States to Shanghai and were on their way to New York—were presumed dead, along with six crew members. Legend had it that the plane was carrying gold bullion. Within days of the crash, however, snow and ice had completely covered the wreckage. For more than fifty years, the mountain had kept the plane's secret.

......

The Most Important Thing I Learned

"How much fun it would be and how gratifying."

......

Until now.

The frozen arm had no tattoos, no rings, no identifying marks of any kind. Some family members of the missing had been waiting for closure on this accident for decades, and everyone wanted to know, Whose arm was it?

In 2007, when the mystery still hadn't been solved, the Armed Forces DNA Identification Laboratory contacted Colleen Fitzpatrick, a nuclear physicist who was building a new career as a forensic genealogist, tracking missing people through vital records, family history, and DNA. If anyone could help break the mysterious "Arm in the Snow" case, it was Fitzpatrick.

At five feet two inches tall, with tousled curls and rimless eyeglasses, Fitzpatrick emanates laser-sharp intelligence and unselfconscious warmth. She favors hugs, not handshakes, and her preferred work clothes are jeans rolled up at the ankles, scuffed black slip-ons, and little makeup. In the Huntington Beach, California, house she shares with her partner, Andy Yeiser, Fitzpatrick keeps a decades-old pet African tortoise named Thing Three (after a character in the Dr. Seuss book *The Cat in the Hat*) and a California desert tortoise dubbed Thing Four. She swings her pet parrot, Sikiru, to sleep every night after feeding it a snack of M&Ms.

Fitzpatrick's personal habits may be eccentric, but her methodical, unyielding style of work has allowed her to build a reputation as one of the best DNA detectives in the country. She combines high-tech DNA analysis with the skills of an old-fashioned gumshoe, combing birth and death certificates, newspaper articles, and church and cemetery records and making calls to distant continents far into the night. Since switching professions in 2005, she has solved a variety of cases, from helping identify the remains of a baby who died in 1912 to locating owners of unclaimed property. "I can usually find anyone around the world in two steps," she boasts today. Yet when the "Arm in the Snow" mystery landed on her desk, it was by far her most complex case.

Fitzpatrick never set out to be a DNA detective, but she's always had a passion for science. As a kid in New Orleans, she was the classic high school geek, more interested in preparing an optical-illusion project for the science fair than in finding a date for the senior prom. "I wasn't Miss Popular," she says. "I pretty much was the science club."

She got her PhD in nuclear physics from Duke University in 1983, then taught at Sam Houston State University in Texas before moving to California to work for a defense firm. In 1989, she started her own optics company. The company flourished, and she hired seven scientists to help her develop and test a range of products, from medical devices to laser measurement equipment for NASA.

Fitzpatrick loved her lab, with its shiny steel optical table and various lasers, mirrors, and lenses. She enjoyed sending beams of light dancing across the table to test the hermetic seals on pace-makers. Most of all, though, she loved the people. "They were like me," she says, "academics, scientists, always looking for new ideas, interested in art, literature, the humanities, and travel."

With these friends, Fitzpatrick pursued numerous eclectic interests. They packed up telescopes and traveled around the globe to witness six solar eclipses. She was a contestant on *Jeopardy!* where she nailed the science questions but finished second to a shirt salesman who beat her on French literature. She took knife-throwing lessons from the Great Throwdini and studied Japanese to add to the foreign languages she already spoke fluently: French, German, and Spanish. (She's also conversant in Italian, Russian, and Chinese and says she can "limp along" in Swedish, Portuguese, and Dutch.)

In 2005, her company seemed to be on the brink of a big break. "We were named to a team designing the next spacecraft to Jupiter," she says. "I was in a position to be the technical manager for all of the environmental sensors on the flight." Then NASA shifted priorities and canceled the Jupiter project. The loss of the contract, along with other setbacks, forced Fitzpatrick to close the company and sell some of her equipment.

"It was pretty rough," she recalls. "That company was my baby."

Discouraged, she kept asking herself, What could I have done differently? She spent her days moping. "I didn't go to the lab," she says. "I felt in despair."

The bad times got worse. Fitzpatrick's best friend died of breast cancer. Her scientist colleagues moved on to other jobs. "There were many days when I felt like the center of my life was gone," she says. "I cried a lot. I felt embarrassed among my peers. When you fail, everyone looks at your flaws."

Fitzpatrick had one island of sanity, though. During her years in the lab, she had dabbled in genealogy, which has interested her ever since she was a child. At thirteen, she'd found a yellowing marriage certificate in her grandmother's house and eventually traced her family's roots to a seventeenth-century French village. In 2002, in her spare time, she began work on a book, *Forensic Genealogy*, and was thrilled when a publisher offered her a contract. The book "was my sedative," she says. A 220-page guide for professionals and amateurs, it explained how to examine old photographs and documents and use public records and DNA databases to trace family history.

When Fitzpatrick's manuscript was ready for publication, "the publisher decided that forensic genealogy was passé," she says. The company canceled the contract, and Fitzpatrick fell back into a depression.

Yeiser, a retired physicist and a computer engineer who has always been her emotional bulwark, didn't let her dwell on it. "Let's just publish it ourselves," he said.

They researched different papers, inks, and distributors and hired a printer. Then they dug into their savings and invested $3,500 to print five hundred copies of *Forensic Genealogy*. Fitzpatrick promoted the book at a genealogy conference in Maine. Sitting at a booth in a convention hall crammed with displays for family tree software, maps, and photo-repair services, she thought, I'm wasting my time; nobody's going to buy my book. Suddenly, a man stopped, thumbed through a copy, and got out his wallet. Fitzpatrick tried to stay calm, but she was ecstatic. She wrote inside the front cover, "This is the first book I ever sold! Colleen Fitzpatrick."

By the end of the conference, she'd found thirty-five buyers and pocketed $1,000.

After that, her new career took off. She set up forensicgenealogy.info, which now gets hundreds of hits a day, and began tracking down missing heirs and owners for an international investment company that specialized in unclaimed property. She wrote a column for *Ancestry* magazine, as well as articles for *Family Chronicle* and *Games*, and created a weekly forensic photo puzzle for her site. She launched a second site, identifinders.com, to promote her business of tracking down missing persons. Her book went into a second and then a third printing, and she wrote and published two more, one of which was funded by a DNA-testing company. She spoke at science, history, and genealogy conferences and gradually patched together a living from book sales, speeches, and the unclaimed-property work.

The process of tracking down a person's identity is like being caught in a "tractor beam," she says. "I'm almost addicted to it. I pick up the thread, and I've got to follow it." By 2007, she had tracked down more than eighty people who owned unclaimed property and had helped identify the remains of the Unknown Child of the *Titanic*, a nineteen-month-old boy whose body was recovered from the sunken ship. Yet most cases have not proved to be as challenging as the "Arm in the Snow" case.

"I didn't ask if I wanted to reinvent myself or not. This just happened. Life just happens, and I follow it."

The Armed Forces lab had access to the DNA sample from the frozen limb, but DNA means nothing unless you can compare it with a living relative's. So Fitzpatrick worked with other scientists to track down as many descendants of the victims of the Northwest Airlines flight as possible. Independent fingerprint experts also worked on the case, and six months later, the team had eliminated twenty-eight of the thirty people on board the doomed plane. That meant the arm could have belonged to either of two remaining passengers. One of them was Frank Van Zandt, a merchant mariner from Bennington, Vermont.

"I turned over every piece of paper in the state of Vermont," Fitzpatrick recalls. "I checked census records, obituaries, newspaper stories. I looked up city directories in Bennington-Arlington. I called churches, searching for marriage records, burial records, baptismal registries, First Communions."

Nothing.

Then she found a marriage certificate for Van Zandt's brother, which said that his mother, Margaret Conway, was born in 1876 in "Timerick," Ireland. Figuring this was a misspelling of Limerick, Fitzpatrick pored over the Irish birth registration and found records for all of the Margaret Conways born from 1872 to 1876. Still nothing.

In bed at night, she kept going over it in her mind: Where *is* this woman?

After weeks of deadends, she suddenly had a hunch: What if Conway had lied about her age? Checking earlier dates, she finally found a birth record for a Margaret Conway born in 1871 to John Conway and Ellen Drum.

The name Drum was extinct in the areas around Limerick, so Fitzpatrick started calling Conways, asking, "Are you related to a family named Drum?" Scores of calls later, she telephoned an elderly machine oiler named Maurice Conway in the village of Askeaton.

"I'm trying to identify the remains of a serviceman. . . . " There was silence on the line. Then Conway's voice replied in a thick Irish accent, "Could you call me back tomorrow?" The next day, the man told her that the Conway cemetery was across from his house and that he'd found a tombstone there dedicated by John Conway to the memory of his wife, Ellen. "The family information on the stone matched everything we knew about the Conways," says Fitzpatrick. Ellen was Maurice's great-great-grandmother's sister. She was also Frank Van Zandt's grandmother.

My Biggest Mistake

"Not realizing how much work it takes to get people to value what I'm doing. Even though I have very unusual services to provide, people don't understand the value, so I don't get paid as much as I should."

"Maurice," Fitzpatrick said with a sigh, "I've been looking for you all over the world."

A few weeks later, a DNA test on Maurice Conway confirmed the link. The arm belonged to Van Zandt. Fitzpatrick cries when she tells the story. "Frank Van Zandt was a serviceman, a real hero," she says.

"A lot of people would have given up," says Mike Coble, the research director of the Armed Forces lab. But Fitzpatrick, he says, was "relentless."

Independent fingerprint experts had concurrently identified the frozen arm, but for Fitzpatrick, this wasn't just about solving a case; she wanted to establish a human connection. In 2008, she visited Ireland and stood at the memorial to Frank Van Zandt's grandmother. "All the spirits were standing there with me. They said, 'It's over. You can go home.' And they all breathed one big sigh," she says.

Since then, Fitzpatrick has become a star in the small field of forensic genealogy, often taking on higher-profile cases pro bono. "It's not lucrative," she says, "but it's satisfying." She traced a man who had fled to Australia after his involvement with the 1920s Teapot Dome bribery scandal that swirled around President Warren G. Harding, and she assisted in uncovering two literary hoaxes connected with the Holocaust. She is currently one of a team of scientists investigating clandestine graves at crime sites, including the ranch of the notorious killer Charles Manson.

What Fitzpatrick values even more than the science, though, is that her work allows her to glimpse both the physical and the spiritual link between all humans. "To see the hand in the snow and know he's connected to someone is the reward," she says. "You're solving a human mystery, and humans are the ultimate mystery."

The MBA Who Became a Matchmaker
Rachel Greenwald

When Rachel Greenwald graduated from Harvard Business School in 1993, she took a prize job as marketing manager for Evian, the high-end French mineral water. At twenty-nine, she was on the business fast track, selling the designer water to supermodels at Fashion Week in New York City and to socialites at ski events in Aspen. It was a high-stress, demanding job with long hours and frequent travel. "At the time, I told myself I was really lucky to have a job with such cachet," she says.

When her son was born in 1995, Greenwald's perspective changed. Her employers declined her request for a part-time position, so she resigned. "I could no longer go into an office and pretend that $5 bottles of water were the most important thing in my day," she says. She took a job as a part-time marketing director at Carolee Jewelry, a family-friendly firm, but after she had a second child, she struggled to find a balance between her work and her family. Three years later, she quit to launch her own marketing consulting company and create a flexible schedule. Yet even that didn't work. Now with a six-year-old, a five-year-old, and a newborn, she found her days too unpredictable to stay on schedule with her work projects. "I threw my hands up," she says. "I wanted to be working, but I didn't see how I could."

-------------------- **My Biggest Mistake** --------------------

"Believing that I had to strike while the iron is hot. I ended up spending less time with my kids, believing I had to chase every exciting opportunity for fear it wasn't going to come around again. If you believe in yourself and you have the stamina to stick it out, another opportunity will come along."

• • • • • •

The Most Important Thing I Did Right

"I took on a long-run view and only worked with clients I genuinely liked. No amount of money will make up for someone being a pain in the neck."

• • • • • •

So Greenwald transferred her work drive into parenting. "I became a neurotic," she says. "It wasn't healthy for my kids, my husband, or me." She skipped her Harvard Business School reunion because she was embarrassed that she wasn't using her degree. After one year at home, she craved mental stimulation. She asked herself, Is there any job on this planet that is truly 100 percent flexible? Her conclusion: becoming an author. Even though she had never had any formal training as a writer, she figured she could pen a book anywhere, any time of the day or night, no matter whether her kids were sick or on a school vacation. She spent $200 on research materials: how to write a book, how to get published, how to find an agent, and how to negotiate a publishing contract. All of the books gave the same bottom-line advice: write about your passion. "That was my stumbling block," she says.

Borrowing from an exercise that she had learned when she lost her last twenty pounds of baby weight, Greenwald set out to uncover a passion. Instead of keeping a food diary where she catalogued everything she put in her mouth, she now kept a "passion journal," writing down events in her day—anything from brushing her teeth to savoring her morning tea, grocery shopping, or kissing her husband—and ranked each action on a scale of one star (*blah!*) to five stars ("*I'm super-passionate about this!*"). At the end of a week, one five-star action stood out: giving dating advice to her forty-one-year-old single friend who was struggling to find Mr. Right. "I had the phone pressed to my ear and tuned out everything around me as I coached her, pacing and waving my arms wildly," she says. "I realized my dating tips were the same strategies I used every day in the business world, centering on branding, packaging, and niche marketing." She had found the topic for a book.

Greenwald sold *Find a Husband after 35 (Using What I Learned at Harvard Business School)* to Random House for the high six figures. In the book, she told the story of her single friend who used her dating advice and was now happily married. "She was my first success story," says Greenwald. The book came out in 2003, became a *New York Times* best-seller, and was translated into eighteen languages. She went on a whirlwind media tour and appeared on *Today*, CNN, *Nightline*, Fox News, ABC News, and NPR. She was also featured in O, *the Oprah Magazine*, *People*, *Fortune*, and the *New York Post*.

Greenwald's matchmaking business was born (rachelgreen wald.com). Private client requests poured in. People who used her book advice e-mailed her their success stories. "I've wallpapered my office with them over the years," she says and claims that she's now responsible for 764 marriages—both private clients and people who have used the advice from her book. She is invited to a couple of dozen weddings a year, sometimes by people she's never met who followed her matchmaking advice. In 2009, she published a second book, *Have Him at Hello: Confessions from 1,000 Guys about What Makes Them Fall in Love or Never Call Back*, which has been translated into ten languages.

Two years ago, Greenwald shifted gears after concluding that the time-crunched deadlines and the promotional tours that came along with book publishing stole time that she wanted for her family. Today, at forty-seven, she is more selective about private clients, charging $500 an hour or $5,000 to $10,000 for a monthly retainer. She trains and certifies dating coaches around the world and takes a percentage of the fees. She reserves her dating seminars for prestigious venues, such as the 92nd Street Y in New York City, high-end destination spas, and meetings of special women's groups. Now that Greenwald's kids are teenagers, she's finally found the work balance that she set out to create when they were young. "I wouldn't have known this is the business model I would end up with," she says. "The passion part was correct, but the means of working in that space turned out to be different than I thought."

Eleven years after that fateful phone call where she doled out dating advice to her single friend, Greenwald gives her career 5-plus stars on the passion scale. "It's one thing to be passionate about an idea, but when it actually works and you see results, there's a whole other depth to it," she says. "I am *in love* with what I do."

············· **Rachel's Key Questions to Ask Yourself** ·············

- What are you truly passionate about? Keeping a passion diary can help you identify passions that feel so natural, you might not even recognize them.

- What is the goal of the reinvention? Money? Flexibility? Doing something meaningful? Your goals have to be aligned for the reinvention to work.

- What kind of budget are you going to put toward this? Reinvention is not free. There's nothing better to invest in than yourself.

Rachel's Success Strategy

"Know the importance of the pivot. For me, it hasn't been one big reinvention but a series of mini reinventions. What you start off thinking your reinvention is focused on may not be where it leads you."

A Chocolate-Coated Life Change
Shelly Mortensen

Growing up, Shelly Mortensen watched her mother, a single mom raising four kids, grudgingly go to her office job at a trucking company. "She worked there twenty-eight years and hated every day of it," says Mortensen, forty-two. Her mother felt trapped but saw the job as the only lifeline to retirement. "I was taught that you work at one company forever, you retire, and then you're happy," says Mortensen. For years, she searched for the job she could one day retire from.

......

The Most Important Things I Learned

"Perseverance, preparation, commitment, and consistency."

......

By the time she was thirty-eight, however, Mortensen had been laid off three times. She had always put in long hours—usually arriving in the morning darkness and getting home in the evening darkness—and never felt rewarded. In the middle of the recession in 2007, she found herself out of work again when her IT project management job was eliminated. "I felt like my self-confidence had received the pink slip," she says. The prospect of another job search deflated her. "I had such a bad experience again and again and again," she says. She swore she wouldn't follow in her mom's footsteps, riding out yet another job that she hated until retirement. "I was yearning for the chance to prove myself and be recognized for my efforts," she says. "I no longer wanted to work for anyone but myself."

Mortensen had dabbled in direct sales on the side while working in IT, selling jewelry at home parties a few times a month. She loved the direct sales party model, where stress levels were low and guests were ready to have a good time. She trolled the Internet to find "the next great product" that she could get excited about. She stumbled on a post about being an independent chocolatier for DOVE Chocolate Discoveries and saw that she might lead chocolate-tasting parties in hosts' homes, where guests would place orders and she would earn commissions. "I thought, Oh, yes, *that* I can be passionate about," says Mortensen, who has always loved chocolate. "The second I saw it, I knew in my soul that I was meant to do this. I knew I was home."

A few days before Mortensen's first party in 2008, she had a horrible meltdown. "I couldn't get my chocolate-tempering equipment to work, and it sent me into a tizzy," she says. "I convinced myself that if I couldn't get the machine to work, I couldn't be successful at this, and I'd have to go back to work for someone else in corporate America." Five minutes before the DOVE home office closed for the evening, she called there to have someone walk her through the problem. A few days later, at her first party, she was a nervous wreck. A Type-A personality who thrives on appearing calm and collected, she fumbled around, relying on note cards to describe the chocolate martinis, brownies, and truffles. "Still, at the end of the night everyone was happy," she says. "I made $75, and I had two more parties booked."

By the end of her first year, Mortensen had held ninety-one parties, earning her a number-one ranking in her company's national sales force. At the annual conference in 2009, just fourteen months after she had signed on as a chocolatier, she garnered awards for first in number of parties, fourth in sales, and fifth in recruiting. She also earned a spot on the prestigious thirteen-member advisory council and an all-expense-paid incentive trip to chocolate school run by Mars Snackfood US, where she witnessed chocolate being made, from bean to bar. "The recognition I received as a result of my efforts was liberating," she says.

Although Mortensen's first year was stellar from a business perspective, it was a nightmare from a medical perspective. She'd been having unexplained symptoms, including problems breathing, since 2007, and they escalated in the spring of 2009. She had weekly doctors' appointments for tests, from CT scans to MRIs, breathing tests, and whooping cough tests. Ultimately, she was

diagnosed with Parkinson's disease. While sitting in hospital waiting rooms, she felt grateful that she had a job with so much flexibility. "If I'd been working a corporate gig, they would have fired
me," she says. "But I was my own boss, and I knew where my heart
was. I didn't question my commitment."

Today Mortensen keeps her symptoms under control with
medication and by minimizing stress and fatigue, which is possible to do with her self-designed schedule. Her business continues
to thrive. She has focused on recruiting more chocolatiers to her
team and helping them build their businesses. She has thirty
chocolatiers directly under her and more than two hundred on
her extended team. "My ability to help others grow and achieve
their goals through my business brings me joy," she says. "I don't
want anyone to have to feel the way my mom felt every day going
to work."

It also brings her additional income because she makes a percentage of their sales (in 2009, she personally sold $36,000 and
her group volume was $324,000). Last year, fewer than three
years after launching her business, Mortensen surpassed the
$75,000 income that she had made in her IT job. She was recently
promoted to senior manager and aims to be the first in the country to reach the top of her company's career path, three more
levels up, by 2012.

Mortensen has rediscovered the confidence that she had lost
when laid off and in the process has ignited career enthusiasm
that she had never before experienced. "It's hard to have a bad
day when you make people smile," says Mortensen. "All you have
to do is say *chocolate*, and people's faces light up. I can't tell you
how many times I've heard, 'You're my new best friend.' To me,
it's a fabulous thing. How can I not love what I do?"

···················· **My Biggest Mistake** ····························
"Pushing myself too hard."

She and her husband recently started a real estate investing company on the side. "There is nothing off limits," Mortensen says. "If I want it and I can imagine it, then I can make it happen. I grew up in an environment where there were all of these limitations. I had myself in a box for so long and didn't even know I was in it."

············ **Shelly's Key Question to Ask Yourself** ············

"If, at the end of your life, you were given an extra twenty-five years, what would you do with that time—and why aren't you doing that now?"

Shelly's Success Strategy

"If you don't have a map, you don't know where you're going, and you're never going to know whether you got there."

6

✌

Seeking Adventure

O ne of the benefits of reinventing yourself is that the change of perspective gives you a new outlook on life. The women in this chapter all achieved that by stepping out of their comfort zone. One city dweller sold her house and moved to the mountains; another took on the risks of becoming a reporter in Iraq. In return, they discovered not only adventure and excitement, but a new belief in their own abilities.

Finding Fulfillment in a War Zone
Shelby Monroe

Shelby Monroe graduated from college with a degree in English literature—and no idea what to do next. So she did a bit of everything: taught classes at a college in Maine; worked in a bookstore; opened her own bookstore. Then she decided to go to library school. "I thought I needed to be practical again," she says, but the classes, at a college in upstate New York, bored her. By the time she hit forty, she says, "I had hoped life would start to happen, and it just wasn't. I felt like I wasn't really living, and there was nothing compelling about the path I was on. I realized I'd have to take charge."

One of her friends was deployed in Iraq with the army's 101st Airborne Division, and he offhandedly suggested that she become an embedded reporter. "It took just a few days for me to start thinking seriously about the idea," she says. The summer after her first year of library school, she contacted the army's public affairs office, but the Department of Defense was not accepting new embeds. The next summer, she called the *Milan Mirror-Exchange*, a newspaper in Tennessee where a friend of a friend worked, and explained her goal. The paper gave her a reporter's press credentials (though no paycheck). This time the military said yes, even asking her where she'd like to go

> "I think there must be a middle ground between the library and Iraq, but I haven't found it. I feel as if I know only the extremes. I'm either holed up by myself in a really quiet safe place, or I'm out there with some guys in a war zone. That would be the trick: finding a middle ground."

and how long she'd like to stay. "As kind of a joke, I said, 'How about 101 days with the 101st?'" she remembers. "They said fine."

Monroe started to file weekly dispatches in May 2006. There were some incidents she will never forget, such as the day a road-

. . . .

The Most Important Thing I Learned

"You really do you have to cherish the time that you have with the people who are important to you. Now I feel as if I couldn't just walk away as I did before, without thinking more about the consequences—what it would put my family through."

. . . .

side bomb exploded just behind the convoy of trucks she was riding in. "I felt like I was a strange case because I wasn't really a professional reporter, and I was spending so much time with one unit," says Monroe. "The reporters I met along the way were all from far more legitimate news sources, but they were always searching for one big bad story, and they didn't stay put for very long in any one place. So I don't really feel as if they got the same full experience that I did, and I don't know that they represented the troops as accurately as I tried to do. I had the privilege of actually getting to know the guys." Monroe extended her stay until the brigade's tour ended and also returned later for a second tour.

Since then, Monroe, now forty-eight, has done a few speaking engagements about her experiences and has written a book proposal. She is also working as a librarian in Augusta, Maine, to pay off the $7,500 in debt she incurred in her travels. She has come to appreciate a new view of herself. "I know now that I'm capable of stepping outside my comfort zone," she says. "It takes a certain amount of bravery to do something you never expected to do, especially having no example to follow. I feel good about having succeeded at that, and I think of myself in some ways as fearless now."

. . . . . .

The Most Important Thing I Did Right

"I set out to really capture a day in the life of the soldiers, and I think I did that. I've heard from a lot of soldiers' families that they were really grateful for my reports because it brought them much closer to the experience."

. . . . . .

Sell Your House, Find a Life
Liz Ward

As the economic crisis escalated in 2008, Liz Ward was on edge. Self-employed in marketing communications, she felt burdened by her living expenses and feared that her client list and income would continue to shrink. One night, she had her first full-blown anxiety attack. "I was in a chair, doubled over, panic gripping my chest and gut," says Ward, fifty-seven. "It was just gnawing at me that something had to be done."

Ward's priority became unloading her Minneapolis home. She no longer felt joy in owning her 1930s three-bedroom Tudor with its monthly mortgage payments and upkeep, both inside and out. "I started looking at it as my albatross," she says. But where would she live? She thought back to a young couple she had met a few months earlier while vacationing in Maine with her adult daughter. As summertime managers of a quaint coastal inn, they lived rent-free in an on-site apartment. Ward went online and searched for seasonal work in resorts and national parks around the country. She filled out applications and discovered that most of the jobs started in late May, so she chose that month as her moving-day target.

Ward knew her home was located in a popular area and would probably sell despite the weak market. To maximize the price, she hired workmen to get it in shape. At the same time, friends helped her purge the place of all but the essentials. She sold and donated almost everything. In the midst of her preparations, she accepted a job offer at a lodge in Wyoming's Grand Teton National Park. Room and board were included. In March 2009, she put her house on the market and after a three-week flurry of open houses, it sold. A week after the deal closed, she set off on a road trip to her new life in the rugged West.

Excited about her adventure, Ward agreed to a seasonal contract with the lodge from May through October. Yet when she moved into her cabin with two twenty-one-year-old roommates, she suddenly felt

· · · · · · · · · ·

**The Most Important
Thing I Learned**

"I didn't consciously recognize that I was reinventing myself. That word was not on my radar. What I was doing, I thought, was finding a solution for my unrest."

· · · · · · · · · ·

very out of place. Many of her coworkers were young enough to be her daughters and knew one another from seasons past. Ward missed her wide circle of close girlfriends. She was frustrated by the new computer application that she was expected to learn quickly to manage the front desk. "All of a sudden, everything hit me," she recalls. *I just sold my house. What have I done?*"

During the next few weeks, Ward longed for the familiar. Yet although she missed her friends, she also felt the anxieties of her former life fade away. She was surrounded by staggering mountain views that she found healing, and she no longer had a mortgage payment or a TV. "News of the world seemed a distant concern," she says. "It didn't rise above the vistas, the crisp air, or the dramatic, craggy mountain peaks across the road." Though she got weepy every time she looked at photos of her friends from her going-away parties, she gained a newfound sense of confidence and resilience from the time that she spent by herself in nature, living simply on a minimum wage.

> "My experience of reinvention has more to do with a sense of spirituality— not the religious kind but 'of the spirit.' It's working its way from the inside out."

Ward reached a turning point in her homesickness when she was out on a solo three-mile hike. "I got to a spot where I heard cars, and I thought, Boy, these people have to go home, but I get to stay," she remembers. "I felt so privileged." She'd drive through the terrain, blaring her stereo to the Dixie Chicks' song "Wide Open Spaces" with the lyrics: "She needs wide open spaces/Room to make her big mistakes." Her rearview mirror reflected awesome, jaw-dropping views of mountains. "My possibilities seemed really big," she says. "I just had this feeling that anything could happen."

Ward's coworkers started to show interest in getting to know her. They ate in the cafeteria together, shared a bottle of wine in their cabins, and enjoyed outings to the local bar. "The biggest decision we had to make was, 'Do you want to come over and sit on the porch at my cabin, or should we sit on yours?'" Ward says.

She developed such a bond with some of her colleagues that when the season ended, her eyes welled up with tears. "I cried when I got there, and I cried when I left," she says with a laugh. "I was really sad to leave."

Ward then traveled around the country and visited family and friends. Sharing her experience with others gave her a new perspective. "People's reactions to my story have been eye opening," she says. "Some commented on my bravery and their own secret wish to be free from their lives of responsibility and financial commitments," she says. "Not once did I hear what I most expected: 'You're a whack job. What do you think you're doing?'"

. . . .

The Most Important Thing I Did Right

"Once the process got rolling, I asked for help when I was overwhelmed."

. . . .

When she moved in with a friend back home and tried to settle down, she felt hemmed in and dreamed of the mountains. So she returned to the lodge for a second season the following May. This time, she went on Match.com and found a man with whom she could share her hikes—and the dance floor. "For twenty years, I'd been wanting to find a man who would take dance lessons with me!" she says.

Ward has decided to go back to Wyoming for a third season and is exploring options for a "portable lifestyle," as she puts it, that will allow her to grow her marketing communications business and build a retirement account while keeping her untethered from the commitments of a home. She writes about her struggles on her blog, Age Appropriate (ageappropriateblog.com), which targets women over 50. "My experience has been unique, and I want my voice to be heard," she says. "Before, I thought my possibilities were limited. Now I know that I have freedom to design my life. I'm standing on the precipice right now. Meryl Streep said something in *Bridges of Madison County* that has always resonated with me: 'We are our choices.' I am pleased with my choices in the last two years."

- What's wrong?
- What do you need?
- Whom can you count on?
- What needs to happen?
- What's stopping you?

A Path in the Wilderness
Mary Emerick

Mary Emerick says that the happiest time of her life was doing seasonal work for the Park and Forest Service after graduating from college. She moved every six months into a new adventure, from planting trees to fighting fires to working as a wilderness ranger. In her early thirties, though, having moved twenty times across eleven states, she finally hunkered down to do what she thought she was supposed to do: move out of the bunkhouse, get settled and secure a permanent job with insurance benefits.

In 1997, at thirty-three, Emerick took a government job as a wilderness specialist with the Bureau of Land Management and moved to a small desert town in eastern Oregon. She was in charge of overseeing a brand-new national wilderness area created by Congress. Yet instead of spending time outdoors, as her job title suggested, she spent most of her hours stuck in meetings. "I was building a national reputation in my field and was on an upward track," she says, but she didn't like the direction her life was going. Her higher-ups at work seemed beaten down, and when she hired new people to fill outdoors wilderness jobs, she realized that she longed to be one of them. "I felt myself becoming old too soon, resigned to a slow slide toward retirement at a computer desk," she says. "I wanted to find that feeling of adventure again."

· · · · · · ·

The Most Important Thing I Learned

"There's a tendency to think you will change completely with a new life. But no—you bring along the person you are."

· · · · · · ·

In 2002, after five years in Oregon—the longest Emerick had lived anywhere as an adult—she applied for a job transfer to Alaska. The position she landed, with the U.S. Forest Service, involved a big cut in pay and prestige, and Emerick's coworkers advised that it would be career suicide, but she decided to pack up and go. "It was the people who were doing adventurous things I admired who told me to go for it," she says.

Emerick moved to Baranof Island, an isolated, rain-drenched part of Alaska where she knew no one. On one of her first weekends there, she sat in the laundry room of a motel and sobbed, thinking, What have I done? "At thirty-eight, I felt like a total beginner," she says. In her new post, where she was responsible for a half-million acres of wilderness, she had to learn how to run a boat, how to handle rip tides and rainy conditions, and how to shoot a gun to protect herself against coastal grizzly bears. "It was overwhelming," she says. She had nightmares about the bears.

Then Emerick bought a kayak, and things started to shift for her. She shared the water with transparent moon jellies, fat purple sea stars, and sea lions. "The first time I slipped inside a kayak, I felt my senses come alive," she says. "I was in charge of my life in a way I had never been. All of the things that made me afraid—bears, capsizing, riptides—also made my skin tingle and my heart beat faster."

When she turned forty, she implemented an official kayak ranger program. Teaming up with a volunteer partner, she set off in a kayak for five days at a time to patrol the wildernesses under

My Biggest Mistake

"Not doing it sooner. I let fear stop me."

her charge, much of which was extremely remote. "After you get dropped off by the powerboat or the float plane, there's this sense of being abandoned," she says. "When you realize you can make it on your own, you can't help but feel changed." At times, sudden shifts in the weather stirred up twelve-foot swells that tossed her kayak around like driftwood. To get through, Emerick invented a persona named Gertrude. "She was a tough cookie who could do anything," she says. "Soon I realized Gertrude wasn't someone separate from me. She was part of me."

The following year, seven years after arriving in Alaska, Emerick finally faced a bear. She and five friends were camping when the animal approached. The friends grouped together to appear bigger and convince the bear not to mess with them. After some tense moments where their barking dog escalated the danger, the griz-

"Before becoming a kayak ranger, I felt myself becoming old too soon, resigned to a slow slide toward retirement at a computer desk."

zly decided to back down and run off. "To be able to do everything right and not scream and run, as I would have in my first year in Alaska, was a culmination of my whole experience," she says.

The following month, Emerick moved back to the mainland, feeling that she had accomplished what she set out to do. Professionally, she left behind a legacy: the kayak ranger program and a partnership she formed with a local environmental group that had been a longtime critic of the U.S. Forest Service. In 2010, that collaboration earned the Bob Marshall Award for Champion of Wilderness, a top national honor, and became a national model. On a personal level, she had redirected the trajectory of her life. "I paused to take stock of things and realized what the second half of my life was going to be," she says.

Today, at forty-seven, Emerick lives in Oregon and works in a high-level wilderness management job that, this time, incorporates her love of the outdoors. During work hours, she has the opportunity to backpack and take small planes and jet boats around what she calls her office, which is made up of mountains, rivers, lakes, and the immense ten-mile-wide Hell's Canyon. On the weekends, she hikes, climbs peaks, skis, and kayaks. She has also returned to writing—she majored in English in college—and just finished a memoir about her seven-year Alaska adventure. "My reinvention was circular," says Emerick. "I used to feel like I had to make sure I wasn't ordinary. I've let go of that. I don't need to have my life at risk all the time. It's a whole other adventure learning to stay in one place."

·············· **Mary's Key Questions to Ask Yourself** ··············

- Why are you really considering doing this? Is it for yourself or for someone else?
- Do you have a plan B if it doesn't work?
- Are you prepared for the fallout (jealousy, lack of support, financial difficulty, etc.)?
- Are you running away from something?
- Do you have one person in your corner who's both a cheer-leader and a shoulder to lean on?

7

Transforming Your Sense of Self

Perhaps the most amazing reinvention of all is setting out to develop the strong, healthy body you've always wished for. The women in this chapter made a commitment to get more physically fit, and in the process they enjoyed an unexpected bonus. Their new physical strength translated into a new mental confidence and the belief that they could do anything they set their minds to. Prepare to be inspired.

The World's Unlikeliest Weight Lifter
Lisa Fisco

After spending eight years contesting the terms of a brutal divorce, Lisa Fisco had racked up more than $800,000 in legal bills and gained 100-plus pounds. "It was like living in a black hole," she says. "You don't think you're worth anything. People sometimes look at themselves and say, 'I'm in my forties; I can't change.' That's exactly what happened to me."

Fisco was an Emmy Award–winning producer of such TV shows as *Leeza* and *Dr. Laura*, but during the years of her court fight, the work dried up. With a mortgage and legal fees to pay, she even visited the welfare office, although she never completed the paperwork. Then in 2008, her children (ages eighteen, thirteen, and eleven at the time) decided to live with their father. "I went into a depression," she says. "But I looked inside myself and said, 'You can either sink or swim. What do you want to do?'"

She had always dreamed of being an entrepreneur, so she signed up for a business course at UCLA. One of her first assignments was to think about what had made her happy as a child. "I had forgotten how much I loved sports," she says. "I played rugby, I was involved in track and field, I lifted weights for fun with my father. And I was obsessed with the Olympics." She decided to look in that direction for her reinvention.

Knowing she would need help rebuilding her body, Fisco went online and found the e-mail address of an Olympic coach in Los Angeles. To get his attention, she decided to brand herself

. . . .

The Most Important Thing I Learned

"How important it is to believe in yourself and then follow through. At this point, I might not be the very best weight lifter, but I still want it more than anybody. I practice and train as hard as I can. There are only two moves in Olympic weight lifting—one is the snatch, and the other is the clean and jerk. The judges add up the total amount of weight you lift in those two moves; that's it. So it really doesn't matter if you're fifty or fifteen. What matters is that you believe in yourself."

. . . .

as the least likely of athletes. "I wrote him and said, 'Hey, how would you like to take a 47-year-old, totally out-of-shape mom and turn her into an Olympic weight lifter who goes for the gold?'" she says. He e-mailed back the same day, and Fisco was floored by his answer. He wrote, "Hell, yes, absolutely."

Since then, she has supported herself by selling ads for Catholic church bulletins so that she can spend about five hours a day at the gym. In January 2011, she began competing locally in preparation for the 2012 Olympic trials. The payoff: At age fifty-one, she can now dead-lift more than 220 pounds. And in three years, she has gone from a size 22—at five feet, two inches tall—to a size 10.

The Most Important Thing I Did Right

"Going with my gut. And not getting discouraged. I've always admired athletes for their tenacity, their desire and drive. Vince Lombardi once said, 'The difference between a successful person and others is not a lack of strength, not a lack of knowledge, but rather a lack of will.' I've used my inner desire, my will, and my tenacity to do the best I could do and not let other people get me down. I have that fire that no one can quash."

If she doesn't make the Olympics? "That doesn't mean I can't go out for the next one," Fisco says. "But my back-up plan for 2012 is that if I don't make the U.S. team, I'll try out for the Italian one because my father was born and raised in Italy. Italy has an Olympic team, but they don't have any female weight lifters!

"I've learned that the biggest killer of dreams is procrastination," she says. "So many women say, 'I'll lose weight tomorrow.' But before you know it, it's been a year or two. Man, you gotta act, you know?"

My Biggest Mistake

"Waiting too long. If I had just a few more years under my belt, boy, I'd kill 'em out there."

A Bike Brought Her Confidence
Diane McAleer

Santa delivered Diane McAleer's first two-wheeler bike, metallic turquoise with plastic streamers flowing from the handlebars, when she was seven. "I loved it and rode it everywhere," she says. As a teenager, however, she outgrew the desire to ride a bike, which suddenly seemed childish compared to walking through the neighborhood with her girlfriends on the chance that a boy she liked would drive by in his car.

Years later, McAleer sometimes rented a bike while visiting the nearby Jersey Shore with her husband and three kids. Though she often said, "I should get a bike," she never did. "Every dime went to the kids and our home," she says. "As a mother, I put *my* wish list at the end." Between taking care of the family and being active in the schools and the community, she had no time for exercise, so as time went by, her weight crept up until she'd gained 35 pounds. "I didn't realize what was happening until I saw a picture of myself taken from behind and didn't recognize my own arm," she says. She started watching what she ate, but it didn't do much good. She tried weight machines, workout classes, walking, but they all felt like drudgery.

. . . . . .

The Most Important Thing I Learned

"If you just take a step, even a very small one, on the path toward your reinvention, you have empowered yourself to do much more."

. . . . . .

McAleer's hectic years as treasurer of the PTA, president of the choral boosters, and vice president of the marching band boosters, among other activities, slowed down as she turned fifty. With one son away at college and her other son and daughter finishing high school, McAleer started to think about what to do with her future. "I thought, The contract is running out in this mothering job; you'd better figure out what you're going to do with yourself," she says.

· ·

The Most Important Thing I Did Right

"I sat by myself to assess my life, figure out what I wasn't happy with, and create a list of things that could make me feel good about myself. I wanted to lose weight, and I wanted to have fun. The bike was an answer for me. The confidence I gained by losing weight and taking control over my life made me know I could do more."

· ·

In the spring of 2007, a friend told her that he'd gotten a bike and really enjoyed riding it. That casual conversation sparked her to action, and during a family dinner, she announced that she was going to buy a used bike. (She didn't want to spend much, she says, because "I wasn't trusting myself to commit.") Her son told her to get on his sister's bike so he could show her a good path near their house. After six miles of trailing her athletic son, McAleer got off the too-small bike and felt her legs buckle. She was red-faced and sweating profusely, but she felt invigorated. "That was it," she says. "Once I did that ride, I said, 'I've got to get my own bike.'"

Within a week, she bought a used bike for $50 and got serious. Every night after dinner, she'd put on her iPod, crank up anything from Van Morrison to Nine Inch Nails, and take to the path. Soon she was riding fifteen to twenty miles daily. "It was time out that I could be by myself and clear my head," she says. "Whenever I came back, I felt so good I wanted to get back on." She lost weight so quickly that in six months, she dropped from a size 12 to a size 4 and developed the lean look of a cyclist in training. "People were asking if I felt okay," she says. "They thought I must be sick since I was suddenly so thin."

She felt great, but not just because she'd lost weight. What she'd gained was confidence that she could do what she set her mind to. "Everything started clicking to help me change from within," she says. Always self-conscious that she hadn't gone to college, she found herself one Saturday morning in a high school corridor waiting to take the SATs along with fifteen hundred teenagers. Six months after she'd first set out on the bike path, she enrolled in college classes. When a professor handed back the class's first writing assignment, she kept it face down so she wouldn't see the grade until she was alone in her car. It was an A+ with the comment, "Great start!" "I had to sit in the parking lot for ten minutes before I could stop crying and drive home," she says. "I felt so validated." A C student in high school, McAleer continued to earn A's in college.

In 2007, she bought a hybrid mountain bike from a shop that was unloading used equipment at the end of the summer season. The next year she stepped up her cycling another notch when her brother-in-law gave her a road bike, one that he had ridden only three times. Because a road bike is lighter and faster than a mountain bike, there was a period of adjustment. The first time she took it out, she made a turn two blocks from home and crashed. She got back on and finished her ride with blood dripping from her knee and elbow scrapes. When a guy who worked at the bike store heard about her accident and asked her if she was okay, another employee chimed in, "Of course, she's okay. She's hard-core!"

"That's when I knew I'd become a real cyclist," says McAleer.

Once adjusted to the lightweight bike, McAleer challenged herself in new ways. "Can I go faster? Can I go longer? It's addictive," she says. She joined an over-fifty online bike forum and began checking in daily. In 2010, she went on a cycling excursion to the Finger Lakes in upstate New York with a group of forum members. A few months later, she joined seven thousand other bikers in a charity event for multiple sclerosis. Her brother, also a cyclist, came in from out of town to visit. "We rode together for the first time since I was nine and used to go with him on his paper route," she says.

McAleer, now fifty-five, graduated in May 2011 with a degree in paralegal studies and plans to eventually work in a real-estate law firm. She's organizing a women's cycling group and is gearing up to do more bike trips, charity events, and solo rides. "After twenty-two years of laundry, cooking, teacher conferences, and volunteering, I finally have something that's all mine," she says. "I really believe that there is a change of life that has nothing to do with menopause. Your children are grown and moved out, and you're at this point where you're saying, 'I feel different. I'm done with the mom thing, and I'm ready to move on. I am changing my life now. *This* is what I am.'"

• •

The Most Surprising Thing about My Reinvention

"I now attract other positive people into my life, and they are happy to help me meet my goals. The high I get from riding in charity events with the purpose of helping others has encouraged me to train for a hundred-mile ride next September. The woman I was would never have believed it possible to do that, but the woman I am now says, 'Okay, I can do this. What's my first step?'"

• •

From Nonathlete to Triathlete
Dani Phillips

Dani Phillips's obsession started small and for the least likely of reasons: she wanted to help someone else lose weight. "My friend's daughter asked me to go running with her mom," she recalls. Even though Phillips had never run a mile in her life, she answered, "Sure, why not?"

Her family couldn't believe she would get up at 5 AM so that she could run and still make it to her job as a quality-testing technician. Her doctor discouraged her, saying that at forty-five she was too old to take up strenuous exercise. Yet Phillips and her friend were determined to get good enough for a 5K race, even though, at first, neither could make it once around a quarter-mile track. "I've started a lot of things in my life and not finished them," Phillips says. "The only reason I kept going was for my friend."

The day she first ran three laps in a row, "I was like, Woo hoo!" she says. "I knew I was getting somewhere." Eventually, the running also became a way for her to work out some of the lingering issues from her marriage, which had ended in divorce four months earlier. Phillips did well for her age in her first 5K race, and although her friend quit running, Phillips kept it up. "That race represented a complete change in my life," she says. "It was my first step in realizing that I still had a lot of life left in me. It was an awakening."

· · · · · ·

The Most Important Thing I Learned

"I can do anything I put my mind to."

· · · · · ·

She had to overcome sciatica, shortness of breath, and hip and knee problems, but by reading books and magazines about running and making regular visits to a physical therapist, Philips worked her way up to 10K races, half-marathons, and eventually a marathon. Then one of the women in Phillips's running group gave her the idea of competing in a triathlon. "There were only two little problems," Phillips says. "I had been on a bike only once in the last twenty-five years, and I couldn't swim." She signed up for lessons at the local recreation center and persisted even though at first she didn't love it. "I had water up my nose constantly, and the whole rest of the day I'd be coughing up crap," she says. "It was gross." Biking wasn't easy at first, either. She dusted off her $30 garage-sale bike and, her first time out, went on a seven-and-a-half-hour adventure. "I could hardly walk the next day, it hurt so much," says Phillips, who soon upgraded to a better bike.

····················· **My Biggest Mistake** ·····················
"Not starting to run sooner."

Four years after she started running, Phillips completed three "sprint distance" triathlons (roughly a half-mile swim, a twelve-mile bike ride, and a three-mile run). The next year she finished three sprints and one Olympic distance (which is twice the sprint distance in each category). In 2007, at fifty-one, she aced her first Half-Ironman, which doubles the Olympic distance. Two years later, she qualified and ran in the Boston Marathon, the twenty-six-mile race she calls her milestone achievement. By 2010, she'd completed two Half-Ironman races and twenty-five triathlons.

"Every time I get a medal, I think, Oh, my God! I can't believe that I can do this! It's such a kick."

Phillips, who recently moved from Colorado to North Carolina, has dropped from a size 12 to a size 4, but what matters much more, she says, is that her social life is active again, and she is enjoying a huge sense of accomplishment. "From the time I started running," she says, "I found 'me' again. It brought my happiness back. I was in a dark room, and now I'm in a room full of light."

· ·

The Most Important Thing I Did Right

"Keeping at it. I had a lot of physical issues because of the running, and doctors told me I needed to quit. The gal I started with did quit. But I told myself that I could get through all of it. I learned how to read my body, and now when I know something's happening, I go directly to the physical therapist. Because of doing all this, my body has become stronger."

· ·

8

※

Reinvention Tips for You from the Trenches

How do I start?" "How much will it cost?" "How do I even figure out what my reinvention should be?" Every woman who wants to give herself a second act faces some basic questions and, in this chapter, *More* magazine experts help answer them. Here is practical advice for those of you just starting out on your journey. Ready, set, reinvent!

Ten Steps to Jump-Starting Your Change

It's a myth that reinventing yourself is a lovely, exciting process that feels good all of the time, says Pamela Mitchell, the founder and CEO of the Reinvention Institute (reinvention-institute.com), based in Miami, Florida. "Reinvention is hard work; it requires a lot of mental ditch-digging, soul-searching, and staying strong in the face of opposition," she says. "It's a process that tests everything we know, everything we thought was true about ourselves and others." Here, Mitchell lists of five things to think about to help you determine what your new career path will be once you embark on your "second act" of life, followed by a list of five hard truths that you'll face once you start down the road to your reinvention.

Five Tips for Planning a Second Act

1. **Start with a mini-reinvention.** The idea of completely overhauling your career can seem daunting. Instead of trying to tackle the big mountain first, start small. Do something that expands your horizon, such as taking a class in a new subject area or tagging along with a friend to an industry event outside your current field. This mini-reinvention doesn't always have to be career-related; things like changing your hairstyle or going skydiving also count. The point is to get used to pushing yourself out of your comfort zone in small ways on a regular basis—a very important skill in reinvention.

2. **Go back to your childhood.** If you're casting about for ideas about what to do next, mine your past for clues. If you were the girl using her Easy-Bake Oven to feed the neighborhood, see how you can integrate that love of cooking into your career. If you led the debate team in high school, see if there's a way to include public speaking in your next gig. The goal is to find elements of what you love and weave them into your reinvention.

3. **Pick up the pennies around you.** What are you currently doing for free that you could get paid for? If your family always fights over your caramel cake at Thanksgiving, tell them that you'll take orders for other holidays. Better yet,

have them spread the word among their friends. If you're constantly being called for advice on the perfect gift, start a small shopping service. Get used to receiving money for the skills you have that people value; it can open a whole new pathway to career reinvention.

4. **Find a buddy.** Reinvention can be a long and lonely road. You'll have a lot more fun if you take a buddy along (just don't drive off a cliff as Thelma and Louise did!). Pick your most supportive, creative, and adventurous friend and see whether she has a project she'd like to get started on. Once you've made a blood-sister pact to help each other along the way, each of you can brainstorm ideas, report your progress, offer encouragement, and keep the other honest. Studies show that those who seek out group support have greater success; the same is true for reinvention.

5. **Give back.** It's very easy to become consumed with what kind of progress you're making in your reinvention, but as your grandma used to say, you won't make a tea kettle boil any faster by hanging over it. You'll feel better if, on a regular basis, you put your focus onto something outside of yourself and your life. Volunteering reminds you that you have something of value to offer, which is one of the most important beliefs you must have in order to reinvent your career

Five Hard Truths to Face, Once You Begin

1. **People will be freaked out by your changes.** When you reinvent , your desire to follow your truth can be very threatening to friends and family. You can expect that some people will be resentful or even angry and will try to block you or shut you down. Sometimes these naysayers are the people who are closest to you, because they have the most to lose if you change. Although you can't let yourself be driven by other people's fear, it's important

that you acknowledge and accept the validity of their feel-ings. You must grant others the freedom to have their own reaction to your reinvention, while not letting that stop you from moving forward.

2. **There will be fallout.** There are consequences to pursuing reinvention: You will have to downsize or restructure your lifestyle; you may have less time for hobbies, friends, or yourself. This doesn't mean that you should drop your quest, but you do need to take responsibility for the results of your decisions while pursuing your goal—often a diffi-cult balancing act.

3. **You must learn to coexist with your fear.** If you're any-thing like the rest of us, the reason you fight so violently against those who freak out about your choices is because they're voicing the fears you'd rather not acknowledge. Martha Beck's wonderful book *Steering by Starlight* calls those fears "the inner lizard." You can't ever fully get rid of the lizard; you must learn to coexist with it and manage it.

4. **Life doesn't stop while you reinvent yourself.** Get over the fantasy of having all of the time in the world to devote to this process. If circumstances arise that cause most of your time to temporarily be diverted (such as a work project or a family trip), don't waste energy on resentment or resis-tance. Just go with it. Even in the midst of busyness, it's still possible to take thirty minutes a day to keep yourself centered on your future, whether you make a phone call, research a piece of information, or do some inspirational reading.

5. **Getting a job "for now" to earn cash *is* reinventing yourself.** Reinvention means doing what it takes to make your dreams happen, and this often means taking a "B" job (as I once did when I temped for several months). Taking a job "for now" doesn't mean you're abandoning your reinven-tion; interim steps can be valuable stepping-stones.

Five Tips from Masters
of Change

On stepping into the unknown:

I reinvented myself in chunks. I had to take small steps to get into TV. I had to give up all the personality traits that worked for me in my first career, like charm.

—Barbara Corcoran, former real estate mogul, now a
popular real estate contributor to NBC's *Today*

On surviving setbacks:

Some of your strongest learning moments come when things aren't working out.

—Trudy Sullivan, CEO of Talbot's

On what to do when you can't decide on a solution:

Flip a coin and think about which way you hope it lands.

—Jean Chatzky, award-winning financial journalist
and *More* contributor

On choosing friends and colleagues:

I needed people around me who had confidence in me, sometimes more confidence than I had in myself. You need cheerleaders for your darkest moments.

—Dawn Lepore, CEO of drugstore.com,
former CIO of Charles Schwab

On knowing what's most important:

I spent so many years thinking the most important thing was to be productive, and now I think it's to be joyful. So I leave parties and events earlier now, to be sure I get seven hours sleep. Our whole culture needs to learn to unplug and recharge. Stop doing what you don't want to do! Saying no gives you more opportunity to say yes.

—Arianna Huffington, president and editor in chief
of the Huffington Post Media Group

How to Afford Your Next Chapter

So you've decided it's time for a new challenge, and you can't wait to open that new boutique, earn your master's degree in physical therapy, or raise honeybees. Ready? Set? *Whoa*. Every transformation has a price—one that many people underestimate. Here's some smart advice from *More* contributor Jean Chatzky on what to do now to prepare for extra costs so that your reinvention can go smoothly later.

- **Save a year of living expenses.** If you're even *thinking* about a reinvention, you should start stockpiling cash. Unless you know you'll immediately generate a decent salary, aim to save at least twelve months' of living expenses, including rent or mortgage, utilities, food, car payment, and any other essentials. How do you accumulate this much money? If you're in a two-income family, see if you can live on one salary and bank the other. If you can't, or if you're on your own, start by tallying up all of your expenses from the last two or three months. Once your expenditures are all specified, you may discover, to your surprise, that you're spending a lot in a certain area that could easily be cut back—for example, you could eat out less or wear a shirt more than once before having it dry cleaned. Another strategy: Find out how much your post-transformation paycheck will likely be, and begin living on that amount now. For an up-to-date salary estimate, check the *Occupational Outlook Handbook* on the Bureau of Labor Statistics' website (bls.gov/oco).
- **Correct your credit report.** You'll need pristine credit to qualify for the best terms on a small business loan or to be able to put any emergency expenses on plastic. To polish up your record, begin by obtaining a copy of your three reports—one from each of the major credit bureaus, Experian, TransUnion, and Equifax; you can download

them all for no fee at annualcreditreport.com. (Note: You'll need to provide your Social Security number.) If you find errors, go to the site of the bureau that issued the flawed data and follow instructions to dispute it electronically. The company should get back to you within forty-five days.

- **Slow down on the way to school.** If you're planning to earn a new degree, don't assume it will automatically pay off. For example, someone with a PhD might earn only a few thousand dollars more annually, on average, than someone with a master's degree—but she has to spend several years longer in school. Again, check the *Occupational Outlook Handbook* (bls.gov/oco), then cross-reference with the time and the money you'd need to spend in order to complete the coursework. Next, evaluate your finances: Can you afford to go full time or would part time be more practical? How much student debt are you comfortable taking on? (Keep in mind that the interest on school loans may be tax deductible.) Also, students of any age qualify for the Federal Lifetime Learning Credit of 20 percent—up to $2,000—of what they spend on education annually. (This is available for individuals with a Modified Adjusted Gross Income of less than $60,000, or $120,000 if married and filing jointly.)

- **Calculate your start-up costs.** Besides your initial inventory, you'll have to shell out for essentials such as incorporation fees, technology, business cards, advertising, and, depending on your business, office space. The U.S. Small Business Administration (sba.gov) and SCORE "Counselors to America's Small Business" (score.org) both provide online worksheets and links to calculators to help you figure out how much money you'll need.

- **Don't quit your day job.** If you're about to launch yourself as an entrepreneur, you should keep your current job "until you can afford to both produce your product and pay yourself," says Nell Merlino, the founder of Make Mine a Million $ Business, which helps women expand their businesses. In other words, moonlight until you're sure your new income is a steady one.

- **Factor in your family.** Do your elderly parents depend on the $1,000 you send them each month? Are your kids insured by your employer-based health care plan? If you're spending money on others, ask yourself: Do I have siblings who could take turns sending money to Mom and Dad? Could the kids be listed on my spouse's health plan? Which brings us to . . .

- **Find health insurance.** If you're leaving a job, it will likely be cheapest to be covered by your spouse's plan. If that's not an option, look into purchasing a policy individually or continuing your coverage through COBRA. To choose a personal policy, start at http://ehealthinsurance.com, the largest online health insurance market for individuals. If you are a small business shopping for yourself and employees, find a broker through the National Association of Health Underwriters at nahu.org.

- **Borrow intelligently.** Exhaust your lowest-interest-rate options first: student loans and loans authorized by the Small Business Administration. Steer clear of home equity loans and lines of credit, because if your new venture doesn't make it, your home will be on the line. Do not even think about robbing your retirement accounts. The potential penalties aren't worth it.

- **Chart your exit strategy.** Before you dive into plan A, make sure you have a plan B. Your success with a new vocation will depend on the economy, as well as on the health of the particular industry you choose, and neither is within your control. So if the seas get rough, can you easily return to your old profession or scale back your original game plan? Understand that not everything will go as expected—regardless of whether you have all of your funding lined up, a supportive family, and a no-brainer proposition. On the other hand, if you *do* have all of that, you're further ahead than most people. Good luck!

Moonlighting Tips

For anyone seeking a little financial security, moonlighting is all the rage, says *More* contributor Jean Chatzky. Here, her advice for doing it the smart way.

According to the Bureau of Labor Statistics, by late 2010 over 6.7 million people held more than one job. Branching out isn't only useful for your bank balance, it can also improve your future job prospects. Like your investment portfolio, your career is more secure when you don't have all of your eggs in one basket, says Marci Alboher, the author of *One Person/Multiple Careers*. "A lot of people who have created second careers are feeling grateful now," she says.

With the unemployment rate close to a twenty-five-year high, some opportunities are tougher to come by than they used to be. If you approach moonlighting shrewdly, however, using your connections and creativity, you might find a way not only to pay down your debts but also to segue into your next career.

Focus on Growth Fields

By targeting the areas that many have called the future of the economy—energy, education, health care—you can narrow your search and improve your odds of finding something. Look at environmentaljobs.com and ecojobs.com for green-sector listings and healthcaresource.com for spots in that field. For teaching opportunities, Google your state's name and "department of education job listings."

Direct selling (à la the Pampered Chef and Lia Sophia, the fashion jewelry company) is another area that is still doing well. During the last three recessions, this field grew 4.5 percent on average, as retail sales fell 3.3 percent. To figure out which direct sales product fits you best, go to directselling411.com.

Target Expert Sites Online

If you have an expertise, you may want to offer yourself as an authority or a coach for pay on a website such as guru.com or liveperson.com. You sign up for these sites, go through a vetting process, and, once approved, hang out a shingle. Customers on the site ask you questions in real time—in live chat rooms—and pay by the minute.

The money can really add up. In July 2008, Teresa Estes, a Florida-based licensed mental health counselor, listed herself on liveperson.com to make up for a softening in her private practice. By September, the online business had become more profitable than her original one, so she decided to make liveperson.com her full-time job. Estes has since raised her rate to $2.25 a minute from $1.59 and (after paying the site its 37 percent commission) takes home more than $1,500 a month. "The convenience really works for me," she says. "So does not being tied to an office."

Watch Out for Conflicts of Interest

Once you start something on the side, should you tell your employer? Although some experts say you should ask permission, others maintain that you'd be better off venturing first and, if necessary, apologizing later. As long as what you're doing doesn't directly compete with your full-time job and you're not working on company time, you are generally not obligated to notify any-one. "Not divulging is not dishonest," says Victoria Colligan, the founder of Ladies Who Launch, a website for women entre-preneurs.

The more successful you become, however, the greater the chance that you'll be found out. So prepare what you'll say if it becomes an issue. Try to find a way to sell what you're doing as a win-win for the company. "I have a Web producer working for me," Colligan says. "I know she's starting her own music website, and she'll go to seminars in search engine optimization. That's great for me."

How to Write a Great Business Plan

Diane Tarshis, a principal at Springboard Business Plans (spring boardplans.com), in Chicago, has been writing plans for clients for more than ten years. Here, in this question-and-answer session, she shares the tricks of her trade.

Q. At what stage should an entrepreneur start thinking about having a business plan?

A. When you ask for funding, whether from a bank, a venture capital firm, angel investors, or family and friends, the first thing they'll typically ask you for is a copy of your business plan. This is a blueprint that lays out your idea, your premise, and how and why your new venture will be successful. Most people don't write a business plan until they're forced to, and they're forced if they need to raise money. Yet it's important to have one even if you don't need to raise funds. Writing a business plan enables you to identify challenges and possible missteps before they affect your business. It's better to avoid obstacles through good planning, rather than waste valuable time, energy, and resources to fix them down the road.

Q. What are the basics of a business plan?

A. It's a road map of what you're going to do and how you're going to do it—profitably. There are two parts: the words and the numbers. You need to tell a coherent story and prepare the numbers to support that story. A business plan needs to answer three major questions: What is the problem or opportunity? What is your solution? Why will customers pay for your solution? If customers won't pay for your solution, then you don't have a viable business idea. There are also several specifics that need to be included in any business plan: a description of the products or the services you're selling, target markets, the competitive landscape, the marketing and/or sales plan, a list of the members of your management team, and, of course, projected financials.

Q. Can you write a business plan if you think you're bad at math?

A. Definitely! You can hire a professional to write it, and if you can't afford that, there are free and low-cost resources available—workshops, books, free counseling—that can help explain which spreadsheets are needed and how to put together strong financial projections yourself. Having said that, I always recommend that my clients arrange for access to a good accountant and a good lawyer.

Q. How long should a business plan be?

A. About forty to forty-five pages is reasonable. I can't tell you how often investors have told me that they roll their eyes when they receive a hundred-page business plan. That typically means the entrepreneur is unfocused and long-winded, so the plan usually ends up in the trash can.

Q. Where can you go for concrete examples of what a business plan should look like?

A. The Small Business Administration (SBA) is an excellent resource. Its website (sba.gov) offers specific information on what needs to be included in a business plan. There are also many Small Business Development Centers located throughout the country. SCORE, a business counseling group (which used to stand for Service Corps of Retired Executives), is another good organization; the counselors are experienced businesspeople and the organization partners with the SBA. It offers free counseling, free and/or low-cost seminars, and numerous helpful pamphlets. I also like *The Business Planning Guide*, by David H. Bangs Jr.; besides explaining each section of a business plan, it offers examples that are especially helpful for those who have never written this kind of document. Your local Chamber of Commerce can be a resource, too. Depending on the size of your city, there may be seminars, counseling, or networking events you can attend. The Chamber of Commerce can often help you put together demographic research for your target market, as can your local library.

Q. Once you write your business plan, how often should you revise it?

A. I recommend that my clients review their business plans annually. It's an important exercise to step back and think about where you are and where you're headed. Once a new business is up and running, the entrepreneur often spends her days fighting fires, so to speak—being reactive instead of proactive. If you step back and look at the big picture every twelve months, you may discover that you've gotten off track without realizing it. Or you'll see that things didn't go the way you expected. Or you could discover that you're spending 80 percent of your resources to bring in 20 percent of your revenues (and, of course, you want that the other way around!). Ultimately, the most valuable part of writing a business plan isn't necessarily the plan itself, but the process you're forced to go through in thinking about every single aspect of your business. That process is invaluable.

Q. What should you avoid when writing your plan?

A. Avoid using too many buzzwords or excess jargon—speak in plain English. Too much jargon is a red flag to investors; they start wondering what you're trying to hide. The most common mistake I see is too many generalizations. Too often, a business plan says, "I'm going to build the best widget ever, and customers will buy it because it's the best." Well, customers aren't standing around waiting for your widget, and if it is the best widget, you've got to let them know about it and why it's worth changing suppliers or taking some other risk to buy yours. How is your widget going to save them time and money, and why should they buy it? And don't rely on being the first to offer a particular product or service as a reason why your business will be a success. Many who were first are not around any longer; it's really about knowing your customers and executing well. Some people make the mistake of trying to write their executive summary first, but how can you summarize what you haven't yet written? A strong business plan is specific. It tells a coherent, specific story and uses realistic, supported assumptions in its financials.

> "I tell clients to imagine that I am a sixty-two-year-old man who has been there, done that, seen it all—very jaded. I'm leaning forward, saying, 'Prove it!' A great business plan answers that challenge."

Q. What is the cost of professional services like yours?

A. I work one of two ways: For those who are pressed for time or would rather have me stare at that blank piece of paper, I charge a flat fee ranging from $6,000 to $15,000 plus, depending on the scope and complexity of the business plan. For those who have tight budget constraints, I can work on an hourly basis at $150 per hour. Under this scenario, the client does more of the writing, while I provide feedback, guidance, and editing. As with hiring any other professional service provider, it's important to consider the person's education and work experience, along with his or her specific experience (in this case, experience in writing business plans). Anyone can hang up a shingle saying, "I can do this because I took a course in school." Ask for a work sample and references.

Mastering the New Job Hunt: How to Stand Out Digitally in Today's Tight Market

If you've always changed jobs by using connections, you may not have conducted a ground search since the first time you dropped a résumé into the corner mailbox. If so, it's time to step away from the Crane's. The rules of the job hunt have changed radically, and you have to market yourself digitally—which involves not only posting your résumé online but also learning to polish your Internet reputation.

Developing this skill is not optional. Almost 90 percent of executive recruiters now use search engines to dig up dirt on candidates—and 48 percent have dropped someone from the running based on information they found online. "You *will* be Googled in your job search," says Kirsten Dixson, the coauthor of *Career Distinction: Stand Out by Building Your Brand*. "Your online identity matters in a whole new way. It's a digital reference check."

Google your name (enclose it in quotation marks) and then take a hard look at what pops up. News clips? An embarrassing video on YouTube? Nothing at all? Ask yourself how your online profile makes you look. Today, it's not enough if the results are neutral; to get a job, you need them to be good.

That isn't a threat. It's an opportunity. Think of the Internet as your own personal publicity machine. "This is your chance to show that you know what's happening out there and that you're not replaceable by some Gen Y person," says William Arruda, the founder and president of Reach, a career management company. To get your job search up to speed, *More* recommends that you create a compelling online presence by putting effort into these four areas:

Your Résumé

Websites have replaced referrals as the best source of new jobs, and to take advantage of them, you'll likely have to paste your work history into an online application form. To make sure you're ready with the right document, have your résumé available in three forms:

- **PDF.** First, create a formatted version, the kind you'd print out and mail if given the option. Then convert that résumé into a PDF. This will open easily on either a Mac or a PC, and the formatting won't change. You'll need access to a full version of Adobe Acrobat; if you'd have to pay for that, download CutePDF Writer (cutepdf.com) for free.
- **Word document.** This should be designed as simply as possible. Use a universal font, such as Times New Roman or Arial, that will reproduce well on virtually any computer. Send the résumé to a friend or two to make sure it opens properly on other people's machines.
- **Text document.** Save a third version of your résumé as unformatted text, which is a .txt file you'd open with an application such as Notepad. The various versions of Word handle the creation of this kind of file differently, but in general, click on "save as," then look for an option that allows you to save as "plain text" or "text only." Unformatted text is free of most everything—no boldface, no

italics—so if you have to cut and paste your résumé into online forms, you'll avoid the invisible coding that exists in Word documents.

Here are some other things to think about when creating your résumé:

- **Scrap the "Objective" line** on your résumé in favor of an executive summary or a summary of qualifications. This may occupy up to a third of your résumé. "Basically, it's how you're distinctive," Dixson says. "An objective focuses on what you want from the position; a summary focuses on what you can contribute." For instance, your objective may have said, "I am seeking an executive director position at a nonprofit, where I can push forward the mission of smart growth." An executive summary, however, could start out listing your years of experience in the field, go on to highlight strengths in "creative problem-solving," then elaborate with "Outstanding communication skills contribute to high effectiveness with staff and stakeholders." (For a detailed example, go to kirstendixson.com/resumes.)
- **Consider a skills-based résumé.** A chronological format is best if you've been consistently employed for years, but if you've taken any sizable breaks or you're trying to switch fields, a skills-based résumé will play up your proficiencies ahead of your work history (Google "skills-based résumé" or "functional résumé" for examples). If you're concerned that your age will work against you, it is acceptable to leave off your college and grad-school graduation dates.
- **Make sure your personal e-mail address seems professional.** Go with first.last@gmail.com. What looks bad: LisaPuppy2010@gmail.com. Include the URL for your site or professional blog and your LinkedIn profile (more on those below).

- **Ditch the résumé photo.** "If you're going for an upper-management position, I find it to be unprofessional," says Deam Roys, the head of a Los Angeles recruiting company. Instead, direct the reader to your website or LinkedIn page, where you should post one. A picture there can, in some cases, be very helpful—if you're concerned that your age may make potential employer see you as behind the curve, a photo that communicates energy and with-it-ness can work in your favor.

Your Website

Having your own site is like wearing a great wristwatch: not strictly necessary, but it conveys a not-so-subtle message about your level of success. Putting up a site will also help you control some of the online content that's out there about you. Yet it's essential that your site have something to say. "If it's basically the same content as your cover letter and résumé, then you shouldn't create one," Arruda says. Your website should provide some kind of demonstration of what you say in your résumé through customer testimonials, case studies, or multimedia clips of your work. If you have that kind of content to contribute, here's how to do it:

- **Register a Domain name.** If possible, buy your own name (for example, JaneSmith.com), because that's where many employers will look first. Search for unclaimed URLs at a site such as GoDaddy.com or Register.com, and expect to pay about $20 a year. Once you have a domain name, find a Web hosting service, such as Homestead.com or GoDaddy.com, that will provide you with Web space for actual pages (fees range from $7 to more than $20 a month). The simplest way to do this is to register your domain with the hosting service, but you don't have to; most hosting sites allow you to transfer your domain to their service. If you're truly clueless, contact their tech support, and they will walk you through the process.

- **Decide whether to build the site yourself or hire someone.** If you're okay with something simple, there is plenty of template software out there—such as Homestead.com's SiteBuilder—to help you create your site. Just choose a style you like, and use the software to fill in the pertinent info (prices usually start at $30 to $50). If you go this route, though, you'll need a good eye. Some sites' templates aren't particularly professional-looking, or they allow so much leeway that it's easy for nondesigners to make unattractive-looking choices.

  If you need a more complicated setup—with multimedia files or a large number of photos, for instance—hire someone to do it for you. When you see a site you love, find out who designed it; many sites provide a way to contact their administrators, or there may be a "designed by" tag on the page. If your budget is tight, call a local college with a Web design program and ask if there's a way to reach out to students about potential work; up-and-comers who need portfolios will often charge less than established professionals. For a three- to five-page site, expect to pay $500 to $800 for an entry-level designer.

  Once the site's up, you'll want to be able to update it without help from the designer, so ask about this before you sign on the dotted line. "Web developers have been known to hold people hostage," says Aliza Sherman, a social media consultant at the marketing company Conversify. "You don't know how to program, and they do; if you want something changed, you'll have to pay them an hourly rate of $25 to $100 or more to do it." A good consultant will provide you with a tool to make the changes yourself, but if DIY is your plan, you should become handy with HTML or Web design software.

- **Organize the content.** Your site should have at least three pages: an introduction, including a brief synopsis of your experience; a more detailed bio or résumé; and evidence of your performance (awards, testimonials, work samples). Include contact info, such as your e-mail address—style it as "name [at] site.com," with the brackets around "at," so that spamming software won't recognize it as an address—and a general idea of your geographic location. Last, include a professional photo. "A potential employer does not need to see you hugging your cats or kids," says Elaine Young, a professor of business at Vermont's Champlain College.

- **Consider a blog.** Although a website is useful to tout your accomplishments, a blog can demonstrate that you are involved in your field. You can create one yourself on sites such as WordPress.com or Blogger.com. "Blogging software is far more user friendly than Web editing tools," Sherman says, so you can and should regularly add content, commenting on recent news or business relevant to your industry.

Your Search-Engine Results

Having a site will help you with what is in many ways the most difficult piece of the new digital marketing: managing your search-engine results page, or SERP. "Dealing with search engines is similar to doing public relations," says Danny Sullivan of Search EngineLand.com. "There are things you can do to get good press, and there are things that you can't control." For instance, you can't change what other people post on their sites, and you may not be able to bury negative press, but you can try to move the positive press into the spotlight. Keep in mind that Google results are fluid and will change over time. If you're actively managing your online image, check back at least once a month to make sure you still know what's out there. Here's how to manipulate your SERP:

- **Join LinkedIn.** You may already have a profile with LinkedIn (linkedin.com), the large business social networking site that lets you "connect" with colleagues and experts in your field. But have you taken full advantage of it? The site allows you to easily promote yourself and your accomplishments without most of the potential embarrassment of other social networking sites. It gives you the opportunity to personalize your profile page link, so that others can find your profile at linkedin.com in your name. (Click on "Profile," look for your "Public Profile" Web address, and click "Edit.") Once you've done that customizing, you can easily list your LinkedIn page on your résumé and website or blog. Bonus: A LinkedIn profile will usually pop up on the first page of Google results. To get the most out of the site, keep your profile updated and go to the Q&A section; you can use your expertise to answer other people's questions, which makes you more visible and lets you demonstrate your knowledge. Also take advantage of your connections' ability to recommend you on the site. A simple way to do this: Recommend others, and they'll automatically be prompted to reciprocate. And link away: there's no downside to accepting invitations from people you don't know well.
- **Create your own content.** Having your own site or blog is a great first step; now you need to get it to pop up to the top of your search results. One thing that will help is using a domain name that has your name in it. "Google puts more weight on keywords if they're in the URL of the page," says Rhea Drysdale, cofounder and acting CEO of Outspoken Media, Inc. So make sure you title each page with your name (instead of, say, "Home Page"), and throw

some text on your main page that explains who you are and what you do. Google searches your site for text and HTML clues to its content, so the more targeted your clues, the higher in search results you'll appear. If you're a landscape photographer in Georgia, for instance, you want to mention the words *landscape*, *photography*, *nature*, and *Georgia*, along with your name, on the intro page.

Text alone won't move you up the SERP list, however. "Google's algorithm is based on links," Drysdale says. "It wants to see relevant links to your site coming from other areas. If you create a Web site and no one ever links to it, it will probably never show up on your SERP." Her suggestion: use the profiles you've created on other sites, such as LinkedIn, Facebook, and ZoomInfo (see below), to link to your site.

- **Contribute to other sites.** Add to the comments sections of industry-related blogs. "It's almost as powerful as having your own blog," Arruda says. "When someone Googles you, those comments will show up." This won't move your personal site up in your SERP, but it will give employers something positive to find when they search your name. Google the topic you're interested in, find the blogs that talk about it, subscribe to them, and contribute your comments, using your real name. You can also access your contacts' blogs via LinkedIn's Blog Link tool—add the application to your LinkedIn account, and it will search your contacts for blogs and websites. In addition, try submitting articles to industry niche sites or more generic sites such as eHow.com, Knol.Google.com, and About.com.

- **Check ZoomInfo.** Even if you've never visited this site, chances are it has created an aggregate profile for you, gleaned from bits and pieces of online data associated with your name—but the information may not be accurate.

Some 50 million people are listed on zoominfo.com, so it's a good idea to visit and find out if you have a write-up. If you do, just click "claim profile," then follow the site's easy edit process to fill in your own professional history and other relevant information. Your own write-up will now replace their inaccurate one. (Other sites, such as Spoke.com, also aggregate data; only worry about fixing the ones that show up in the first few pages of your Google results.)

- **Be smart about Facebook.** You may be on Facebook already, but the jury is still out on whether it has business advantages. If you work in an industry that thrives on social connections, you may find that a Facebook profile is an invaluable networking resource. But don't panic: you won't be penalized if you haven't joined the crowd yet. In fact, there are so many pitfalls associated with Facebook, you might be better off without a page, unless you become a master of its privacy settings. "You don't have control over what someone writes on your wall, and you can't manage every photo of you that gets tagged," Young says. You can, of course, delete wall posts and untag yourself in other people's photos, but you may tire of keeping a constant eye on your Facebook content. You also may not have time to react before someone else finds a photo, as was the case for a White House speechwriter who was tagged in a photo that showed him cupping the breast of a cardboard cut-out of Hillary Clinton. (For a lesson on privacy, search for "How to set your Facebook privacy settings" on CIO.com.)

  If you have a Facebook page, decide whether it's professional or personal—and stick with that. If you're using it for business relationships, don't "friend" every member of your college sorority or post photos of your kitchen renovation. If you're using it for social purposes (most experts agree that's its best use), use privacy settings to make your page unfindable on search engines. Tell business-only contacts that you value the connection but that you're using your Facebook account for very close friends and family. Ask if you can connect with them via LinkedIn instead.

- **Tie up loose ends.** A couple of last notes: if you're wondering about using Twitter, the social messaging site, you can relax. While it can be used for professional gain (by following the feeds of well-respected people in your industry, for example), there may not be enough hours in the day for you to maintain a job hunt, a professional blog, a Facebook profile, a LinkedIn profile, and a Twitter account. So unless you're fascinated by the concept, let it go.

  Also be aware that search engines can find content in your online file collections, such as YouTube videos and photos on Flickr. If you have content posted that you would rather a potential employer not see, now's the time to make those profiles private.

- **The final step: get out there.** While your online identity is important, don't forget about face-to-face networking. Just because you've posted to every job site, updated all of your online profiles, and e-mailed every contact you know, that doesn't mean you can stay home in your jammies. "You still need to go out to events and pound the pavement and have a cup of coffee," Dixson says. "The more virtual rapport you build up front, the more your time isn't going to be wasted. But nothing replaces in-person connections."

The Ten Best Jobs for Women Now

Perhaps you're inspired by the idea of reinvention but wonder how to switch tracks in an economy like this one, in which jobs are hard to find. What field can you choose that will pay you enough to rebuild your 401(k) and won't leave you scrambling again in ten years? Here are some answers.

With the help of the Polling Company, a Washington, D.C.–based research firm, *More* conducted an exclusive nationwide telephone survey and asked mid-career women to define the most important elements of a great job, besides good salary and benefits. Their answers:

Meaning, to feel that you're contributing positively	98%
A job in a growing field with a bright future	89%
A high level of control or freedom	87%
A job that's appropriate for a woman over forty	79%
A chance to work a flexible schedule	73%

Armed with these criteria, *More* scoured the statistics and grilled the experts to find careers that deliver. A variety of data were examined, including from the U.S. Bureau of Labor Statistics, the Department of Labor Women's Bureau, the Center for Women's Business Research, the Families and Work Institute, Catalyst, and the MetLife Mature Market Institute. The jobs on this ranked list come in well above the national average salary for women ages thirty-five to fifty-four ($37,908), and if the salaries aren't enough to attract you, consider that for career changers, financial sacrifices are usually offset by lifestyle improvements, such as more reasonable hours or the option to telecommute. Plus, career changers tend to shoot up the ladder; their passion turns quickly into promotions—and an increase in pay. "You have more maturity and more knowledge, and a great many of the skills you pick up in one industry are transferable," says Amelia Warren Tyagi, the cofounder of the Business Talent Group, a nationwide firm that places senior-level independent consultants.

1. Community Service Coordinator/Manager
(Volunteer Coordinator, Program Director)

This title could mean managing educational programs, organizing volunteers or even soliciting community services for a government agency. "You're finding help for people in need," says Ira Madin, the executive vice president of the staffing agency Professionals for NonProfits (nonprofitstaffing.com). "You need to either have a passion for a cause or find something that speaks to you as a member of society."

Ellen Vaughn, fifty-one, started working with volunteers after a bout with leukemia in her twenties. A stream of helpers watched her son while she was sick, and she promised herself that when she could, she would give back to the community. Now she works as a volunteer services coordinator for the Rosamond Gifford Zoo, in Syracuse, New York. "I love working with people who enjoy being where they are and doing what they're doing," Vaughn says. "It's less money than I've made at other jobs, but I'm a lot more excited about what I do. This job uses all of my skills."

Salary: $40,780 to $70,890, top 10% make $92,000+

Why now?: The field is expected to grow 48% by 2016.

What you'll need: BA, passion for a cause.

Entrepreneur opportunities: Most people in this field work for nonprofits or the government.

2. Personal Financial Planner

"People are looking for good, unbiased financial advice right now," says Ellen Turf, the CEO of the National Association of Personal Financial Advisors. "It's not the kind of job where you have to be there from eight to five, and you get an hour for lunch. You can do it on your own terms. We see a lot of career changers."

Renée Weese, fifty-six, was a vice president for Hartford

Financial Services Group when her division was sold in 2006, and she decided to make the break she'd been thinking about for years. "I'd always worked with the financial aspects of the business and enjoyed it," she says. She'd gotten her MBA in 2002, so she started working to become a certified financial planner (which takes at least three years), then joined a small financial planning practice in Atlanta. She's now preparing to take the CFP Board Exam which is the final step in her quest to become a certified financial planner. "When I was younger, I was motivated to be successful, make a good living, and build financially," she says. "As I've gotten older, passion has come more into play. I want to feel like I'm doing what I want, like I'm contributing."

> **Salary:** $44,890 to 117,260, top 10% make $166,000+
>
> **Why now?:** One of the 10 fastest growing occupations, it's projected to boom 41% by 2016.
>
> **What you'll need:** A solid business background, plus education in the field. you'll probably also need series 7 and series 63 or 66 licenses.
>
> **Entrepreneur opportunities:** 30% are self-employed.

3. Environmental Scientist

(Hydrologist, Environmental Ecologist, Environmental Chemist, Ecological Modeler)

"Becoming an environmental scientist could mean studying changing agricultural practices, investigating chemicals in the environment, or understanding how ecosystems behave," says Linda Sheldon, sixty-four, a scientist and an associate director of the National Exposure Lab at the Environmental Protection Agency. It's also geographically specific: you have to go where the research is being done.

Robbie Morris, forty-seven, is an air pollution specialist for the state of California. Prior to her current job, she did soil and water cleanup with a state agency, which required a lot of time in the field. She now spends her days in an office, implementing regulations for air quality. "It was a lifestyle choice," she says. "I got tired of the driving. The great thing is that I have that choice—I could always go back to an outside job." For now, she analyzes reports, meets with truck fleet owners, and educates the public about regulation changes. "I enjoy being a part of the implementation of things," she says. "I get up every day and love going to work."

> **Salary:** Most earn $46,520 to $86,490, top 10% make $116,000+.
>
> **Why now?:** The field is expected to grow 25% by 2016.
>
> **What you'll need:** Most positions require a master's degree in environmental science, hydrology, or a related natural science.
>
> **Entrepreneur opportunities:** About 2% are self-employed.

4. Registered Nurse
(Critical Care, Emergency, Oncology, Clinical)

Nursing is intense physical and mental work. "Shifts are typically eight to twelve hours, and you're on your feet most of the time," says Cheryl Peterson, the director of nursing practice and policy for the American Nurses Association. "But the beauty of the profession is that there are so many different kinds of places to work and types of working arrangements."

During the last twenty years, Gen Olivas, forty-five, has been on staff at a neonatal intensive care unit, a psychiatric ward, a cardiac step-down unit, and a nursing home. She is now the nursing director at a home hospice in Moorpark, California. "I'm not stuck doing one thing," she says. Having recently moved cross-country from Pennsylvania, Olivas also appreciates how transferable her nursing skills are. "Nurses are always needed. Every place we move, I've been able to find a job."

Salary: $52,800 to $78,080, top 10% make $94,000+.

Why now?: A projected 587,000 new nursing jobs will be created by 2016.

What you'll need: A BS in nursing (four years), an associate's degree in nursing (two to three years), or a diploma from an approved nursing program.

Entrepreneur opportunities: Although some nurses provide care as independent contractors or wellness coaches, most are employees.

5. Computer And Information Systems Manager
(Chief Technology Officer, Management Information Systems [IMS] Director, Information Technology [IT] Director)

This growing field offers some obvious lifestyle advantages. "You may be able to telecommute, and the work doesn't necessarily have to be done between eight and five," says Leslyn Broughton, the regional vice president of the national tech staffing firm Modis (modis.com). "And when it comes to jobs in technology, there just aren't enough people out there."

Carla Ventrano, forty-four, carved out a niche for herself as an information technology director at various law offices, and she currently holds the position for a firm in Miami. She manages the company's network, file system, e-mail, Internet connectivity, data backup, and remote access. "You name it, I do it," she says. She also handles employee training and tech support calls, and she often works late. Despite the hours, she loves it. "I enjoy the authority," she says. "I love being able to make decisions about where the firm is headed technology-wise and helping the firm do what it does."

Salary: $73,800 to $113,670, top 10% make $135,000+.

Why now?: This field will add 43,000 jobs by 2016.

What you'll need: A bachelor's degree and sometimes a

master's degree—consider an MBA with a focus on technology.

Entrepreneur opportunities: These tend to be leadership positions within a company.

6. Education Administrator
(Principal, Assistant Principal, Provost, Dean Of Students, School District Administrator, Director Of Student Services)

Education administrators are generally the first to arrive at work and the last to leave, and it's not a profession for someone who needs to make it home for dinner every night. "Administration involves a 24/7 year-round commitment," says Mark King, the director of Fairfield Teachers' Agency, an educational placement firm. "It's a commitment that goes well beyond when the bell rings."

Linda Rudes, sixty, was an elementary school teacher in Kings Park, New York, for six years before leaving to raise her children. After rejoining the field at age forty-four as a reading teacher, she decided to take some administrative courses. "I fell in love with the law, the what-ifs, the problem solving," she says. She got a degree in educational administration in eighteen months, logged four hundred hours as an intern, and landed a position as an assistant administrator. From there, she moved on to assistant principal and then principal for six years until retiring in June 2010. "Being a principal was by far the best job of my life," she says. "When I retired, my parting words were 'I won't cry because it's over. I'll smile because it happened.'"

Salary: $55,140 to $95,970 (elementary and secondary school), top 10% make $122,000+.

Why now?: Many will retire in the next decade.

What you'll need: Experience as a teacher or in a field such as recruiting. some positions require a master's degree.

Entrepreneur opportunities: Most work for school districts or universities.

7. Strategic/Crisis Communication Professional
(Crisis Manager, Strategic Communications Specialist)

With the advent of social media and the twenty-four-hour news cycle, specialists who manage companies' reputations have become increasingly important. "Crisis communication professionals are constantly putting out fires," says Lindsay Olson, a partner at Paradigm Staffing (paradigmstaffing.com). "Someone who is adrenaline-charged, who likes to focus on a company's problems—this would be a good career for her."

Sixteen years ago, Davia Temin, now in her late fifties, used her marketing and crisis-management experience at big firms to open her own company. Now her clients include biotech and pharmaceutical firms, investment banks, and politicians. Translation: She's available all of the time. "Forget this 24/7 business," says Temin, who sleeps with two BlackBerrys, an iPad, and an iPhone on her pillow. "Try 25/8." Although her life is hectic, she thrives on the pace and the energy. "You can really positively impact an organization, a stock price, a drug coming back into the marketplace," she says. "I don't think somebody fresh out of college would have any way of succeeding in crisis management. There are some things you have to have accumulated wisdom about. You have to have lived through it."

Salary: $39,420 to $66,470, top 10% make $82,000+.

Why now?: The field is expected to create 43,000 new jobs by 2016.

What you'll need: Public relations experience.

Entrepreneur opportunities: With the right expertise, it's possible to provide this service as an independent contractor.

8. Accountant

(Public Accountant, Management Accountant, Government Accountant, Internal Auditor)

"Most accounting careers include a lot of autonomy once a person is past the training and staff levels," says Mary Bennett, a member of the American Institute of Certified Public Accountants. "There's a lot of flexibility. Some people work part time, and many start their own practices."

Melanie Shaw, forty-nine, made the jump into accounting seven years ago after working sixteen years as a civil engineer. She'd been taking classes as part of an MBA program, and a personal tax class sparked her interest. "Taxes are a puzzle, with all sorts of arcane rules, twists, and turns," she says. Because she'd already taken a handful of business classes and plenty of math, Shaw, who lives in Marin County, California, enrolled in an intensive full-time summer program and received her certification. Three years ago, after working for a tax firm since 2005, she opened her own practice. "If you need to be independent, it's a fabulous field," she says. "I work hard, but I like to do it on my own terms."

> **Salary:** $41,110 to $64,430, top 10% make $78,000+.
>
> **Why now?:** The field will grow 18% by 2016.
>
> **What you'll need:** A degree in accounting or a related field. you have to pass an exam to become a CPA.
>
> **Entrepreneur opportunities:** 10% are self-employed.

9. Human Resources Specialist

(Job Analyst, Compensation Manager, Training and Development Manager, Recruiter)

About 55 percent of HR specialists began their careers in a different area. "There isn't the same barrier to entry for HR that there is for other fields," says Deb Cohen, of the Society for Human Resource Management. "You can really decide to change careers to get into HR." Even when companies downsize, most still need HR staff. The field breaks down into generalists, who handle a little of everything, and specialists, who have expertise in such areas as benefits or training. Certain subspecialties, including labor relations and recruitment, are now growing rapidly, according to the Bureau of Labor Statistics.

April Bettencourt, fifty-two, from Lodi, California, started to specialize in benefits seventeen years ago. "I liked that things were changing constantly and that you have to continue to learn and grow, because benefits are a very personal thing for people," she says. "Benefits and payroll can get a bit scary because they're so visible. They impact every single employee, and if they're not done flawlessly all the time, everybody sees it. You have to have a thick skin."

> **Salary:** $44,400 to $66,000, top 10% make $80,000+.
>
> **Why now?:** There will be 147,000 new specialist jobs created by 2016.
>
> **What you'll need:** To specialize, you may need an MBA with a focus in HR management.
>
> **Entrepreneur opportunities:** About 2% are self-employed.

10. Small-Scale Niche Farmer

Farmers rarely get a day off, but the work is rewarding. "There's a call for local food," says Deborah Stockton, the executive director of the National Independent Consumers and Farmers Association. "The farmers I know who provide for their communities cannot keep up with demand."

Robin Follette, forty-seven, used to work in county government. "I would go to the office and look out the window and think, I could be outside," she says. Twenty-one years ago, Follette quit her job and started gardening. Now she uses three thousand square feet of greenhouse space on her forty-five acres in Talmadge, Maine, to grow vegetables year round. "I keep succession planting going," she says. "As soon as a crop comes out, I have to put something in its place." When her husband lost his job two years ago, the couple did fine on Robin's income. "I'm passionate about this," she says. "I get to feed my family and feed a lot of other people, too."

Salary: $21,970 to $57,300, top 10% make $98,000+

Why now?: Small farms are growing at a rate of 10,000 a year.

What you'll need: Nothing—training is done on the job.

Entrepreneur opportunities: 80% are self-employed.

Contributors

Kate Ashford: "From Flight Attendant to Fashionista"; "The Million-Dollar Coupon Clipper"; "She Found Her Inner Publicist"; "Mastering the New Job Hunt; "The Ten Best Jobs for Women Now"

Jean Chatzky: "How to Afford Your Next Chapter"; "Moonlighting Tips"

Susan Crandell: "Call of the Wild"

Dalia Fahmy: "She's a Wrap Star"

Gabrielle Frank: "How to Write a Great Business Plan"

Elizabeth Gehrman: "From Entrepreneur to Best-Selling Novelist"; "Finding Fulfillment in a War Zone"; "She Discovered She Was a Leader"; "The World's Unlikeliest Weight Lifter"; "From Nonathlete to Triathlete"

Jan Goodwin: "She Dreamed of Africa"; "She Saves Wild Cats"

Patti Greco: "Cancer Wigged Her Out"

Marc Herman: "Soul Survivor"

Dana Hudepohl: "From Wags to Riches"; "Skills from the Past Can Create a Future"; "From Executive Assistant to Master Chef"; "A Headhunter Rediscovers Painting"; "Fashion Saved Her Life"; "How a Beading Class Set Her Free"; "Handbags Helped Her Heal"; "Write What You Know"; "Sell Your House, Find a Life"; "A Path in the Wilderness"; "Discovering the Art of Instruction"; "Miracle in the Ladies Room"; "Reinventing via Inventions"; "The MBA Who Became a Matchmaker";

"A Chocolate-Coated Life Change"; "Reinventing Mrs. Oregon"; "A Bike Brought Her Confidence"

Aileen Jacobson: "Giving Up Money for Music"; "A Suburban Mom's Road to TV Stardom"; "The Cop Who Became a Comedian"

Joanne Kaufman: "A Sea Change"

Jean Hanff Korelitz: "An Artful Business Plan"; "She Ditched the Corner Office"

Jennifer Margulis: "Her Restaurant Breaks All of the Rules"; "Wife for Hire"

Maryn McKenna: "The Earthquake Avenger"

Pamela Mitchell: "Ten Steps to Jump-Starting Your Change"

Alison Overholt: "Her New Life Was in the Cards"

Amanda Robb: "Mika's Do-Over"

Lynn Rosellini: "The DNA Detective"

Jenny Rough: "The Beekeeper"; "The Sheep Farmer"

Carin Rubenstein: "Not Too Late for a New Degree"; "A Dream Built on China"; "She De-stressed in a New Career"; "Furnishing Her Life with Meaning"

Karen Schwartz: "Shipping Help from America"

Salley Shannon "The Book Farmer of Botswana"; "Crisis Is Her Business"

Rebecca Adler Warren: "The Egg Banker"

Acknowledgments

Women sharing their stories with other women is the heart and soul of *More* magazine, and that's where this book began. So most of all we thank the women who agreed to be interviewed about their reinventions for the magazine's Second Acts column, or who wrote their own histories for More.com.

Enormous thanks also go to Janet Chan, who shaped and edited the book, and Dana Hudepohl, who brought her reporter's eye for detail to many of these stories. This project also benefited greatly from the work of the following editors and writers at *More*: features editor Stephanie von Hirschberg, who culled the best reinvention stories from the magazine and website; assistant art director Susanne Bamberger; and Beatrice Hogan, the magazine's head of research, whose finely honed storytelling instincts and devotion to accuracy kept us on track every step of the way. Assisting her, and drawing out many of our reinventors' helpful tips and success strategies, were Cheryl Alkon, Aliyah Baruchin, Michelle Ciarrocca, Cathy Garrard, and Michelle Memran.

And at Meredith Corporation, we thank Katherine Surprenant and Simone Procas, whose advice has been, as always, invaluable.